AUTO-BIOGRAPHY

This page enables you to compile a list of useful data on your car, so that whether you're ordering spares or just checking the tyre pressures, all the key information - the information that is 'personal' to your car - is easily within reach.

Registration number:..

Model: ....

Body colour:..

Paint code number: ....

Date of first registration: ....

Date of manufacture (if different): ....

Chassis or 'VIN' number: ....

Engine number:..

Gearbox number: ....

Overdrive unit number (if fitted): ....

Front axle casing number: ....

Rear axle casing number:....................................

Tyre size

   Front: ....Rear:......................

Tyre pressure (normally laden)

   Front:..........................Rear:......................

Tyre pressure (fully laden)

   Front: ....Rear:......................

Ignition key number: ....

Door lock key/keys number: ....

Fuel cap lock key number (if fitted):....................

Alarm remote code (if fitted): ....

Alarm remote battery type: ....

Radio code no. (if appropriate): ....

Insurance

   Name and address of insurer:...

   ....

   Policy number:..

Modifications

   Information that might be useful when you need to purchase parts:...

   ....

   ....

Suppliers

   Address and telephone number of your garage and parts suppliers:...

   ....

A PORTER PUBLISHING book

First Published 1994

PORTER PUBLISHING

Published and Produced by

Porter Publishing Ltd
The Storehouse
Little Hereford Street
Bromyard
Hereford
England HR7 4DE

British Library Cataloguing in Publication Data

A catalogue record for this book is available from the British Library.

ISBN 1-899238-03-4

Series Editor: Lindsay Porter
Design: Lindsay Porter and Lyndsay Berryman, Pineapple Publishing
Printed in England by The Trinity Press, Worcester

Other Titles in this Series
MGB, (including MGC, MGB GT V8 and MG RV8) Service Guide
Mini (all models 1959-on) Service Guide
VW Beetle (all models to 1980) Service Guide

- With more titles in production -

Every care has been taken to ensure that the material contained in this Service Guide is correct. However, no liability can be accepted by the authors or publishers for damage, loss, accidents, or injury resulting from any omissions or errors in the information given.

Step-by-Step Service Guide to the Land Rover

FOREWORD

Of all the vehicles on the road, the Land Rover must be the ultimate for DIY! It was designed to be easy to assemble, take apart and put back together again, in all kinds of places, from desert to farmyard, so a couple of sturdy ramps in the front drive will seem like luxury to these tough beasties.

Every part of the Land Rover can be got at; every part can be serviced and maintained by human beings rather than computers, but that's only part of the appeal. Another is the incredible strength and unstressed longevity of the vehicles. But even Land Rovers will wear out and even break if neglected for too long - while the sheer strength and size of the parts means that they are often more expensive than those for ordinary passenger cars. It pays to maintain your Land Rover and to do it well, using only parts that are as reliable as the parts that were originally fitted - and in the majority of cases, that means paying up and buying genuine Land Rover parts.

And that leads me to another part of the appeal of DIY Land Rover servicing. So many have been built over the years that the supply of parts is excellent. There are Land Rover dealers in every part of the UK and independent specialists abound. In addition, most general parts stockists either keep spares or can obtain them in next to no time.

This is my second book on the Land Rover Series I, II and III vehicles, the first being a restoration guide for Haynes. If this book proves to be as useful as readers tell me that the first has been, I'll be well pleased. If its contents are followed with care, it will certainly put back the day when restoration will be required!

Lindsay Porter

CONTENTS

	Auto-Biography	*1*
	Foreword	*4*
	Introduction and Acknowledgements	*6*
	Using This Book	*7*
CHAPTER 1:	*Safety First!*	*8*
CHAPTER 2:	*Buying Spares*	*12*
CHAPTER 3:	*Service Intervals, Step-by-Step*	
	Using the Service Schedules	*15*
	500 Miles, Weekly or Before a Long Journey	*18*
	1,500 Miles - or Every Month	*23*
	3,000 Miles - or Every Three Months	*25*
	6,000 Miles - or Every Six Months	*46*
	12,000 Miles - or Every Twelve Months	*62*
	Spark Plug Conditions	*65*
	24,000 Miles - or Every Twenty Four Months	*72*
	36,000 Miles - or Every Thirty Six Months	*75*
CHAPTER 4:	*Repairing Bodywork Blemishes*	*77*
CHAPTER 5:	*Rustproofing*	*81*
CHAPTER 6:	*Fault Finding*	*85*
CHAPTER 7:	*Getting Through the MOT*	*89*
CHAPTER 8:	*Facts & Figures*	*99*
CHAPTER 9:	*Tools & Equipment*	*105*
APPENDIX 1:	*Lubrication Chart*	*108*
APPENDIX 2:	*American & British Terms*	*109*
APPENDIX 3:	*Specialists & Suppliers*	*110*
APPENDIX 4:	*Service History*	*111*

Keep a record of every Service you carry out on your car.

Lindsay Porter
Porter Publishing Ltd

Introduction

O ver the years, each of us involved with this project has run any number of cars, from superb classic cars, modern cars, to those with one foot in the breaker's yard. And we know only too well that any car is enjoyable to own only if it's reliable, safe and basically sound - and the best way of ensuring that it stays that way is to service it regularly. That's why we have set about creating a series of books which aim to provide you, the owner, with all the information you might need in order to keep your car in tip-top condition. And if your car is not as reliable as it might be, you will be able to give your car a 'super service', using the information contained in the Servicing section of this book, and bring it back to good, reliable order.

Porter Publishing Service Guides are the first books to give you all the service information you might need, with step-by-step instructions, along with a complete Service History section for you to complete and fill in as you carry out regular maintenance on your car over the months ahead. Using the information contained in this book, you will be able to:

◆ see for yourself how to carry out every Service Interval, from weekly and monthly checks, right up to longer-term maintenance items.

◆ carry out regular body maintenance and rustproofing, saving a fortune in body repairs over the years to come.

◆ enhance the value of your car by completing a full Service History of every maintenance job you carry out on your car.

We hope you enjoy keeping your car in trim whilst saving lots of money by servicing your car yourself, with the help of this book. Happy motoring!

Acknowledgements

T his book has been a real team effort, with lots of people contributing time, expertise and no little brain-ache to ensure that it is full of good stuff whilst being easy and straightforward to follow. That the project has worked is due in no small measure to Kim Henson who helped with the research for several sections of this book, and my assistant Zoe Palmer who helped with much of the research for the book, as well as having spent countless hours on the original concept behind this series of books. Dave Pollard and John Mead (Technical Editor) have all also provided a highly valued input. It's a pleasure to work with such people, professionals all and thoroughly nice folk, to boot.

In fact, one of the great things about this project is the positive, enjoyable spirit in which the whole thing has taken place. Highly valued expertise also came from Keith Gott, the Land Rover specialist of Alton, Hampshire, who put workshop and staff at our disposal while Chapter 3 was in preparation - and thanks are due to Ben and Charlie for all their help. Dave Bingley of Perris Garage, Llanrhystud, Dyfed kindly shared some of the knowledge which he has gained during many years of experience of Land Rovers and of servicing and repair work in general in his rural garage business. Colin Beever of Holden Vintage and Classic Ltd. gave willing assistance in providing quantities of information on electrical equipment fitted to Land Rovers and the Land Rover Series II Club and Frank King, of the Land Rover Series III Owners Club supplied the information about clubs which appears in Appendix 3.

Others who have provided invaluable assistance include 'Trish Giles, who helped to ensure that the servicing information flowed logically, Peter Stant, who demonstrated the bodywork repair techniques seen in this book and my wife Shan who put her great experience in book-matters to excellent effect.

Specialist expertise also came from Dunlop/SP Tyres, Roger McNickle of Dinol GB Ltd, Gunson's who supplied the very useful DIY test equipment, Kamasa tools, who supplied almost all of the great range of tools used here and from David's Isopon who supplied expertise on bodywork repair and body filler that is second to none, with more from Partco and AP Lockheed. And of course, there are our old friends Richard Price and Dawn Adams at Castrol whose advice we are always pleased to receive and whose products we can always unhesitatingly recommend.

Many thanks to everyone listed here as well as to anyone else whom we might inadvertently have missed.

Using This Book

Everything about this book is designed to help you make your car more reliable and long-lasting through regular servicing. But one requirement that you will see emphasised again and again is the need for safe working. There is a lot of safety information within the practical instructions, but you are strongly urged to *read and take note of Chapter 1, Safety First!*

To get the most from this book, you will rapidly realise that it revolves around two main chapters. *Chapter 3, Service Intervals, Step-by-Step* shows you how to carry out every service job that your car is likely to need throughout its life. Then, the final Section, *Service History*, at the back of this book, lists all of the jobs described in *Chapter 3*, and arranges them together in tick-lists, a separate list for each Service interval, so that you can create your own *Service History* as you go along. When you have completed the three years of *Service History* included in this book, continuation sheets can be purchased from Porter Publishing.

Keeping your car in top condition is one thing; getting it there in the first place may be quite another. At the start of *Chapter 3*, we advise on carrying out a 'catch-up' service for cars that may not have received the de-luxe treatment suggested here. And then there are four other chapters to help you bring your car up to scratch. *Chapter 4, Repairing Bodywork Blemishes* and *Chapter 5, Rustproofing* show how to make the body beautiful and how to keep it that way - not something that is usually included in servicing information but bodywork servicing can save you even more money than mechanical servicing, since a corroded body often leads to a scrapped car, whereas worn out mechanical components can usually be replaced. *Chapter 6* shows you how to carry out *Fault Finding* when your car won't start, and *Chapter 7* describes *Getting Through the MoT*, an annual worry - unless you follow the approach shown here. With *Chapter 2, Buying Spares* describing how you can save on spares and *Chapter 8, Facts and Figures* giving you all the key vital statics, we hope that this book will become the first tool you'll pick up when you want to service your car!

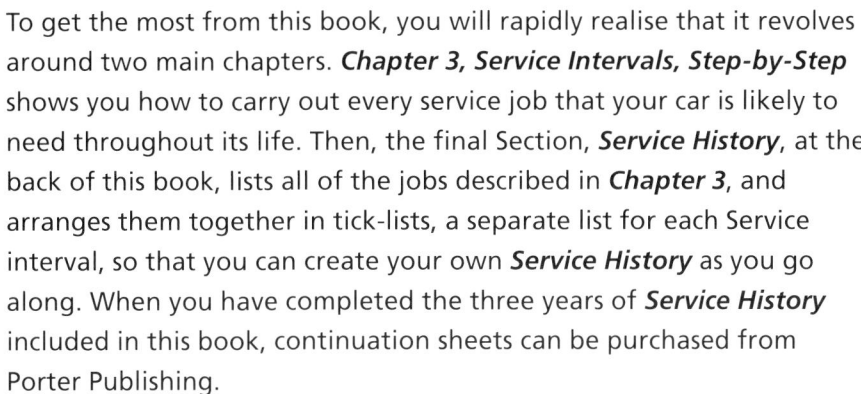

This book is produced in association with Castrol (U.K.) Ltd.

"Cars have become more and more sophistated. But changing the oil and brake fluid, and similar jobs are as simple as they ever were. Castrol are pleased to be associated with this book because it gives us the opportunity to make life simpler for those who wish to service their own cars.
Castrol have succeeded in making oil friendlier ane kinder to the environment by removing harmful chlorine from our range of engine lubricants which in turn prolong the life of the catalytic convertor (when fitted), by noticeably maintaining the engine at peak efficiency.
In return, we ask you to be kinder to the environment too... by taking yor used oil to your Local Authority Amenity Oil Bank. It can then be used as a heating fuel. Please do not poison it with thinners, paint, creosote or brake fluid because these render it useless and costly to dispose of."

Castrol (U.K.) Ltd

CHAPTER 1 - SAFETY FIRST!

It is vitally important that you always take time to ensure that safety is the first consideration in any job you do. A slight lack of concentration, or a rush to finish the job quickly can often result in an accident, as can failure to follow a few simple precautions. Whereas skilled motor mechanics are trained in safe working practices you, the home mechanic, must find them out for yourself and act upon them.

Remember, accidents don't just happen, they are caused, and some of those causes are contained in the following list. Above all, ensure that whenever you work on your car you adopt a safety-minded approach at all times, and remain aware of the dangers that might be encountered.

Be sure to consult the suppliers of any materials and equipment you may use, and to obtain and read carefully any operating and health and safety instructions that may be available on packaging or from manufacturers and suppliers.

IMPORTANT POINTS

ALWAYS ensure that the vehicle is properly supported when raised off the ground bearing in mind that Land Rovers are much heavier than most cars. Don't work on, around, or underneath a raised vehicle unless axle stands are positioned under secure, load bearing underbody areas, or the vehicle is driven onto ramps.

DON'T suddenly remove the radiator or expansion tank filler cap when the cooling system is hot, or you may get scalded by escaping coolant. Let the system cool down first and even then, if the engine is not completely cold, cover the cap with a cloth and gradually release the pressure.

NEVER start the engine unless the gearbox is in neutral and the hand brake is fully applied.

NEVER drain oil, coolant or automatic transmission fluid when the engine is hot. Allow time for it to cool sufficiently to avoid scalding you.

NEVER attempt to loosen or tighten nuts that require a lot of force to turn (e.g. a tight oil drain plug) with the vehicle raised, unless it is properly supported and in a safe condition. Wherever possible, initially slacken tight fastenings before raising the car off the ground.

TAKE CARE to avoid touching any engine or exhaust system component unless it is cool enough so as not to burn you.

ALWAYS keep antifreeze, brake and clutch fluid away from vehicle paintwork. Wash off any spills immediately.

NEVER syphon fuel, antifreeze, brake fluid or other such toxic liquids by mouth, or allow prolonged contact with your skin. There is an increasing awareness that they can damage your health. Best of all, use a suitable hand pump and wear gloves.

ALWAYS work in a well ventilated area and don't inhale dust - it may contain asbestos or other poisonous substances.

WIPE UP any spilt oil, grease or water off the floor immediately, before there is an accident.

MAKE SURE that spanners and all other tools are the right size for the job and are not likely to slip. Never try to 'double-up' spanners to gain more leverage.

SEEK HELP if you need to lift something heavy which may be beyond your capability.

ALWAYS ensure that the safe working load rating of any jacks, hoists or lifting gear used is sufficient for the job, and is used only as recommended by the manufacturer.

NEVER take risky short-cuts or rush to finish a job. Plan ahead and allow plenty of time.

BE meticulous and keep the work area tidy - you'll avoid frustration, work better and loose less.

KEEP children and animals right away from the work area and from unattended vehicles.

ALWAYS wear eye protection when working under the vehicle or using any power tools.

BEFORE undertaking dirty jobs, use a barrier cream on your hands as a protection against infection. Preferably, wear thin gloves, available from DIY outlets.

DON'T lean over, or work on, a running engine unless strictly necessary, and keep long hair and loose clothing well out of the way of moving mechanical parts. Note that it is theoretically possible for fluorescent striplighting to make an engine fan appear to be stationary - check! This is the sort of error that happens when you're dog tired and not thinking straight. So don't work on your car when you're overtired!

REMOVE your wrist watch, rings and all other jewellery before doing any work on the vehicle - especially the electrical system.

ALWAYS tell someone what you're doing and have them regularly check that all is well, especially when working alone on, or under, the vehicle.

ALWAYS seek specialist advice if you're in doubt about any job. The safety of your vehicle affects you, your passengers and other road users.

FIRE

Petrol (gasoline) is a dangerous and highly flammable liquid requiring special precautions. When working on the fuel system, disconnect the vehicle battery earth (ground) terminal whenever possible and always work outside, or in a very well ventilated area. Any form of spark, such as that caused by an electrical fault, by two metal surfaces striking against each other, by a central heating boiler in the garage 'firing up', or even by static electricity built up in your clothing can, in a confined space, ignite petrol vapour causing an explosion. Take great care not to spill petrol on to the engine or exhaust system, never allow any naked flame anywhere near the work area and, above all, don't smoke.

Invest in a workshop-sized fire extinguisher. Choose the carbon dioxide type or preferably, dry powder but never a water type extinguisher for workshop use. Water conducts electricity and can make worse an oil or petrol-based fire, in certain circumstances.

FUMES

In addition to the fire dangers described previously, petrol (gasoline) vapour and the vapour from many solvents, thinners, and adhesives is highly toxic and under certain conditions can lead to unconsciousness or even death, if inhaled. The risks are increased if such fluids are used in a confined space so always ensure adequate ventilation when handling materials of this nature. Treat all such substances with care, always read the instructions and follow them implicitly.

Always ensure that the car is outside the work place in open air if the engine is running. Exhaust fumes contain poisonous carbon monoxide - even if the car is fitted with a catalytic converter, since 'cats' sometimes fail and don't function with the engine cold. Never have the engine running with the car in the garage or in any enclosed space.

Inspection pits are another source of danger from the build-up of fumes. Never drain petrol (gasoline) or use solvents, thinners adhesives or other toxic substances in an inspection pit as the extremely confined space allows the highly toxic fumes to concentrate. Running the engine with the vehicle over the pit can have the same results. It is also dangerous to park a vehicle for any length of time over an inspection pit. The fumes from even a slight fuel leak can cause an explosion when the engine is started.

MAINS ELECTRICITY

Best of all, use rechargeable tools and a DC inspection lamp, powered from a remote 12V battery - both are much safer! However, if you do use a mains-powered inspection lamp, power tool etc, ensure that the appliance is wired correctly to its plug, that where necessary it is properly earthed (grounded), and that the fuse is of the correct rating for the appliance concerned. Do not use any mains powered equipment in damp conditions or in the vicinity of fuel, fuel vapour or the vehicle battery.

Also, before using any mains powered electrical equipment, take one more simple precaution - use an RCD (Residual Current Device) circuit breaker. Then, if there is a short, the RCD circuit breaker minimises the risk of electrocution by instantly cutting the power supply. Buy one from any electrical store or DIY centre. RCDs fit simply into your electrical socket before plugging in your electrical equipment.

THE IGNITION SYSTEM

Extreme care must be taken when working on the ignition system with the ignition switched on or with the engine cranking or running.

SAFETY FIRST!

Touching certain parts of the ignition system, such as the HT leads, distributor cap, ignition coil etc, can result in a severe electric shock. This is especially likely where the insulation on any of these components is weak, or if the components are dirty or damp. Note also that voltages produced by electronic ignition systems are much higher than conventional systems and could prove fatal, particularly to persons with cardiac pacemaker implants. Consult your handbook or main dealer if in any doubt. An additional risk of injury can arise while working on running engines, if the operator touches a high voltage lead and pulls his hand away on to a conductive or revolving part.

THE BATTERY

Never cause a spark, smoke, or allow a naked light near the vehicle's battery, even in a well ventilated area. A certain amount of highly explosive hydrogen gas will be given off as part of the normal charging process. Care should be taken to avoid sparking by switching off the power supply before charger leads are connected or disconnected. Battery terminals should be shielded, since a battery contains energy and a spark can be caused by any conductor which touches its terminals or exposed connecting straps.

Before working on the fuel or electrical systems, always disconnect the battery earth (ground) terminal.

When charging the battery from an external source, disconnect both battery leads before connecting the charger. If the battery is not of the 'sealed-for-life' type, loosen the filler plugs or remove the cover before charging. For best results the battery should be given a low rate 'trickle' charge overnight. Do not charge at an excessive rate or the battery may burst.

Always wear gloves and goggles when carrying or when topping up the battery. Even in diluted form (as it is in the battery) the acid electrolyte is extremely corrosive and must not be allowed to contact the eyes, skin or clothes.

BRAKES AND ASBESTOS

Whenever you work on the braking system mechanical components, or remove front or rear brake pads or shoes: i) wear an efficient particle mask, ii) wipe off all brake dust from the work area (never blow it off with compressed air), iii) dispose of brake dust and discarded shoes or pads in a sealed plastic bag, iv) wash hands thoroughly after you have finished working on the brakes and certainly before you eat or smoke, v) replace shoes and pads only with asbestos-free shoes or pads. Note that asbestos brake dust can cause cancer if inhaled.

Obviously, a car's brakes are among its most important safety related items. Do not dismantle your car's brakes unless you are fully competent to do so. If you have not been trained in this work, but wish to carry out the jobs described in this book, it is strongly recommend that you have a garage or qualified mechanic check your work before using the car on the road.

BRAKE FLUID

Brake fluid absorbs moisture rapidly from the air and can become dangerous resulting in brake failure. Castrol (U.K.) Ltd. recommend that you should have your brake fluid tested at least once a year by a properly equipped garage with test equipment and you should change the fluid in accordance with your vehicle manufacturer's recommendations or as advised in this book if we recommend a shorter interval than the manufacturers. Always buy no more brake fluid than you need. Never store an opened pack. Dispose of the remainder at your Local Authority Waster Disposal Site, in the designated disposal unit, not with general waste or with waste oil.

ENGINE OILS

Take care and observe the following precautions when working with used engine oil. Apart from the obvious risk of scalding when draining the oil from a hot engine, there is the danger from contaminates that are contained in all used oil.

Always wear disposable plastic or rubber gloves when draining the oil from your engine. i) Note that the drain plug and the oil are often hotter than you expect! Wear gloves if the plug is too hot to touch and keep your hand to one side so that you are not scalded by the spurt of oil as the plug comes away. ii) There are very real health hazards associated with used engine oil. In the words of one manufacturer's handbook, "Prolonged and repeated contact may cause serious skin disorders, including dermatitis and cancer". Use a barrier cream on your hands and try not to get oil on them. Where practicable, wear gloves and wash your hands with hand cleaner soon after carrying out the work. Keep oil out of the reach of children. iii) NEVER, EVER dispose of old engine oil into the ground or down a drain. In the UK, and in most EC countries, every local authority must provide a safe means of oil disposal. In the UK, try your local Environmental Health Department for advice on waste disposal facilities.

PLASTIC MATERIALS

Work with plastic materials brings additional hazards into workshops. Many of the materials used (polymers, resins, adhesives and materials acting as catalysts and accelerators) readily produce very dangerous situations in the form of poisonous fumes, skin irritants, risk of fire and explosions. Do not allow resin or 2-pack adhesive hardener, or that supplied with filler or 2-pack stopper to come into contact with skin or eyes. Read carefully the safety notes supplied on the tin, tube or packaging.

JACK AND AXLE STANDS

Throughout this book you will see many references to the correct use of jacks, axle stands and similar equipment - and we make no apologies for being repetitive! This is one area where safety cannot be over stressed - your life could be at stake!

Special care must be taken when any type of lifting equipment is used. Jacks are made for lifting the vehicle only, not for supporting it. Never work under the car using only a jack to support the weight. Jacks must be supplemented by adequate additional means of support, positioned under secure load-bearing parts of the frame or underbody. Axle stands are available from many discount stores, and all auto parts stores. Drive-on ramps are limiting because of their design and size but they are simple to use, reliable and the most stable type of support, by far. We strongly recommend their use.

Full details on jacking and supporting the vehicle will be found in Raising a car - Safely! near the beginning of Chapter 3.

FLUOROELASTOMERS

MOST IMPORTANT! PLEASE READ THIS SECTION!

If you service your car in the normal way, none of the following may be relevant to you. Unless, for example, you encounter a car which has been on fire (even in a localised area), subject to heat in, say, a crash-damage repairer's shop or vehicle breaker's yard, or if any second-hand parts have been heated in any of these ways.

Many synthetic rubber-like materials used in motor cars contain a substance called fluorine. These materials are known as fluoroelastomers and are commonly used for oil seals, wiring and cabling, bearing surfaces, gaskets, diaphragms, hoses and 'O' rings. If they are subjected to temperatures greater than 315 degrees C, they will decompose and can be potentially hazardous. Fluoroelastomer materials will show physical signs of decomposition under such conditions in the form of charring of black sticky masses. Some decomposition may occur at temperatures above 200 degrees C, and it is obvious that when a car has been in a fire or has been dismantled with the assistance of a cutting torch or blow torch, the fluoroelastomers can decompose in the manner indicated above.

In the presence of any water or humidity, including atmospheric moisture, the by-products caused by the fluoroelastomers being heated can be extremely dangerous. According to the Health and Safety Executive, "Skin contact with this liquid or decomposition residues can cause painful and penetrating burns. Permanent irreversible skin and tissue damage can occur". Damage can also be caused to eyes or by the inhalation of fumes created as fluoroelastomers are burned or heated.

After fires or exposure to high temperatures observe the following precautions:

1. Do not touch blackened or charred seals or equipment.

2. Allow all burnt or decomposed fluoroelastomer materials to cool down before inspection, investigations, tear-down or removal.

3. Preferably, don't handle parts containing decomposed fluoroelastomers, but if you must, wear goggles and PVC (polyvinyl chloride) or neoprene protective gloves whilst doing so. Never handle such parts unless they are completely cool.

4. Contaminated parts, residues, materials and clothing, including protective clothing and gloves, should be disposed of by an approved contractor to landfill or by incineration according to national or local regulations. Oil seals, gaskets and 'O ' rings, along with contaminated material, must not be burned locally.

WORKSHOP SAFETY - GENERAL

1. *Always have a fire extinguisher of the correct type at arm's length when working on the fuel system - under the car, or under the bonnet.*

    If you do have a fire, DON'T PANIC. Use the extinguisher effectively by directing it at the base of the fire.

2. *NEVER use a naked flame near petrol or anywhere in the workplace.*

3. *KEEP your inspection lamp well away from any source of petrol (gasoline) such as when disconnecting a carburettor float bowl or fuel line.*

4. *NEVER use petrol (gasoline) to clean parts. Use paraffin (kerosene) or white (mineral) spirits.*

5. *NO SMOKING! There's a risk of fire or transferring dangerous substances to your mouth and, in any case, ash falling into mechanical components is to be avoided!*

6. *BE METHODICAL in everything you do, use common sense, and think of safety at all times.*

CHAPTER 2 - BUYING SPARES

Reliable though the Land Rover undoubtedly is, there are, of course, occasions when you need to buy spares in order to service it and keep it running. There are a number of sources of supply of the components necessary when servicing the car, the price and quality varying between suppliers. As with most things in life, cheapest is not necessarily best - as a general rule our advice is to put quality before price - this policy usually works out less expensive in the long run! But how can you identify 'quality'? It's sometimes difficult, so stick with parts from suppliers with a reputation, those recommended to you by others and parts produced by well-established brand names. But don't just pay through the nose! The same parts are often available at wildly different prices so, if you want to save money, invest your time in shopping around.

In any event, when buying spares, take with you details of the date of registration of your car, also its chassis (or VIN) and engine numbers. These can be helpful where parts changed during production, and can be the key to a more helpful approach by some parts salespeople! You may, by now have entered this key information on the Auto-Biography pages at the front of this book, for ease of reference. The line drawings on these pages show you where to find the relevant information on your car.

IDENTIFICATION NUMBERS

The most important identification number on your Land Rover is the vehicle number (also known as chassis number) and it is this number which provides a positive identification for your vehicle when it comes to buying spares.

1. The vehicle number on all Land Rovers up to an including Series IIA, can be found beneath the dash on the bulkhead, behind the gear change knobs except on earliest vehicles, whose number is on the engine side of the bulkhead.

INSIDE INFORMATION: This plate is only screwed or (usually) pop-riveted in place. The same number can also be found stamped on the chassis, on the left-hand rear spring shackle bracket on early vehicles and on the right-hand side of the chassis adjacent to the road spring front mounting on all later vehicles.

2. On all later Land Rovers, the vehicle number is stamped to a plate pop-riveted to the bulkhead on the engine side, adjacent to the brake master cylinder and just above the throttle cross-shaft.

3. Here you can see the general direction in which to look for the vehicle number on later vehicles and the position of the engine number on all vehicles except V8s. V8 engines have their engine number stamped on a cast pad on the cylinder block between numbers 3 and 5 spark plugs and behind the engine oil dipstick.

4. On all other cars, the engine number is stamped to the block at the front of the engine on the left-hand side.

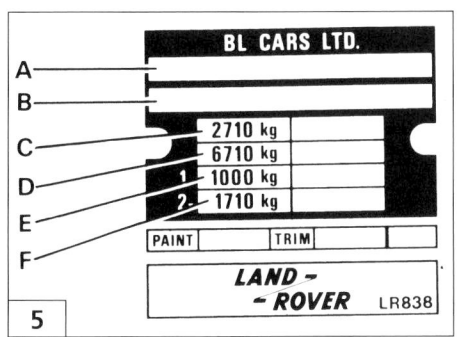

5. From 1980-on, all vehicles in the UK were fitted with a Vehicle Identification Number (VIN). Its location is similar to that for all Series III vehicles and the VIN number is also stamped to the front right-hand side of the chassis. The top number (A) is the vehicle's type approval number (not needed when ordering spares), the second number (B), with a minimum of 14 digits is the official VIN number and this is your cars formal identification number. The four rows of numbers beneath indicate successively: C. Maximum permitted laden weight; D. Maximum vehicle and trailer weight; E. Maximum road weight - front axle; F. Maximum road weight - rear axle. At the bottom of this plate is the paint code and trim colour which are of great benefit when ensuring that touch-up paint and replacement parts match the originals. (Illustration, courtesy Land Rover)

MAIN DEALERS

Always consider your local main dealership as a source of supply of spares. One benefit is that the spares obtained will be 'genuine' items and it has to be said that the only way to be totally certain of 'as new' quality and reliability is to buy Land Rover main dealer parts for your car.

In addition, the parts counter staff are likely to be more familiar than most with the vehicles, and are only too pleased to help owners identify the spares required - but you can only expect such help if you go to the trouble of taking with you all the data on your car that will be required. (The best way is by filling in the Auto-Biography page at the start of this book and taking it along with you.) Sometimes parts departments will go to the trouble of contacting other dealers, on your behalf, in search of an elusive part, and this can usually be delivered within a day or so, if located at another dealer within the same group of companies, for example.

Prices are occasionally reduced and on 'special offer' from the usual retail level - watch for special deals which are sometimes listed at the parts counter. Try to avoid Saturday mornings when buying - weekends are often very busy for parts counters, and you may find the staff have more time to help you if you visit early on a weekday morning, or in the evening, while on your way to or from work. At these times you are also less likely to have to queue for a long time! However, even with a main dealer, there may be parts that just won't be in stock when you want them. Try to find out how long they are likely to take to arrive or you could even ring around your local main dealerships, if you have a choice in your area - to find out whether the parts you need are currently held in stock.

PARTS FACTORS/MOTOR ACCESSORY SHOPS

Local parts factors and motor accessory shops can be extremely useful for obtaining servicing parts at short notice - many 'accessory' outlets open late in the evening, and on both days at weekends. Most servicing parts for the Land Rover are readily available, so, for example, requests for 'routine' items such as brake shoes, spark plugs, contact points, rocker cover gaskets, and oil filters, are unlikely to draw a blank look from the sales assistant! Some outlets supply 'original' equipment spares, but in many cases the components are 'pattern' parts. In this case, if there is a choice, opt for well-known, respected names, even if the prices are a little higher than those required for possibly dubious 'cheap import' items. This is especially important when shopping for safety-related items such as brake shoes. In this example, experience has shown that cheap brake shoes can be subject to excessive brake fade under enthusiastic driving, and in any case, they often wear rapidly.

Don't overlook the 'trade' motor factors outlets in the UK. You will find them all over the country, but look for them in Yellow Pages, since they are invariably situated in out-of-town areas, such as on trading estates.

LAND ROVER SPECIALISTS

There are a multitude of spares suppliers catering for the needs of Land Rover owners. They are particularly useful when buying components needed for restorations, but of course will also be pleased to help you with regard to servicing components. Most of the major suppliers run mail order services, and 'next day' deliveries are usually available. The spares supplied are often original specification items (this is not always the case, though, so enquire when buying), and prices are competitive. The only drawback is that you will have to pay postage and packing charges, on which V.A.T. is also levied, in addition to the cost of the spares if you're buying by mail order.

LAND ROVER SPECIALISTS

Many Land Rover specialists advertise regularly in magazines such as those published by the clubs and the highly popular Land Rover specialist and (more general) four wheel drive magazines. There are large numbers of such specialists, most of them offering a mail order service: so much so that it would also be worthwhile looking in your local Yellow Pages to see whether you have one or more such specialists in your area. In their magazine advertisements, many include lists of the parts they have on offer, and the prices they are asking. Again, watch out for special offers which can save you money. If you plan ahead, often you can buy spares at a preferable rate, keeping them 'in stock' until needed.

The overwhelming advantage of buying from a Land Rover dealer or specialist (also, see 'Clubs', below) is that a good retailer will have the best stock of parts and the most useful fund of specialised knowledge to be found anywhere.

CLUBS

There are a number of clubs catering for Land Rover owners (see Appendix 3: Specialists and Suppliers) and members can usually benefit from general spares information provided by the organisations, while the Club magazines, as well as conversations with other club members, often provide helpful pointers with regard to spares availability.

Club meetings, and the large 'jamborees' often run by the Land Rover magazines, are an excellent way of buying spares, both new and second-hand, at lower cost than normal. They're invariably enjoyable events in their own right and they can save you more money than you spend in getting there!

BUYING SECONDHAND

We would strongly advise against buying secondhand brake, suspension, and steering components, unless you know the source of the parts, and really are sure that they are in first class condition. Even then, be sure that you see the vehicle they have been taken from, and avoid any such parts from accident-damaged cars. On the other hand, it might make sense to buy, say, a distributor, or carburettor which you know to be 'low mileage' units, to replace your worn out components. Such moves can help your car run more sweetly but for less expense than buying new! In every case, ensure that the components you are buying are compatible with your particular vehicle, and carry out basic checks to ensure that they too are not badly worn. In particular, on distributors, ensure that the main spindle cannot be moved from side to side more than just perceptibly (if it can, the bearings are worn and properly setting the points gap/dwell angle and ignition timing will be impossible). With regard to carburettors, similarly check to make sure that there is minimal sideways play between the throttle spindle and the body of the unit. If there is excessive movement, the carburettor is worn, the result being air leaks and erratic running.

CHECKS ON RUNNING GEAR COMPONENTS

Always take very great care when purchasing 'hardware' for the steering, suspension and braking systems, which are obviously vital for safety.

Although many outlets sell 'reconditioned' components on an 'exchange' basis, the quality of workmanship and the extent of the work carried out on such units can vary greatly. Therefore, if buying a rebuilt unit, always check particularly carefully when buying. It has to be said that, wherever possible, reconditioned units are best obtained from main agents, or from reputable specialist suppliers. Always talk to fellow owners before buying - they may be able to direct you to a supplier offering sound parts at reasonable prices. When buying, always enquire about the terms of the guarantee (if any!).

In any event, the following notes should help you make basic checks on some of the commonly required components:

BRAKES (NEW parts ONLY): Look for boxes bearing the markings of your car's manufacturer, or one of the few top-notch brake companies such as AP Lockheed or Girling. If buying at an autojumble or car boot sale, inspect the contents of the box and reject any obviously rusty stock.

STEERING AND SUSPENSION: Again, buy new, rejecting any moisture-damaged stock if you come across 'new-old' stock at an autojumble. The major steering components are expensive to buy new but, if you buy second-hand, there's a good chance that you will buy something as worn as the ones you want to replace. (In any case, vague steering is the curse of most Land Rovers and the best way to start improving matters is to replace all of the minor components, in particular the various ball joints, as well as checking tightness of components, including spring mountings.) If you do feel that the steering box is worn, try having your main dealer or specialist adjust it first and then look for a more economical reconditioned unit.

Never buy shock absorbers second-hand. They are not too expensive when new but their condition can never be guaranteed when used and, in any case, you should always replace them in pairs; both fronts or both rears together. Much the same applies to springs which will invariably sag and soften during their working life. Do note, however, that when a Land Rover's springs are as good as new, the driver's side should be higher than the passenger side, to allow for settlement later in life.

TYRES: For the ultimate in long life, roadholding and wet grip, brand new radial tyres from a reputable manufacturer offer the best solution by far. Remoulds are available at lower initial cost, but life expectancy is not as long as with new tyres. Even low price 'budget range' tyres seem usually not to last as long as tyres with major brand names. Take advice from your tyre supplier on which tyres are expected to give most wear and remember that the cheapest in the short run may not be the cheapest over the longer term. If you use the vehicle mostly off-road, your needs will be different to those of the mainly on-road user, while there a number of manufacturers who offer what they consider to be the best compromise between on-road and off-road driving. Take advice from your Land Rover or off-road specialist in these cases, rather than your tyre supplier, since he will be more likely to have the experience you need to be able to call on.

It is true that secondhand tyres can offer an inexpensive short-term solution to keeping a car on the road, but beware. Such tyres may have serious, hidden faults. Hundreds of thousands are rumoured to be imported from the continent, from places where tyre laws are more stringent than in the U.K. However, if you purchase such covers, you are taking a risk in that you have no knowledge of the history of the tyres or what has happened to them, how they have been repaired, and so on. Our advice - very strongly given - is to stick to top quality, unused tyres from a reputable manufacturer. They may cost a little more, but at least you will have peace of mind, and should be able to rely on their performance in all road and weather situations. After all, your life - and those of other road users - could depend on it!

SAVING MONEY

Finally, if you want to buy quality and save money, you must be prepared to shop around. Ring each of your chosen suppliers with a shopping list to hand and your car's personal data from the Auto-Biography at the front of this book in front of you. Keep a written note of prices, whether the parts are proper 'brand name' parts or not and - most importantly! - whether or not the parts you want are in stock. Parts expected 'soon' have been known never to materialise. A swivel pin in the hand is worth two in the bush! (Bad pun!)

CHAPTER 3
SERVICE INTERVALS STEP-BY-STEP

Everyone wants to own a Land Rover that starts first time, runs reliably and lasts longer than the average. And there's no magic about this; it's all a question of thorough maintenance! If you follow the Service Jobs listed here - or have a garage or mechanic do it for you - you can almost *guarantee* that your Land Rover will still be going strong when others have fallen by the wayside... or the hard shoulder. Mind you, we would be among the first to acknowledge that this Service Schedule is just about as thorough as you can get; it's an amalgam of all the maker's recommended service items plus all the 'Inside Information' from the experts that we could find. If you want your Land Rover to be as well looked after as possible, you'll follow the Jobs shown here, but if you don't want to go all the way, you can pick and choose from the most essential items in the list. But do bear in mind that the Jobs we recommend are there for some very good reasons:

◆ *body maintenance* is rarely included in most service schedules. We believe it to be essential.

◆ *preventative maintenance* figures very high on our list of priorities. And that's why so many of our service jobs have the word "Check..." near the start!

◆ *older vehicles* need more jobs doing on them than new ones - it's as simple as that - so we list the jobs you will need to carry out in order to keep any vehicle, old or new, in fine fettle.

USING THE SERVICE SCHEDULES

At the start of each Service Job, you'll see a heading in bold type, looking a bit like this:

☐ **Job 34. Adjust spark plugs.**

Following the heading will be all the information you will need to enable you to carry out that particular Job. Please note that different models might have different settings. Please check *Chapter 8, Facts and Figures.* Exactly the same Job number and heading will be found in the Service History chapter, where you will want to keep a full record of all the work you have carried out. After you have finished servicing your Land Rover, you will be able to tick off all of the jobs that you have completed and so, service by service, build up a complete Service History of the work carried out.

You will also find other key information immediately after each Job title and in most cases, there will be reference to an illustration - a photograph or line drawing, whichever is easier for you to follow - usually on the same page.

If the Job shown only applies to certain vehicles, the Job title will be followed by a description of the type of vehicle to which the Job title applies. For instance, Job 18 applies to **DIESEL MODELS ONLY** - and the information in bold tells you so.

Other special headings are also used. One reads **OPTIONAL,** which means that you may wish to use your own discretion as to whether to carry out this particular Job or whether to leave it until it crops up again in a later service. Another is **INSIDE INFORMATION.** This tells you that here is a Job or a special tip that you wouldn't normally get to hear about, other than through the experience and 'inside' knowledge of the experts who have helped in compiling this Service Guide. The third is **SPECIALIST SERVICE,** which means that we recommend you to have this work carried out by a specialist. Some jobs, such as setting the tracking or headlamp alignment are best done with the right measuring equipment while other jobs may demand the use of equipment such as an exhaust gas analyser. Where we think you are better off having the work done for you, we say so!

We are grateful to Keith Gott, the Land Rover specialist in Alton, Hampshire for his kind assistance with this Chapter. Almost all of the work was photographed at his premises.

Throughout the Service Schedule, each 'shorter' Service Interval is meant to be an important part of each of the next 'longer' Service Interval, too. For instance, under *1,500 Mile Mechanical and Electrical - Around the Vehicle*, Job 20. you are instructed to check the tyres for wear or damage. This Job also has to be carried out at 3,000 miles, 6,000 miles, 9,000 miles, and so on. It is therefore shown in the list of extra Jobs to be carried out in each of these 'longer' Service Intervals but only as a Job number, without the detailed instructions that were given the first time around!

SAFETY FIRST!
The other special heading is the one that could be the most important one of all! SAFETY FIRST! information must always be read with care and always taken seriously. In addition, please read the whole of Chapter 1, Safety First! before carrying out any work on your Land Rover. There are many hazards associated with working on a motor vehicle but all of them can be avoided by adhering strictly to the safety rules. Don't skimp on safety!

The 'Catch-up' Service

When you first buy a used Land Rover, you never know for sure just how well it's been looked after. Even one with a full service history is unlikely to have been serviced as thoroughly as one with a Porter Publishing *Service Guide* history! So, if you want to catch-up on all the servicing that may have been neglected, just work through the entire list of Service Jobs listed for the *36,000 miles - or Every Thirty Six Months service*, and your Land Rover will be bang up to date and serviced as well as you could hope for. Do allow several days for all of this work, not least because it will almost certainly throw up a number of extra jobs - potential faults that have been lurking beneath the surface - all of which will need putting right before you can 'sign off' your Land Rover as being in tip-top condition.

The Service History

Those people fortunate enough to own a new Land Rover, or one that has been well maintained from new will have the opportunity to keep a service record, or 'Service History' of their vehicle, usually filled in by a main dealer. Until now, it hasn't been possible for the owner of an older vehicle to keep a formal record of servicing but now you can, using the complete tick list in *Appendix 4, Service History*. In fact, you can go one better than the owners of those new models, because your vehicle's Service History will be more complete and more detailed than any manufacturer's service record, with the extra bonus that there is space for you to keep a record of all of those extra items that crop up from time to time. New tyres; replacement exhaust; extra accessories; where can you show those on a regular service schedule? Now you can, so if your battery goes down only 11 months after buying it, you'll be able to look up where and when you bought it. All you'll have to do is remember to fill in your Service Schedule in the first place!

RAISING A LAND ROVER - SAFELY!
You will often need to raise your Land Rover off the ground in order to carry out the Service Jobs shown here. To start off with, here's what you must never do - never work beneath a vehicle held on a jack, not even a trolley jack. Quite a number of deaths have been caused by it slipping off the jack while someone has been working beneath. On the other hand, the safest way is by raising the Land Rover on a proprietary brand of ramps. Sometimes, there is no alternative but to use axle stands. Please read all of the following information and act upon it!

When using car ramps:

(**I**) Make absolutely certain that the ramps are parallel to the wheels of the vehicle and that the wheels are exactly central on each ramp. **Always** have an assistant watch both sides of the vehicle as you drive up. Drive **up to** the end 'stops' on the ramps but never over them!

Apply the hand brake firmly and put the vehicle in first or reverse gear.

(**II**) Chock **both** wheels remaining on the ground, both in front and behind so that the vehicle can't move in either direction.

INSIDE INFORMATION: Wrap a strip of carpet into a loop around the first 'rung' of the ramps and drive over the doubled-up piece of carpet on the approach to the ramps. This prevents the ramps from skidding away, as they are inclined to do, as the vehicle is driven on to them.

On other occasions, you might need to work on the Land Rover whilst it is supported on an axle stand or a pair of axle stands. These are inherently less stable than ramps and so you must take much greater care when working beneath them. In particular: ensure that the axle stand is on flat, stable ground, never on ground where one side can sink in to the ground. before using the jack, ensure that the Land Rover is on level ground and that the hand brake is off and the transmission in neutral.

Raise the Land Rover with a trolley jack - invest in one if you don't already own one; the wheel changing jack is often too unstable. Ensure that the floor is sufficiently clear and smooth for the trolley jack wheels to roll as the Land Rover is raised and lowered, otherwise it could slip off the jack.

(**III**) Jack one side of the Land Rover at a time (because the differentials aren't central). For example, at the front jack the right-hand side under the spring shackle plate - and put the axle stand under the axle tube.

(**IV**) Jack the left-hand side under the differential casing and put the axle stand under the shackle plate.

As a general rule, locate the jack under a low point on the vehicle rather than a higher point and avoid extending the jack to its full height if possible. Trolley jacks are, of necessity, quite narrow tools and they become less stable quite quickly as the lifting arm gets higher.

If, for any reason, you can't use the location points recommended here, take care to locate the top of the axle stand on a strong, level, stable part of the Land Rover's underside. A chassis member is ideal but never use the floor of the vehicle, which is just too weak.

Just as when using ramps - only even more importantly! - apply the hand brake firmly, put the Land Rover in first or reverse gear and chock both wheels remaining on the ground, both in front and behind.

Be especially careful when applying force to a spanner or when pulling hard on anything while the vehicle is supported off the ground. It is all too easy to move the vehicle so far that it topples off the axle stand or stands. And remember that if it falls on you, YOU COULD BE KILLED!

Whenever working beneath a vehicle, have someone primed to keep an eye on you! If someone pops out to see how you are getting on every quarter of an hour or so, it could be enough to save your life!

Do remember that, in general, a vehicle will be more stable when only one wheel is removed and one axle stand used than if two wheels are removed in conjunction with two axle stands. You are strongly advised not to work with all four wheels off the ground, on four axle stands. Any vehicle is very unstable and dangerous in this situation even when the ground is level and firm.

When lowering the Land Rover to the ground, remember first to remove the chocks, release the hand brake and place the transmission in neutral.

500 Miles, Weekly, or Before a Long Journey

These are the regular checks that you need to carry out to help keep your Land Rover safe and reliable. They don't include the major Service Jobs but they should be carried out as an integral part of every 'proper' service.

500 Mile Mechanical and Electrical - The Engine Bay

INSIDE INFORMATION: i) It will be convenient to lean over the Land Rover's wings for some of the Jobs in this section of each service interval. You can protect the paintwork on both wings with a soft cloth or 'bubble pack' plastic, held on with masking tape.
ii) Disconnect the bonnet steady and tie back the bonnet, giving much better access!

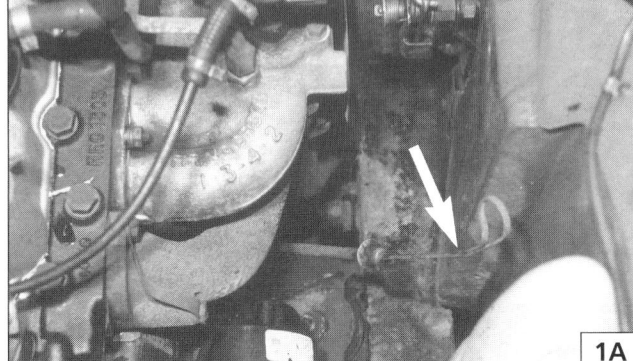

☐ **Job 1. Engine oil level.**

Check the engine's oil level with the vehicle on level ground.

1A. The oil dipstick is on the right-hand side of the engine in all Series I petrol engines and on the left hand side, as shown here, in all other petrol engines (including V8s) and all diesels.

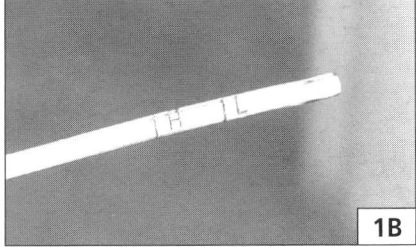

1B. The oil level should be somewhere between the H (HIGH) and L (LOW) levels. Make sure that the dipstick is pushed right back when replacing it and when dipping it to discover the oil level.

Series I, very early Series II, and six-cylinder petrol engines have their oil filler caps at the left-hand front of the engine at the top of a filler tube. On all diesels and on Series II, IIA and III four-cylinder petrol engines the oil filler is at the right-hand front of the engine, and on the V8 it is on top of the right-hand rocker cover near the front.

1C. Filler caps may be of the type shown here (arrowed), which unscrew, or the more basic twist and lift type (similar in external appearance to a radiator cap), or they may serve the dual purpose of filler cap and engine breather and look just like the breather shown next to the filler cap here - in which case they twist and lift, or simply pull off the top of the filler tube. Some engines have both a breather/filler cap and a separate breather.

Also, check the ground on which the Land Rover has been parked, for evidence of oil or other fluid leaks. (If any leaks are found, do not drive the vehicle without first establishing where the leaks have come from - they could come from a major failure in the braking system.)

☐ **Job 2. Clutch fluid level.**

NOT SERIES I VEHICLES

> *SAFETY FIRST!*
> **If clutch fluid should come into contact with the skin or eyes, rinse immediately with plenty of water.**

Series II and IIA 4-cylinder models have a combined brake and clutch fluid reservoir on the engine side of the bulkhead in front of the driving position. The level is correct when it is at the top of the inner reservoir.

2. Check/top up the clutch fluid reservoir. The six-cylinder-engine models and all Series III models have a combined reservoir and master cylinder as shown here in which the level should be about a quarter of an inch (5 to 6 mm) below the top edge of the reservoir.

INSIDE INFORMATION: i) Check the ground on which the Land Rover has been parked, especially beneath the engine bay and inside each road wheel, for evidence of oil, clutch or brake fluid leaks. If any are found, investigate further before driving the vehicle.. ii) Clutch fluid will damage painted surfaces if allowed to come into contact. Take care not to spill any, but if there is an accident, refit the master cylinder cap and wash off any accidental spillage immediately with hot soapy water.

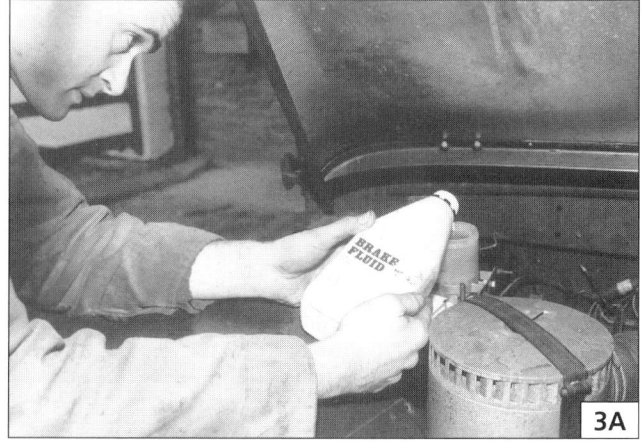

3A

Job 3. Brake fluid level.

SAFETY FIRST!

i) If brake fluid should come into contact with the skin or eyes, rinse immediately with plenty of water.

ii) The brake fluid level will fall slightly during normal use, but if it falls significantly, stop using the vehicle and seek specialist advice.

iii) If you get dirt into the hydraulic system it can cause brake failure. Wipe the filler cap clean before removing.

iv) Use only new brake fluid from an air-tight container. Old fluid will absorb moisture and this could cause the brakes to fail when carrying out an emergency stop or other heavy use of the brakes - just when you need them most and are least able to do anything about it, in fact!.

3A. On Series II and IIA, four-cylinder models there is a combined brake and clutch fluid reservoir in the location shown here.

On Series I models the brake fluid reservoir is within the seat box on the right-hand side and the reservoir should be three-quarters full.

3B

3B. 6-cylinder, V8 and all Series III 4-cylinder models have a reservoir similar to this one in which the correct level is at the bottom of the filler neck or as marked on the reservoir.

INSIDE INFORMATION i) Check the ground on which the Land Rover has been parked, especially beneath the engine bay and inside each road wheel, for evidence of oil, clutch or brake fluid leaks. If any are found, investigate further before driving the vehicle. ii) Brake fluid will damage painted surfaces if allowed to come into contact. Take care not to spill any but if there is an accident, refit the master cylinder cap and wash off any accidental spillage immediately with hot soapy water.

Job 4. Battery electrolyte.

The location of the battery or batteries varies from model to model. It may be under the bonnet, under the left-hand front seat as shown here or, in the case of diesels with two batteries, both of them under the bonnet, or one of them under the seat and the other under the bonnet.

SAFETY FIRST!

i) The gas given off by a battery is highly explosive. Never smoke, use a naked flame or allow a spark to occur in the battery compartment. Never disconnect the battery/ies (it can cause sparking) with the battery caps removed.

ii) Batteries contain sulphuric acid. If the acid comes into contact with the skin or eyes, wash immediately with copious amounts of cold water and seek medical advice.

iii) Do not check the battery levels within half an hour of the battery/ies being charged with a separate battery charger because the addition of fresh water could then cause the highly acid and corrosive electrolyte to flood out of the battery.

4. Unless the battery is a 'sealed for life' unit, remove the battery cap or caps and, with the Land Rover on level ground, check the level of the electrolyte - the fluid inside each battery cell. You often can't see it at first, so use an inspection lamp or flashlight and tap the side of the battery to make the surface of the electrolyte ripple a little, so that you can see it. The plates inside the battery should just be covered with electrolyte. If the level has fallen, top up with distilled water, NEVER with tap water! Dry off the top of the battery. If the battery terminals are obviously furred, refer to Job 89. This is the under-bonnet battery position.

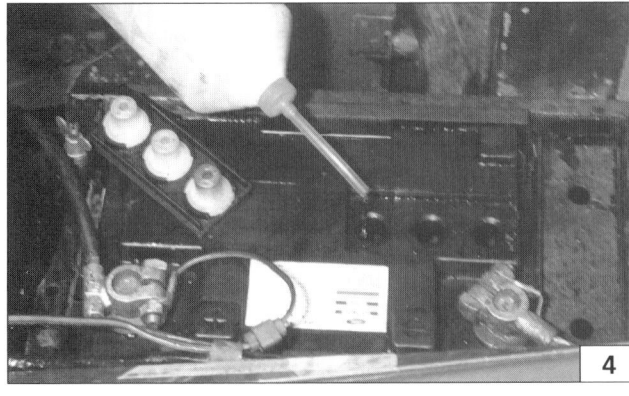

INSIDE INFORMATION i) When water is mixed with the acid inside the battery, it won't freeze. So, after topping up in extremely cold weather, run the engine (out of doors) so that you put a charge into the battery and this will mix the fresh water with the electrolyte, cutting out the risk of freezing and a cracked battery case.. ii) Here's how to check the strength, or specific gravity, of the battery electrolyte. You place the end of a hydrometer into the battery electrolyte, squeeze and release the rubber bulb so that a little of the acid is drawn up into the transparent body of the hydrometer and the float or floats inside the tube (small coloured beads are sometimes used) give the specific gravity. However, only water evaporates out of a battery, not acid, so topping up with distilled water is invariably sufficient. If a battery goes flat because it has been left standing for too long, use a small battery charger to top up the battery, following the instructions and disconnecting the battery/ies on your Land Rover first. A battery that goes flat too rapidly can be checked by a garage - they may well check the specific gravity of the electrolyte in each cell in order to establish whether one or more has failed. Some garages tell you that you need a new battery anyway, so it might be worth investing in a hydrometer and testing the cells yourself if your battery appears to have failed. Otherwise, you could try disconnecting the battery and seeing if it still goes flat. If not, suspect a wiring fault allowing the current to drain away.

☐ **Job 5. Washer reservoir.**

5. Check/top up the windscreen washer reservoir (if fitted). Remember that, in cold weather, a greater proportion of screen wash fluid provides an increased measure of frost resistance.

☐ **Job 6. Cooling system.**

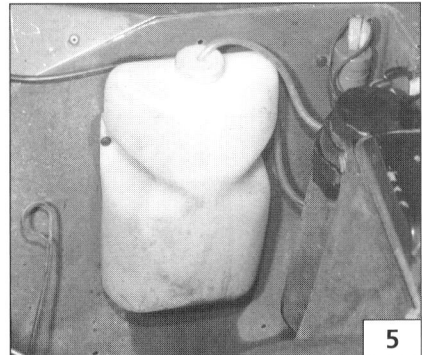

SAFETY FIRST!
i) The coolant level should be checked WHEN THE SYSTEM IS COLD. If you remove the pressure cap when the engine is hot, the release of pressure can cause the water in the cooling system to boil and spurt several feet in the air with the risk of severe scalding. ii) Take precautions to prevent anti-freeze coming in contact with the skin or eyes. If this should happen, rinse immediately with plenty of water.

6A. Top up with a mixture of 50% anti-freeze and water until the level is just beneath the filler neck on the radiator, or on V8 engine models, up to the maximum level marked on the expansion tank.

6B. Later models are fitted with an overflow bottle connected by a hose to the radiator filler neck. Ensure that there is just enough coolant in this bottle to cover the end of the hose.

Carry out a visual check on all cooling system and other hoses in and around the engine bay for leaks.

500 Mile, Mechanical and Electrical - Around the Vehicle

☐ **Job 7. Check horns.**

Try the horn button. If the horn fails to work, examine the fuse and then the wiring to the horn itself - located behind the front grille (which is attached by four screws) on Series III model vehicles.

SPECIALIST SERVICE: Horn wiring and connections are more complex than they appear at first. If there is no obvious problem with wiring connections, have the horn circuitry and switches checked over by a specialist.

☐ Job 8. Windscreen washers.

Check the operation of the windscreen washers (if fitted). If one of them fails to work, check that pipes have not come adrift and then check the jet - clear it with a pin. Some jets are adjustable by inserting a pin and twisting the jet inside its rubber housing; others are turned with a screwdriver. Also, check that the pick-up pipe and valve inside the reservoir has not become blocked or faulty.

☐ Job 9. Windscreen wipers.

Check that the wiper blades are not torn, worn or damaged in any way. Give each blade a wipe clean with methylated spirit (industrial alcohol). On most models lift the whole wiper assembly clear of the screen then a flat spring has to be lifted clear of a peg before the wiper blade assembly can be pulled clear of the arm. This is the most common type of blade assembly although other types may be encountered.

☐ Job 10. Tyre pressures.

SAFETY FIRST!
Incorrectly inflated tyres wear rapidly, can cause the vehicle's handling to become dangerous and can even cause a noticeable increase in fuel consumption.

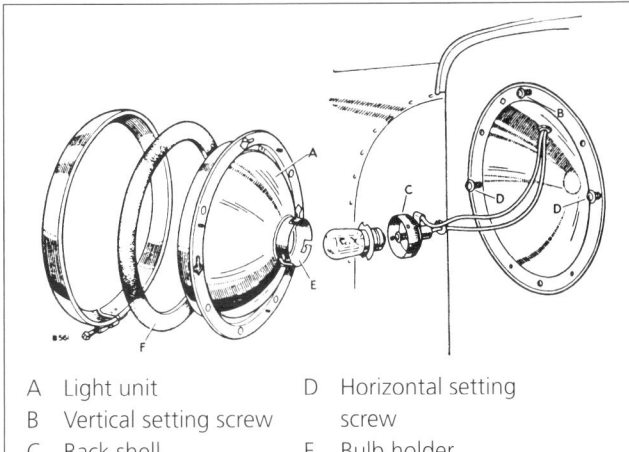

A Light unit
B Vertical setting screw
C Back shell
D Horizontal setting screw
E Bulb holder
F Dust excluder

11A

Use a reliable tyre pressure gauge to check the tyre pressures but never after driving the vehicle, which warms up the tyres considerably and increases their pressures. Check tyre pressures including the spare wheel.

☐ Job 11. Check headlamps.

SPECIALIST SERVICE: It is not possible to set headlamps accurately at home. In *Chapter 7, Getting Through The MoT*, we show how to trial-set your headlamps before going to the MoT Testing Station (in the UK) but this method is not good enough, unless you are going to have the settings checked by a garage with proper beam checking equipment.

Early Land Rovers had their headlamps mounted in the front grille panel, later models had them in the front wings. Replaceable bulb or sealed beam type headlamp units may be encountered in most versions.

11B

11A. For access to the bulb on early models, undo the screw at the bottom of the headlamp rim and lift off the rim together with the rubber seal. Turn the lamp unit anticlockwise while at the same time pushing it inwards to release it from the spring-loaded beam adjusters. Turn the back shell anticlockwise to release it, then lift out the bulb.

Where a sealed beam unit is fitted, after removing the three screws holding the headlamp rim, the unit inside will slip to the floor and break, if you're not careful! Sealed beam units just plug straight out and in again. (Illustration, courtesy Land Rover)

11B. On later models with the headlamps in the front wings, it will be necessary to remove the bezel which is attached by four screws. This is not necessary in order to adjust the lamps. The adjusting screws can be reached through two cutaways in the bezel one of which can be seen on the left of the lamp here - and see 11C.

11C. The headlamp unit is held in place by a removable outer rim which appears to be secured be several screws. In fact the screws at 9 o'clock and 12 o'clock (as indicated here) are for adjusting the direction of the beam. The remaining screws secure the rim and may need to be dosed with penetrating oil or easing fluid for a few minutes before they can be undone. Steady the headlamp unit as the rim comes away, then ease it out gently and disconnect the wiring plug (sealed beam type) or release the wiring cap and remove the bulb (replaceable bulb type).

11C

500 MILE/WEEKLY SERVICE

☐ Job 12. Check front sidelamps.

Check the front sidelamp and indicator bulbs and replace if necessary. If you have to remove a lens, clean it inside and out by washing in soapy water - it makes a big difference!

On Series I models, prise out the rim and pull the lens away from the rubber base. The bayonet type bulb is removed by pushing in slightly and twisting out. Replacing the lens can be a little tricky as the rim will be extremely reluctant to return to its seat. A little water and washing-up liquid helps promote a smooth action when persuading the rubber lip to engulf the rim edge.

12A

12A. Later models use more conventional screws. Simply release the two securing screws...

12B. ...and remove the bulb in the same fashion as described above.

Clean the sealing ring before replacing the lens and smear it lightly with a little rubber grease or a suitable type of rustproofing fluid. This will help to preserve the ring and improve its sealing capability.

INSIDE INFORMATION: If a bulb refuses to budge, try gripping with a piece of cloth - it provides a lot more grip and reduces the risk if the bulb glass breaks. If the bulb comes free of its brass ferrule, carefully break it away and push one side of the ferrule in with a screwdriver (lights/indicators turned off!). Spray releasing fluid behind the bulb base and leave for a while. Then work the base free by gripping the side that you have pushed in, with a pair of pliers.

12B

☐ Job 13. Check rear sidelamps.

13. Check/replace rear sidelamps/stop lamps and indicators and clean the lenses. On Series I models with a metal body type lamp unit, turn the complete unit anticlockwise approximately 50 degrees and lift off. On all other models, the red and amber lenses of the sidelamps/stop lamps and indicators respectively are each secured by two screws.

The bulbs are removed in the same way as for the front ones. Details of the correct bulbs for various applications are given in *Chapter 8, Facts and Figures* and if buying new bulbs locally it is worth having the old ones with you for comparison. Note that side/stop lamp bulbs have offside pegs so that they can be fitted one way round only.

13

☐ Job 14. Number plate lamps.

14A. On models with a separate number plate lamp unit, check and clean the lamp and replace the bulbs if necessary. Slacken the central screw to release the outer cover. The glass lens is likely to remain stuck to its sealing gasket - but don't let it drop off!

14B. Two bulbs (arrowed) are readily accessible once the glass lens has been removed. Other types of rear number plate lamps have either one or two screws to be undone to release the lens and give access to the bulb.

☐ Job 15. Reversing lamps.

Check the reversing lamps (if fitted), replace bulbs if necessary and clean the lenses. Also check any auxiliary lamps, such as fog lamps, that may have been fitted as original equipment or as accessories, in which case they are still supposed to function correctly, by law.

14A

14B

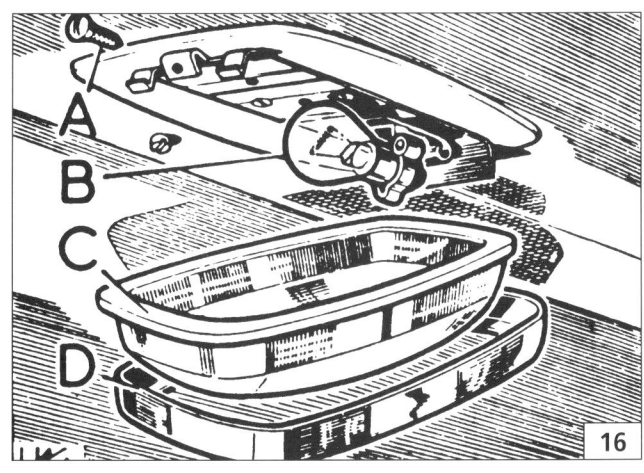

Job 16. Interior lights.

16. Check the interior light (if fitted) and replace the bulb if necessary. Various non-original lights have been fitted to Land Rovers. In the original type shown here, undoing the single screw (16.A) releases the rim and lens (16.D and C respectively) to give access to the bulb (16.B). Take care not to drop the lens when the rim is released. (Illustration, courtesy Land Rover)

500 Mile Bodywork and Interior - Around the Vehicle

Job 17. Clean bodywork.

17. Wash canvas top (if fitted), paintwork and exterior glass with water and a suitable car wash detergent, taking care not to get 'wax-wash' on the glass. Finish by washing the wheels and tyre walls. Leather the paintwork dry and then polish. Use a separate leather on the glass to avoid transferring polish from the paintwork.

LAND ROVERS WITH CANVAS TILT COVERS
Use a soft brush to remove dust and flaking dirt prior to washing. Do not use strong cleaning agents on the canvas. A mild detergent washed off with plenty of clean water should be sufficient.

INSIDE INFORMATION: If the canvas or the seams leak, buy a suitable waterproofer from your Land Rover specialist or camping specialist store. Paint it on and your interior will stay dry-ish!

1,500 Miles - or Every Month, Whichever Comes First

1,500 Mile Mechanical and Electrical - The Engine Bay

Job 18. Drain sedimenter.

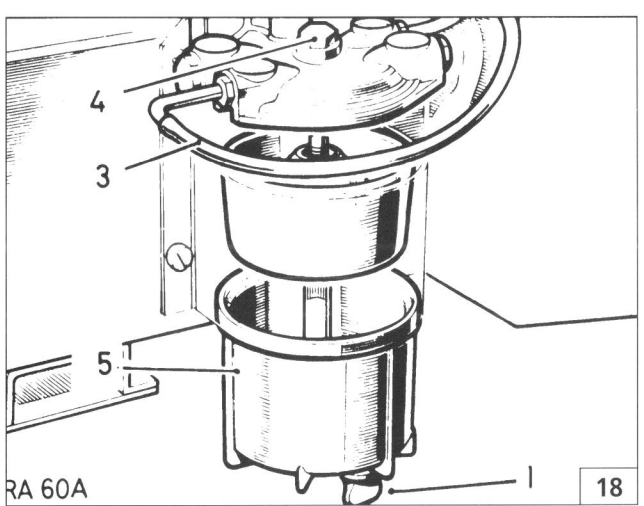

DIESEL MODELS ONLY
18. The sedimenter (where fitted) is attached to the right-hand chassis rail on later models and can be drained by slackening the drain plug (18.1) at the base of the unit. Use a container to catch the fluid which drains out. Allow water to run out but tighten the drain plug as soon as clean diesel fuel is emerging. Also shown here are the fuel pipe, lower bowl and retaining bolt (18.3, 4 and 5 respectively). (Illustration, courtesy Land Rover)

On certain Land Rovers, the sedimenter takes the form of a second fuel filter mounted alongside the main fuel filter on the engine compartment bulkhead. The procedure for draining is the same as for the chassis rail mounted unit.

Job 19. Drain fuel filter.

DIESEL MODELS ONLY

19. Diesel fuel filters are mounted either on the right-hand chassis rail, on the engine compartment bulkhead (as shown here) or on the front right-hand side of the engine. The method of draining the water accumulation is the same as described in Job 18.

1,500 Mile Mechanical and Electrical - Around the Vehicle

Job 20. Check tyres.

Check the tyres for tread depth, using a tread depth gauge and note that in the UK, the minimum legal tread depth is 1.6 mm. However, tyres are not at their safest at that level and you might want to replace them earlier. Also check both tyre walls as well as the tread of each tyre for uneven wear, cuts, bulges or other damage in the tyre walls and remove stones etc., embedded in the tread. Raise each wheel off the ground, using an axle stand, otherwise you won't be able to see the inside of each tyre properly and nor will you be able to check that part of the tyre that is in contact with the ground.

SAFETY FIRST!

Tyres that show uneven wear tell their own story, if only you know how to speak the language! If any tyre is worn more on one side than another, consult your specialist Land Rover centre or tyre specialist. It probably means that your suspension or steering is out of adjustment - probably a simple tracking job but conceivably symptomatic of suspension damage, so have it checked. If a tyre is worn more in the centre or on the edges, it could mean that your tyre pressures are wrong, but once again, have the vehicle checked.

Job 21. Check spare tyre.

Check the tread depth and the wear pattern and look for damage. Check the tyre pressure on the spare wheel and keep this at the highest recommended pressure - when you need the spare it will be easier to let some air out, if necessary, than to put some in.

Job 22. Tighten wheel nuts.

22. Check tightness of the road wheel nuts using the wheelbrace from the vehicle's toolkit (or a similar tool) and applying hand pressure only. Do not use foot pressure or additional levers to tighten the nuts as this could overstress the wheel studs. The correct torque setting is 75 to 85 lb ft (10.3 to 11.7 kg m) and it would be worth checking your handiwork with a torque wrench (but do make sure that the nuts run freely up and down each stud). Over tightening the wheel nuts could prove dangerous.

INSIDE INFORMATION: Normally - that is, in the absence of rust and corrosion - the torque required to loosen a nut is far less than that which was used to tighten it. Therefore, the only way to check whether you have tightened a nut sufficiently is NOT to undo it with a torque wrench but, instead, to undo it and then re-tighten it with the torque wrench at the required setting.

1,500 Mile Bodywork and Interior - Around the Vehicle

Job 23. Touch-up paintwork.

Treat stone chips or scratches, especially where this will prevent or eliminate rust on steel parts of the vehicle. Allow ample time for new paint to harden before applying polish.

Job 24. Aerial/antenna.

24. Clean the sections of an extending, chrome plated aerial mast. Wipe a little releasing fluid (not oil - it will hold on to dirt) onto the surface and work in and out a few times.

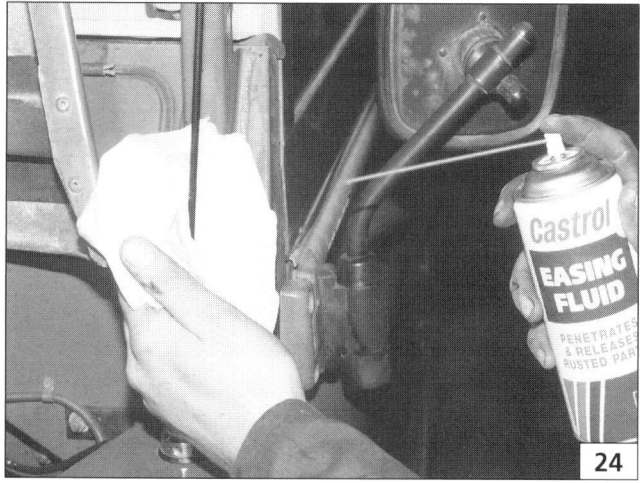

Job 25. Clean out interior.

25. Land Rovers are made to be hosed out if necessary, with no steps on the outer edges of the floors. When dry, use a vacuum cleaner to remove dust and grit from the interior trim and carpets. Those cheap 12 volt vacuum cleaners are generally a waste of money so if you can't get your domestic cleaner to the Land Rover, drive to a garage with a self-service valeting facility. Proprietary upholstery cleaners can be surprisingly effective and well worthwhile if the interior has become particularly grubby. Very bad stains, caused by grease, chocolate or unidentified flying brown stuff are best loosened with white spirit or methylated spirit before bringing on the upholstery cleaner - but first test a bit of upholstery that you can't normally see, just in case either of the spirits removes upholstery colour.

Seat belts should be washed only with warm water and a non- detergent soap. Allow them to dry naturally and do not let them retract, if they're the inertia reel type, until completely dry.

Job 26. Improve visibility!

Use a proprietary brand of windscreen cleaner to remove built-up traffic film and air-borne contaminants from the outside of the windscreen and smears from the inside. Wipe wiper blades with white spirit to remove grease and contaminants.

25

1,500 Mile Bodywork - Under the Vehicle

SAFETY FIRST!
Wear goggles when clearing the underside of the Land Rover. Read carefully the information at the start of this Chapter on lifting and supporting the vehicle.

Job 27. Clean mud traps.

Hose the underside (if particularly muddy) and allow to dry before putting the vehicle in the garage, or scrape off dry mud. Wear gloves because mud can force itself painfully behind finger nails! Note that the insides of the front wheelarches, at the rear, are among the worst areas: rust-prone steel can be found in these areas.

3,000 Miles - or Every Three Months, Whichever Comes First

3,000 Mile Mechanical and Electrical - The Engine Bay

First carry out Jobs 1 to 6, 18 and 19 as applicable

Job 28. Drain engine oil.

Warm the engine up just a little, but not so much that the oil becomes scalding hot - running the engine for just so long that it will idle off the choke (petrol engines) should do it - so that the oil becomes warm and will therefore run more freely.

SAFETY FIRST!
Refer to the section on ENGINE OILS in Chapter 1, Safety First! before carrying out the following work. Wear rubber or plastic gloves.

*Oil drain plugs are often so tight that they seem to have been fitted by a gorilla with toothache. i) Take care that the spanner does not slip causing injury to hand or head. (Use a socket or ring spanner - never an open ended spanner - with as little offset as possible, so that the spanner is near to the line of the bolt.) ii) Ensure that your spanner is positioned so that you pull **downwards,** if at all possible. iii) There is usually sufficient clearance under a Land Rover to drain the oil with the vehicle on the ground. If you do need extra clearance, refer to the information at the start of this Chapter on **Raising a Land Rover Safely!** Take great care that the effort needed to undo the drain plug does not cause the vehicle to fall on you or to slide off ramps - remember those wheel chocks!*

*INSIDE INFORMATION: Note that a 5 litre plastic oil can with one side cut out of it will make a useful container for oil drained from a differential, gearbox or transfer box but will not be big enough for draining the engine sump. Refer to **Chapter 8, Facts and Figures** to find out how large a container you will need.*

28A. Place an oil drain container in place beneath the sump with several sheets of newspaper beneath and protecting the surrounding area. Unscrew the oil drain plug with a socket or ring spanner but beware! especially if the plug is so tight that you have to use an extension on your spanner - an unsafe thing to do but something that is occasionally unavoidable.

28B. Remove the oil drain plug - watch it; it will be hot! - and drain out the oil.

28C. Allow several minutes for the oil to drain fully. Replace the plug but be certain to use a new drain plug washer, available from your accessory shop or parts specialist, otherwise you'll leave oil drips wherever you park.

IMPORTANT NOTE: If working on the V8 engine, refill the sump with fresh engine oil as described in Job 31 BEFORE removing the oil filter. If this is not done the engine oil pump may not re-prime when the engine is started.

☐ Job 29. Remove engine oil filter.

Before removing the oil filter, move the oil drain container so that it is situated beneath the oil filter. Land Rover oil filters come in two broad types: the renewable element canister type with a steel casing which is fitted to 4- and 6-cylinder engines, and the disposable type which is fitted to the V8.

If working on the V8 engine, refer to the note at the end of the previous Job before proceeding.

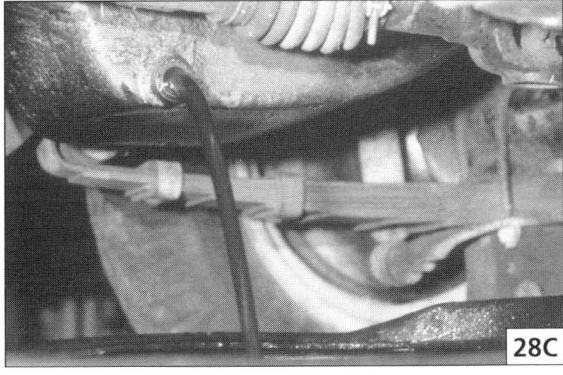

A single bolt passes through the centre of the canister type of oil filter, the bolt head being either above or below the filter casing.

29A. Release the long retaining bolt that passes through the centre of the canister type of oil filter. You may find that the steel casing will remain 'glued' to the filter housing. If so, give the casing a slight nudge but be ready to support it when it does release and be prepared for a lot of dripping oil. Lift away the assembly and pour any residual oil into the drain container. Remove the long bolt from the filter casing complete with its outer sealing washer.

29B. Lift out the filter (29B.B) and discard it safely. In the majority of cases, the rubber sealing ring (29B.C) between the casing (29B.A) and housing will remain in the housing and will need to be prised out. A point from an old school drawing compass is ideal, as is a sharpened dart point. Scrape out any hardened or glued-in sealing ring that may remain. (Illustration, courtesy Land Rover)

INSIDE INFORMATION: Disposable oil filters rarely come off by hand so a number of tools are available on the market to assist. One type is a belt wrench, but they come in other forms such as chain or three pronged finger. Most fit a 1/2 inch socket drive. It only needs a jolt to free the seal and then the filter will spin off.

A   Container
B   Element
C   Gasket

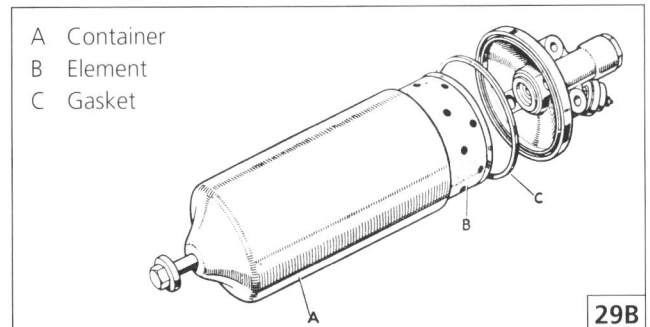

Job 30. Fit new oil filter.

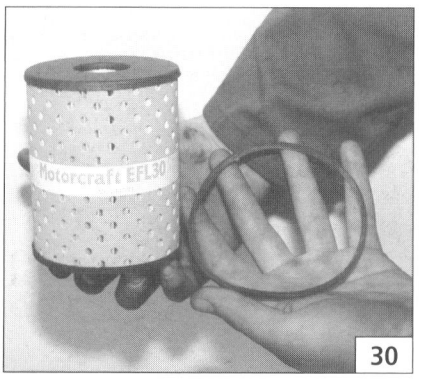

30. Here's the new canister type filter together with the new sealing ring that comes with it, ready for fitting. Thoroughly clean all components then place the new filter in the canister. Apply a little grease or engine oil to the sealing ring and place it in the lip of the housing. Grease should help the ring with the battle against gravity. Push the container against the sealing ring and make sure that the lip sits squarely before finally tightening the long centre bolt.

When fitting a disposable type of oil filter, wipe the sealing ring with a little grease or fresh engine oil. Fit the new filter using firm hand pressure only. Using the removal tool may distort the filter and render the sealing qualities useless.

Job 31. Pour fresh engine oil.

31. Pour in fresh oil but note that it's easy to overfill the rocker cover, allowing oil to run down the engine in which case it invariably gets all over the exhaust manifold with horrendous results when the engine gets hot and puts up a smokescreen! Keep checking the oil level as the oil goes in to the rocker cover so that this does not happen.

Job 32. Check oil level.

Run the engine for a minute or so and then turn it off. Check the engine oil level and top up as necessary. See Job 1 if you need to understand the dipstick markings. Also, while the engine is running, check for oil leaks, especially around the drain plug and oil filter.

Job 33. Clean oil bath air cleaner.

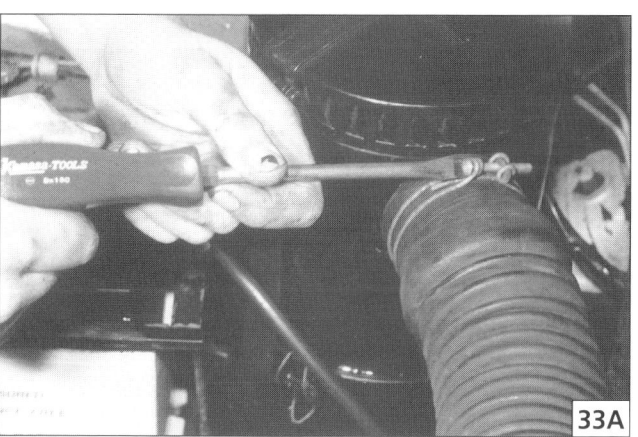

With the exception of the V8, all Land Rover engines receive their filtered intake air through an oil bath type air cleaner assembly. The obvious advantage of this system is that there are no new parts to buy when servicing is necessary and the full efficiency of the system can be restored by a routine cleaning operation.

Some Land Rover owners may wish to carry out the following procedures more frequently, particularly if the vehicle is used in very arduous conditions. The manufacturers actually state that vehicles used under dusty road or field conditions may require attention to the air cleaner daily (or even twice daily!).

33A. The design of the oil bath air cleaner is virtually unchanged since 1948, and in all cases it is retained in place by clips or by a strap and wing nut type clamp. Release the outlet hose from the side of the casing.

33B. Now slacken the wing nut or release the clips...

33C. ...and lift away the complete assembly from the engine bay.

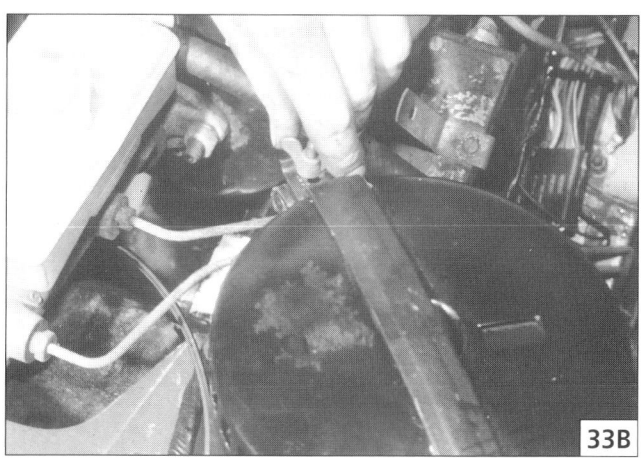

33D. Undo the wing nut and take off the top cover.

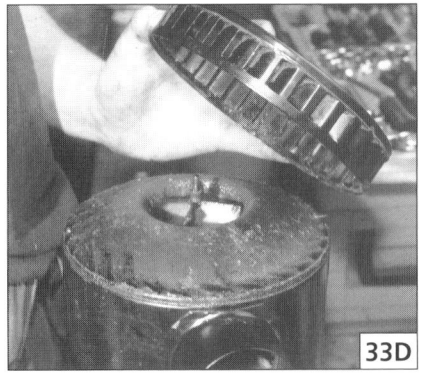

33D

33E

33E. Spring back the clips around the side of the casing and separate the upper part from the lower oil bath. Remove the wire mesh filter element, safely pour away the old oil from the oil bath and thoroughly clean all the parts. Wash the wire mesh element in paraffin and shake off any surplus. Also make sure that you remove all the sludge that will have collected in the bottom of the oil bath.

33F. Pour fresh engine oil into the oil bath until the level is up to the line indicated by a ring formed in the pressing. It will take approximately 1.5 pints (0.85 litres).

Reassemble all the parts and refit the unit in the vehicle.

33F

☐ Job 34. Adjust spark plugs.

34A. Number the spark plug HT leads to avoid confusion when refitting, then carefully pull them off the plugs. Remove the spark plugs using a proper plug socket with a rubber insert. This prevents the plug from dropping on the floor and breaking and also prevents the socket from leaning over and breaking the plug's insulator as it is unscrewed.

Check the spark plugs to ensure that they are in acceptable condition (see colour illustrations on Page 65) and also check that i) the round terminal nut is tight - tighten with pliers - and ii) the gap is correct. Clean them up with a brass bristle wire brush applied vigorously!

34A

34B. Check the gap with a feeler gauge - the end of the gauge should just go in, making contact and meeting just the smallest resistance from both sides, but without being forced in any way. Lever the longer electrode away to open the gap - but take great care not to move or damage the centre electrode or its insulation and tap the electrode on a hard surface to close it up again. If in doubt, throw the plugs away and buy new. Running with damaged or worn out plugs is false economy - although having said that, don't just change them for the sake of it. Look for evidence of electrode erosion, insulator staining, damage - or just old age.

Make sure that the threads are clean then screw the plugs back by hand. Finally tighten them to the torque setting given in *Chapter 8, Facts and Figures*. Carry out the next Job before refitting the HT leads.

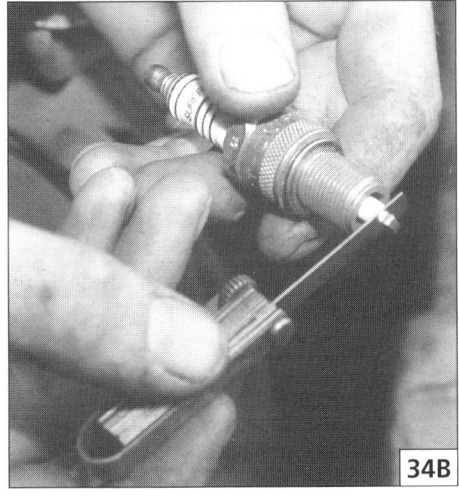

34B

Job 35. Check distributor cap and rotor arm.

35A. Check distributor cap for cracks and tracking and clean it. Tracking shows up as faint lines on the surface of the cap (inside or outside) where dampness or dirt has caused the high tension circuit to find its way to earth across the surface of the cap rather than through the appropriate HT lead and spark plug. A new distributor cap is the best solution. On this 4-cylinder engine the trunking between the air cleaner and carburettor has been removed to give easier access to the distributor.

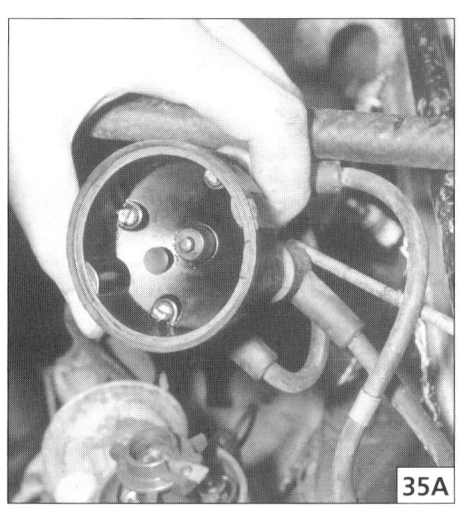

35A

35B. Check the rotor tip for burning or brightness. If it's bright, it suggests that the distributor bushes have worn out and that means that it's reconditioned distributor time - available from your Land Rover specialist. If the distributor rotor can move about, allowing its tip to brush against the contacts inside the distributor cap, the distributor's accuracy is also way out of line, which means that your Land Rover will run badly, uneconomically and may fail the emissions part of the MoT test. If this has been happening, the contacts will also be bright and you can expect to see quite a bit of brass or aluminium dust inside the distributor cap. Black dust in any quantity suggests that the top (carbon) contact has worn away - it should protrude from the centre of the cap and move in and out freely under light spring pressure.

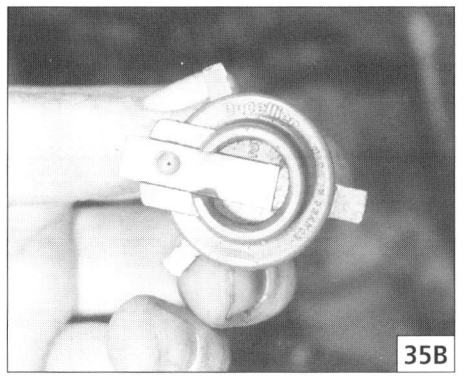

35B

Incidentally, to remove a distributor cap, try levering the tops of the retaining clips with a screwdriver, but take care that the bottom of the clip doesn't jump off the distributor body, possibly losing the clip somewhere. Try to hold it on with your other hand as the screwdriver goes to work. Leave the plug leads in place on the cap so that you can't confuse where they go. Disconnect the HT lead that comes from the coil if you want to take the cap away and into the daylight.

Job 36. Check HT circuit.

36. Check that the HT leads (those are the thick ones that connect the distributor to the spark plugs and to the coil) are clean, dry and undamaged. Check each one for signs of corrosion at the end contacts and deterioration of the insulation. If in doubt fit a new set (not just one!). Also check the low-tension lead between the distributor and the coil (the much lighter-grade cable, arrowed).

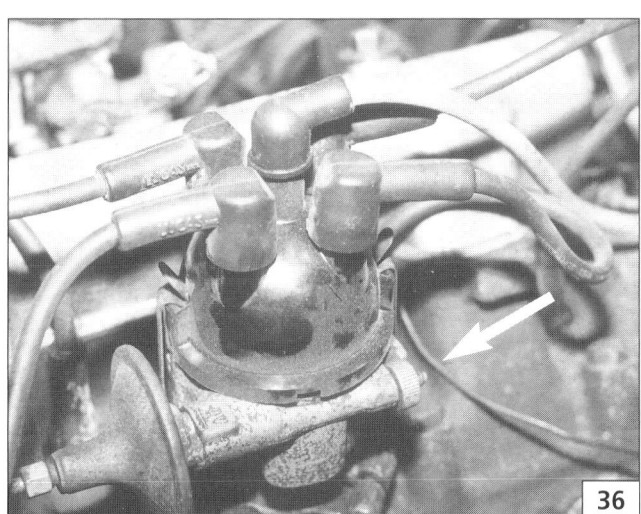

36

Job 37. Check CB points.

37A. If they haven't already been removed from the previous Jobs, remove the distributor cap and rotor arm, and on Ducellier distributors, the dust shield. You're not changing the points at this stage; that comes later in the service schedule but with the ignition turned off, use a screwdriver to open the points up and see if they are badly pitted or burned. If there is any evidence of such marks, replace the points as shown in Job 82. and replace the condenser as well because a faulty condenser will cause the points to burn.

Since the heel on the points can wear down, you'll have to adjust the points gap to compensate for this. Turn the engine over with the starting handle (transmission in neutral), which will rotate the distributor shaft cam. Stop turning when the heel on the points is at the top of the cam lobe and the points are fully open.

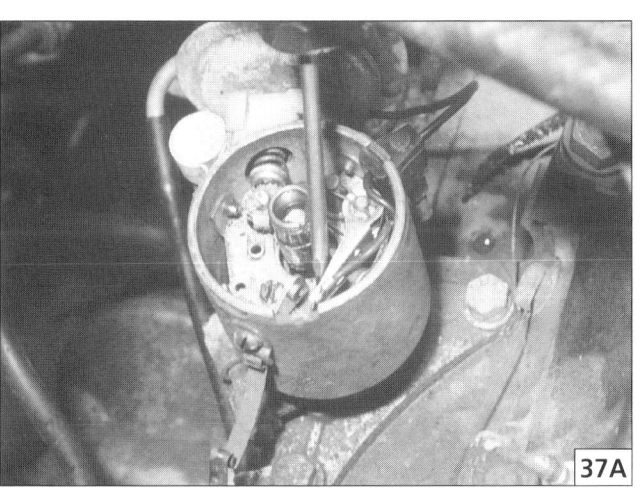

37A

37B. On early Lucas distributors, with the retaining screw (37B.B) slackened, you will be able to open and close the points gap by inserting a screwdriver between the 'V'-shape slot in the base plate and the 'V' slot in the points (37B.A). Later distributors have a peg against which to twist your screwdriver. (Illustration, courtesy Land Rover)

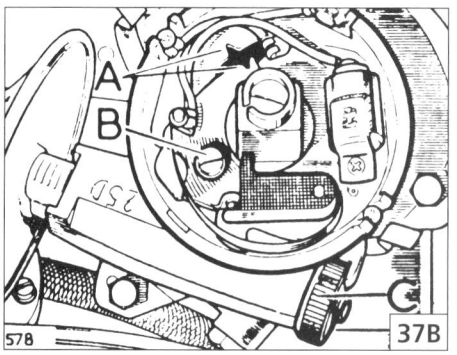

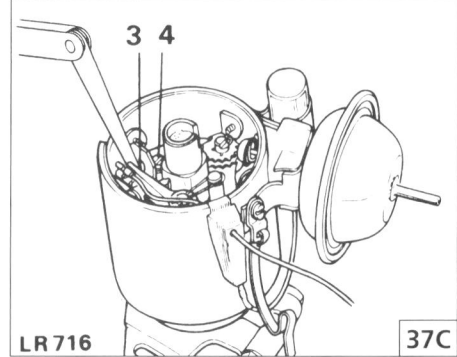

37C. The (latest) Ducellier-type distributor is best set to a 57 degree dwell angle. In an emergency, after lifting off the distributor cap, rotor arm and dust shield, set the points gap (37C.3) to 0.014 to 0.022 in. (0.35 to 0.55 mm). If necessary, slacken the screw (37C.4) which secures the adjustable contact, retightening afterwards. (Illustration, courtesy Land Rover)

37D. Here, in the 'real world', you can see a feeler gauge inserted into the points gap. Adjust the gap until the feeler gauge makes contact with both sides of the points at once - a tricky business, because it's easy to close the points up too far so that they snap shut as you pull out the feeler gauge and it's equally easy to leave them too far apart because it's difficult to discern when the feeler gauge is actually in contact. Still, you have to persevere!

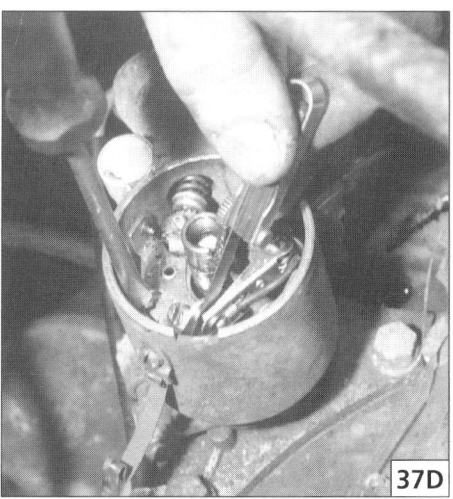

37E. The V8 distributor is on the front of the engine at the top and the points gap is particularly easy to adjust. The procedure is the same as described previously, but instead of slackening the retaining screw and moving the points by means of the 'V'-slot, you just use a spanner on the hexagonal nut sticking out of the side of the distributor body (arrowed), until the correct points gap is obtained.

37F. The most accurate way of setting the points gap on all engines is by using a dwell meter - they can be bought quite inexpensively from motor accessory stores. See the instructions with the meter for its correct use. The Gunsons Autoranger shown here is an easy-to-use multi-function meter.

Job 38. Lubricate distributor.

You should also take this opportunity to lubricate the distributor taking enormous care not to get grease or oil on to the distributor points or any other electrical components.

38A. Here you can see the lubrication areas on the later type Lucas distributor. With the rotor arm (38A.2) removed, add a few drops of oil to the felt pad (38A.5) in the top of the cam spindle (the felt pad is sometimes missing but add a few drops of oil anyway). Very lightly smear the cam (38A.4) with a small amount of grease or petroleum jelly but *do not lubricate the cam wiping pad if one is present*. If accidentally get any oil or grease onto the contact breaker points (38A.3), wipe them clean with a cloth dampened with methylated spirits. Add another three or four drops between the contact plate and the cam spindle (38A.7) so that the oil runs down into the body of the distributor beneath the base

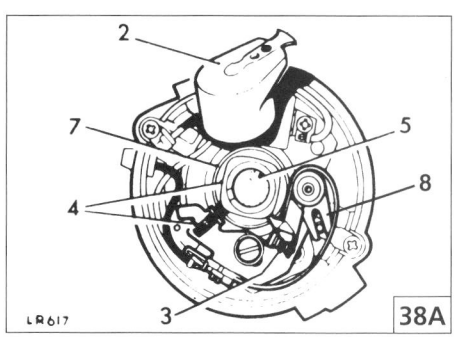

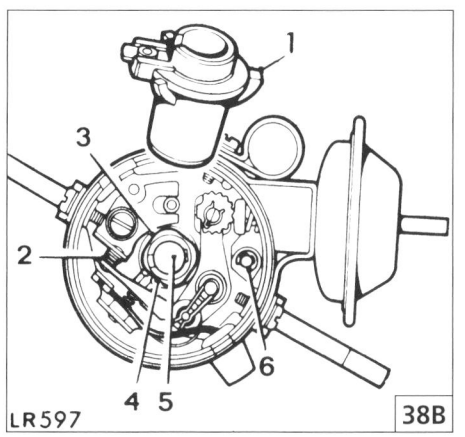

LR597 · 38B

plate. If this hasn't been done for some time, it's a good idea to use a can of releasing fluid with an injector nozzle to spray a small quantity beneath the base plate and into the body of the distributor. The centrifugal weights inside the distributor can seize and this causes the engine to lose power. Lubricate the sliding contact mechanism (38A.8). (Illustration, courtesy Land Rover)

LATER MODELS ONLY
38B. Here are the lubrication areas on the Ducellier distributor. Again with the rotor arm (38B.1) and the anti-dust cover removed, you can lubricate the felt pad (38B.5) in the top of the cam spindle. Smear the cam (38B.3) and the heel on the points arm (38B.4) with grease or petroleum jelly also making sure that no oil or grease gets onto the points (38B.2). Finally, turn the engine over until the centrifugal advance weight pivot post is visible through the cut-out in the baseplate (38B.6). Add a few drops of oil to the pivot post, then turn the engine over again until this can be repeated when the other pivot post is accessible. Refit the anti-dust cover (where applicable), the rotor arm and the distributor cap then reconnect the HT leads. (Illustration, courtesy Land Rover)

☐ Job 39. Check drive belts.

39A

Usually there is just the fan belt, unless an air pump is fitted as part of an emission control system. Belts need to be tight enough to drive pulleys without slipping, yet not so tight that they wear rapidly and cause wear in water pump and generator bearings. As a rough guide, it should be possible to move the belt in and out between pulleys around 0.25 to 0.30 in. (6 to 8 mm.) for every 10 in. (25 cm.) between pulleys.

INSIDE INFORMATION: Normally, belt tension is checked at the middle of the longest belt run between pulleys but if this part of the belt is hidden by the fan cowling (it is on many Land-Rovers) then check the bit that you can see!

39A. The generator belt should also be checked carefully for wear. If you see (or feel along its inner edge) any signs of cracking or fraying, or if the driving surfaces of the belt look polished, renew it.

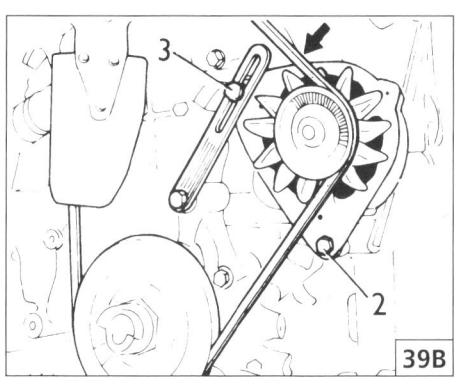

39B

39B. There are slight differences in the mountings on different models of Land Rover and slight differences between alternators and dynamos and their positions vary, but the basic principles of adjusting belts are the same. Slacken off all of the mounting bolts (39B.2) and the adjusting nut (39B.3). So that you don't cause any damage to an alternator, use a piece of wood rather than metal to lever the generator until the belt has the correct degree of tension and do not exert too much force against an aluminium generator casing - you might break it! (Illustration, courtesy Land Rover)

INSIDE INFORMATION: If you slacken off all of the bolts and nuts just far enough for the generator to move when levered, you should be able to place a socket spanner on the adjuster nut, holding it in place with one hand while you lever on the piece of wood between the generator and engine block with the other. The socket spanner should stay in place while you check the tension of the belt and then you can rapidly tighten the adjuster nut, holding the generator in place. The remaining bolts can then be tightened separately. DO NOT OVER TIGHTEN the belt because all that will do is cause the generator bearings and possibly the water pump bearing to fail prematurely and the belt will become stretched.

40

☐ Job 40. Check air pump drivebelt.

6-CYLINDER 'EMISSIONS' MODELS ONLY
40. On 6-cylinder models fitted with emission control equipment, check the condition of the air pump drivebelt in the same manner as for the generator drivebelt, described previously.

Check the adjustment of the belt at a point midway between the water pump and air pump pulleys (arrowed). There should be approximately 0.25 in. (6.3 mm) of movement at this point. If adjustment is necessary, slacken the mounting bolts (40.2) and the adjustment bolt (40.3) and move the pump to obtain the correct drivebelt tension. Tighten the adjustment bolt to hold the pump in position, then tighten the mounting bolts. (Illustration, courtesy Land Rover)

☐ Job 41. Pipes and hoses.

Carry out a visual check on all pipes and hoses, both flexible and rigid, in the engine compartment. Look for leaks, loose connections, inadequate pipe supports, chafing or other damage, corrosion of rigid pipes and deterioration of flexibles. Appropriate spanners (for unions) or screwdrivers (for Jubilee clips) will be needed to check the tightness of joints. Leaks may not be conspicuous but, eventually, even a slight seepage will leave a stain or other evidence.

☐ Job 42. Lubricate accelerator controls.

42. Check the throttle pedal for smooth operation. Lubricate the throttle linkages in the engine compartment and at the pedal inside the vehicle. If the throttle does not operate smoothly, check for worn or damaged pivot bushes, bent or distorted control rods and worn balljoint sockets. Where a cable is incorporated in the linkage, check for any fraying of the inner cable or kinks in the outer cable. Renew any parts that are found to be worn.

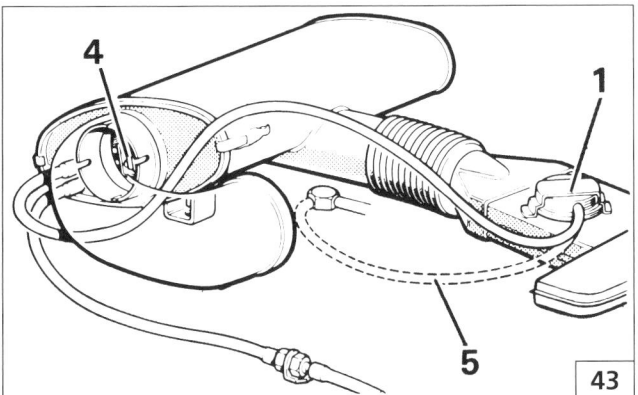

☐ Job 43. Check heated air intake valve.

V8 ENGINES ONLY.
43. Check the operation of the mixing flap valve in the air cleaner - not fitted to every vehicle. The flap is intended to divert warm air into the intake in cold weather, preventing icing-up and improving economy. If the valve does not open slowly when the engine is started from cold, connect a pipe as shown in (43.5) direct from the manifold tapping. If movement of the flap valve (43.4) can be seen, the sensor is faulty. If no movement can be seen, the vacuum capsule (43.1) is faulty. Replace faulty parts.

☐ Job 44. Set carburettors.

Land Rovers have been fitted with various carburettors since the start of production including a twin carburettor installation on V8 engined models. Balancing and tuning twin carbs is an art form and extremely time-consuming. As this installation has only been fitted to V8 engines, most of which have emission control equipment fitted as well, this is a SPECIALIST SERVICE operation, or refer to your manual.

Therefore, the two basic adjustments open to you are the idle speed and the mixture, but don't tinker with your carburettor for the sake of it - remember the old adage - if it ain't broke, don't fix it! For the most part, this is likely to be true. If the condition of your spark plugs indicates that the mixture is OK (with light grey/brown deposits with no obvious damage to the electrodes) then leave this adjustment alone.

Before touching your carburettor, you should ensure that the spark plugs, points, valve clearances and ignition timing are absolutely right and that the air cleaner oil has been changed. Always warm the engine thoroughly before tuning the carburettor.

INSIDE INFORMATION: An excellent and inexpensive tool for judging when the carburettor's mixture is set right is the Colortune, available from most motorist's stores. (See Chapter 9, Tools and Equipment). Alternatively, you can use the less accurate but traditional method described here and have your local garage, with an exhaust gas analyser, carry out fine tuning later.

SAFETY FIRST!
Carburettor adjustment has to be carried out with a warm, running engine. Watch out for rotating cooling fan and belt and do not wear loose clothing or jewellery and tie back long hair. Take care that you do not burn yourself and always work out of doors. DO NOT perform this check in your garage or any confined space - exhaust gases are dangerous and can KILL within minutes! If you're not (justifiably) confident, give the job to someone who is fully competent.

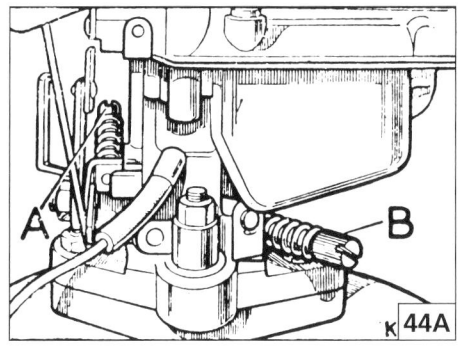

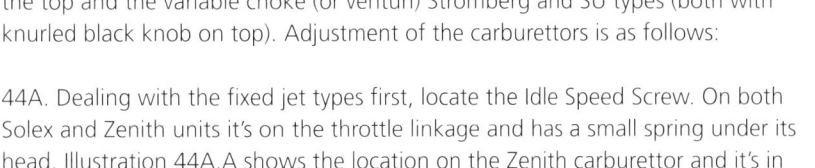

Basically there are two carburettor types fitted to Land Rovers, the fixed jet Solex and Zenith units, each with a large-bore black inlet pipe and elbow mounted on the top and the variable choke (or venturi) Stromberg and SU types (both with knurled black knob on top). Adjustment of the carburettors is as follows:

44A. Dealing with the fixed jet types first, locate the Idle Speed Screw. On both Solex and Zenith units it's on the throttle linkage and has a small spring under its head. Illustration 44A.A shows the location on the Zenith carburettor and it's in roughly the same place on the Solex. Turning it clockwise increases the idle speed, turning it anti-clockwise decreases it. Adjust the engine speed to around 500 RPM - a normal tick-over speed.

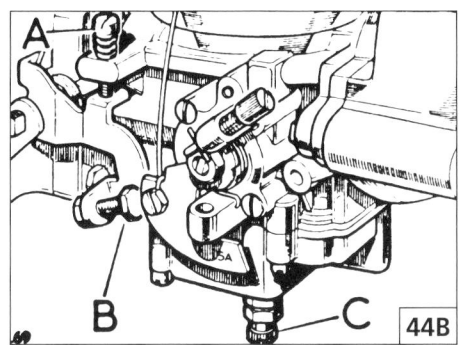

Now locate the Mixture Screw - it's on the lower part of the carburettor body and also has a spring under its head. Again, illustration 44A.B shows the Zenith location with the Solex being similar. Screw this clockwise (the screw will go in) until the engine revs start to stutter then back it off until the engine is running at its smoothest and fastest. Then, it's back to the Idle Speed Screw. Adjust it until you've got the correct tickover speed and that's the job done. (Illustration, courtesy Land Rover)

44B. Now for the variable choke carburettors, Stromberg and SU. As far as the Stromberg unit goes, we're really only concerned with pre-Series III vehicles. On later models the carburettor is 'tamperproofed' to meet emission regulations and should not be disturbed. It is possible, however, that an early carburettor may have been fitted to a later vehicle by a previous owner, so refer to Illustration 44B and see if you can find the adjustment screws A, B and C, shown. You may have some, but not all of them depending on the version of carburettor fitted.

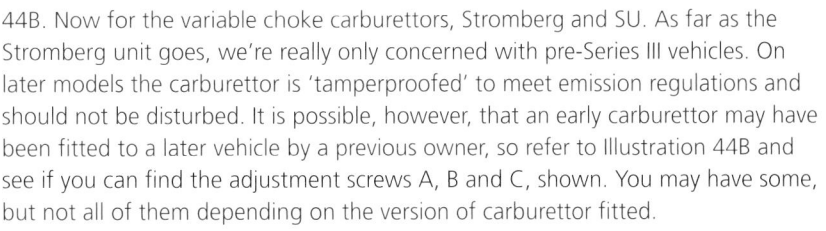

Start with the idle speed first. Turn the Idle Speed Screw (44B.A) clockwise to increase the idle speed and turn it anti-clockwise to decrease it. Set the engine speed to a standard tick-over of around 500 RPM. (Illustration, courtesy Land Rover)

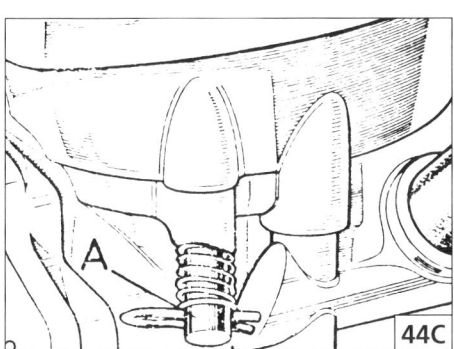

44C. Before adjusting the mixture, locate the carburettor lifting pin which protrudes downwards from under the carburettor upper body, and press this pin upwards until slight resistance is met as it contacts the piston. Now press it up a further 0.03 in (1 mm) (not all the way!) and see what happens to the engine speed as you do this. Ideally, the engine should hesitate briefly then return to even running. If it speeds up, the mixture is too rich and if the engine stops immediately, the mixture is too weak.

If the mixture is too rich, turn the Jet Adjustment Screw (mixture screw) (44B.C) at the base of the carburettor anti-clockwise, when viewed from above, to weaken the mixture. Turn the screw clockwise to enrichen it. A coin inserted in the slot in the screw makes turning it easier. Only turn the screw about half a turn at a time and try the piston lifting pin each time to see what difference the adjustment is making. When the engine runs smoothly and evenly, with very little difference when the piston lifting pin is pressed, you've got it right.

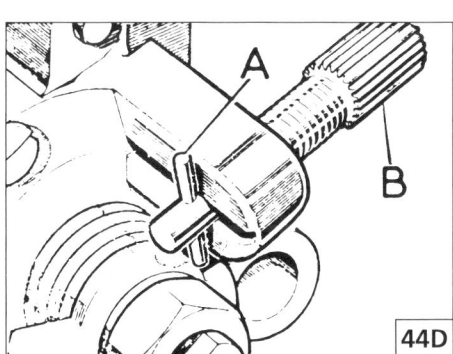

The final adjustment on the Stromberg carburettor is to do with fast idle speed and cold starting. Normally, the Fast Idle Speed Screw (44B.B) will not require adjustment, but if you find that the engine fast idle speed is too fast or too slow when starting from cold with the choke fully on, turn the screw as necessary until you feel it's about right. (Illustration, courtesy Land Rover)

44D. The choke adjustment screw has two positions according to the temperature range that the vehicle is operating in. For cold starting at temperatures down to 0°F (-18°C) push and turn the spring-loaded choke adjustment screw (44D.B) so that the peg on the screw (44D.A) is at right angles to the slot on the carburettor body, as shown in the illustration. For cold starting at temperatures below 0°F (-18°C) turn the adjustment screw so that the peg lies within the slot.

The SU carburettor fitted to Land Rovers is slightly unusual in comparison to the 'standard' SU type fitted to so many BMC/BL/Rover cars over the years. Don't go looking for the familiar jet adjusting nut underneath the carb because it isn't there on this model! This does, however, make adjustment quite easy, just by turning the adjuster screws. (Illustration, courtesy Land Rover)

44E. First adjust the idle speed by means of the Slow Running Valve. This is a spring loaded screw located just in front of the piston suction chamber. The valve components comprise a spring, washer, and gland (44E.A,B and C) which are fitted into the carburettor body (44E.D), but you'll only see the screw and spring when it comes to adjustment. Turn the screw as necessary until the idle speed is approximately 500 rpm.

The mixture is adjusted by means of the Mixture Adjustment Screw which is a small spring loaded screw next to the choke operating arm. Turn the screw a small amount at a time, in either direction until the engine speed falls and the tickover becomes rough and irregular. Now turn the screw the other way until the smoothest, fastest speed is obtained. The mixture should now be correct. If necessary re-adjust the idle speed by means of the slow running valve. (Illustration, courtesy Land Rover)

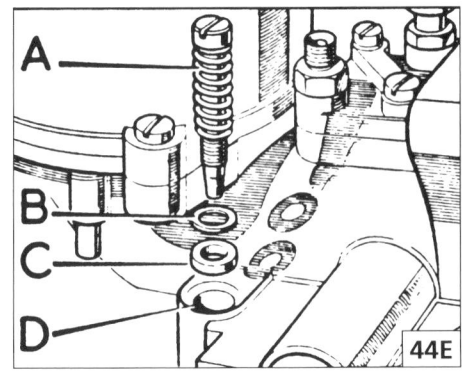

3,000 Mile Mechanical and Electrical - Around the Vehicle

First carry out Jobs 7 to 16 and 20 to 22 as applicable

☐ **Job 45. Check fuel pipes.**

SAFETY FIRST!
Before inspecting fuel pipes take all precautions against fire. No smoking, of course, and extinguish, switch off or remove to a safe distance, all naked lights or sources of flames or sparks.

INSIDE INFORMATION: Most corrosion takes place beneath the pipe clips where it cannot easily be seen. Examine carefully.

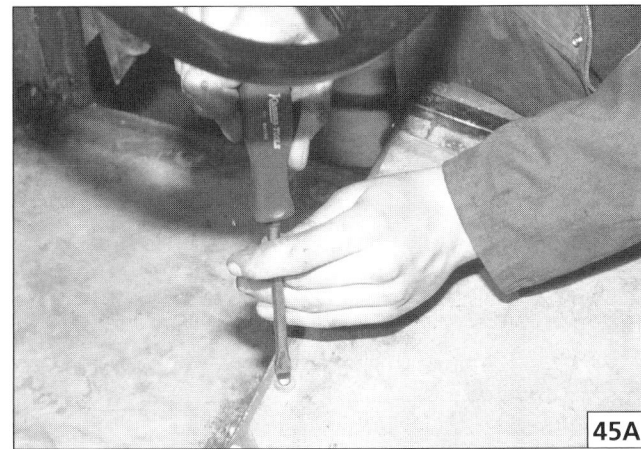

45A. On vehicles with a front-mounted fuel tank, access to the fuel pipe at the tank end calls for the removal of the cover under the driver's seat.

45B. It looks as if there is a slight seepage of fuel here where the pipe is secured to the tank - and it may not be long before it is seeping through pin-holes caused by rust on the tank! If you remake any joints, use new gaskets, where appropriate.

If the tank is mounted at the rear on your Land Rover, carry out the same checks but inspect the pipe runs carefully especially around the chassis pipe clips.

46A

Job 46. Fuel filler pipe.

Check the fuel filler pipe connections for leaks and tightness.

46A. Parts of the fuel tank filler and breather pipes can be seen behind the drivers seat on this front-mounted tank installation.

46B. This panel in the rear of the Land Rover (behind the drivers seat and secured by screws in this Series III) hides the greater part of the filler and breather pipes.

46B

Job 47. Top-up steering relay.

47. Remove the front grille for access to the steering relay. Just below the steering arm on the relay unit top cover you will see four bolts (one is arrowed here) that hold the top cover in place. Remove two of these bolts, diagonally opposite one another (see below), one to act as a filler hole, the other to act as a breather during filling. Observe the oil level by looking through one of the holes and check that it is up to the bottom of the hole. If not, add oil (see Appendix 1 for the correct oil type) through one of the holes, until the level is correct. Do this slowly allowing time for the oil to settle and for all air to escape through the other (breather) hole. Do not let an oily air bubble emerging through the breather hole give you the impression that the relay is full; it might not be. Wait for the bubble to disperse and check again, adding more oil if necessary. When the job's done, refit the two bolts and the grille.

SAFETY FIRST!
Do not, under any circumstances, remove more than two steering relay bolts at a time and be sure that they are diagonally opposite one another. The relay contains an enormously strong spring. If the top is removed or its fixing weakened, the unleashed power of this spring is quite enough to kill: this is NOT an exaggeration! If you have the slightest doubts about carrying out this work, make it SPECIALIST SERVICE: leave it to your dealer or Land Rover specialist.

47

Job 48. Front wheel alignment.

SPECIALIST SERVICE: Have the front wheel alignment checked and tested. Wheel alignment will go 'out' through regular use, causing the vehicle to become less stable, while also causing increased tyre wear. This is not work that can be carried out at home; special alignment equipment is required.

3,000 Mile Mechanical and Electrical - Under the Vehicle

SAFETY FIRST!
Raise the front of the Land Rover off the ground after reading carefully the information at the start of this chapter on lifting and supporting the vehicle.

Job 49. Check wheel hubs.

49. Check for oil leaks from the front wheel hubs. If the swivel pin housing is leaking there will be a mixture of oil and mud in the area indicated here. Unless there is severe wear of the swivel pins themselves, causing excessive free play, then any leakage is likely to be due to wear of the large oil seal around the swivel pin housing. Replacement of this is a SPECIALIST SERVICE operation.

Job 50. Top-up swivel pin housings.

50A. Each swivel pin housing has an oil level/filler plug. Clean the plug and the area around it before removing it so that dirt will not get into the housing. If any oil runs out when the plug is removed, then there's no problem - the level is correct and the plug can be refitted.

50B. If no oil runs out when the plug is removed, a plastic bottle with a thin tube for a spout makes an ideal dispenser for injecting new oil until it reaches the level of the hole. Wipe the area clean and refit the plug.

49

50A

Job 51. Steering joints.

Grease all steering joints fitted with grease nipples. Work your way systematically through the steering linkages to ensure that all have been greased. The number of grease nipples encountered varies according to the model. In general, the later the Land Rover (and the more that modern replacement parts have been fitted), the fewer the grease nipples.

51A. There are six steering joints/track rod ends in total on the steering linkages of the Land Rover, each with a rubber gaiter to protect the balljoint within from grit and dust which could quickly cause serious wear. Check that the rubber gaiters are present and undamaged. This is the steering joint directly in front of the steering relay. (Note the grease nipple at the base of this joint.)

51B. There are two steering joints at the left-hand front wheel. If the rubber boots are damaged renew the complete track rod end. In theory, you can replace the boot but it's false economy for the following reasons: i) chances are that the old track rod end will be worn because the boot has split and because of the resulting absence of lubricant, and ii) the track rod end has to be removed from the steering arm in any case. This can be such a pig of a job to carry out that you might as well get it over with and fit a relatively inexpensive, new track rod end while you're at it.

50B

51A

51B

51C. This track rod end is at the right-hand front wheel. Each track rod end comprises a balljoint attached to the track rod by a tapered shank with a threaded end for a nut. The tapered shank system gives a very positive location but it also makes the ball joint very difficult to remove. There are balljoint removal tools available from your local motorists' store and there is the traditional way of doing the job. With the latter, you hold one hammer against one side of the eye (on the end of the steering arm, fitted over the taper) and hit the other side sharply with another hammer. This deforms the eye enough to loosen it on the taper. Theoretically! In practice, you may have to use a removal tool and a pair of hammers - and to strike the eye repeatedly until a good, sharp blow shocks the joint free. You will probably cut the rubber bellows on the balljoint as you hammer, so you will probably have to renew it even if you are just dismantling for another job.

Don't forget to check the steering joints at either end of the drag link which connects the steering box to the relay unit.

INSIDE INFORMATION: Alternatively, forget about special tools, repeated heavy hammering etc. and start by placing an old kitchen bowl under the track rod end. Then pour freshly boiled water on to the end of the steering arm or track rod from which you want to remove the tapered shank. Try to direct the water on to the eye of the arm rather than the balljoint or shank. As the heat from the water expands the eye (before it reaches the taper), the taper should become loose enough to be tapped out with a hammer. SAFETY FIRST! Keep out of the way of that freshly boiled water!

Job 52. Adjust front brakes.

SAFETY FIRST! and SPECIALIST SERVICE: Obviously, a vehicle's brakes are among its most important safety related items. Do not dismantle your Land Rover's brakes unless you are fully competent to do so. If you have not been trained in this work, but wish to carry out the work described here, we strongly recommend that you have a garage or qualified mechanic check your work before using the vehicle on the road. See also the section on BRAKES AND ASBESTOS in Chapter 1, for further important information. Also read Raising a Land Rover - Safely! towards the start of this Chapter.

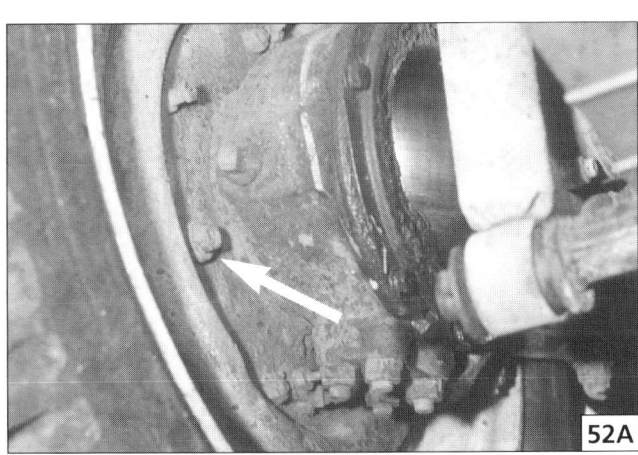

52A. Front brake adjustment is carried out by turning the hexagon shaped adjuster (arrowed in this photo) located on the brake backplate. As a general rule all SWB Land Rovers have a single brake adjuster for each front wheel and LWB models have two. There are exceptions on some models, so see how many you have before starting. If there are two adjusters, the second one will be diagonally opposite the first one. Before starting to check the brake adjustment, spray a little releasing fluid on to the back of the brake adjuster and wipe off any loose dirt. Check first of all that the wheel can be rotated by hand - it won't be all that easy because of the drag of the differential and gearbox (unless you have freewheeling hubs fitted) but it will turn freely, bearing in mind all the mechanical stuff that is having to be rotated at the same time.

First, wire brush the backplate clean. Try turning the brake adjuster in a clockwise direction (when looking at the brake back plate) until a little resistance is found. Now come out from underneath and try turning the road-wheel again. Continue turning the adjuster until the wheel is locked up and can't be turned by hand but DON'T force the adjuster. Once the wheel is locked, apply the footbrake firmly to centralise the brake shoes. Now turn the adjuster in an anti-clockwise direction until the road-wheel can just be rotated freely without any sense that the brakes are binding. If two adjusters are fitted, repeat the procedure on the second adjuster.

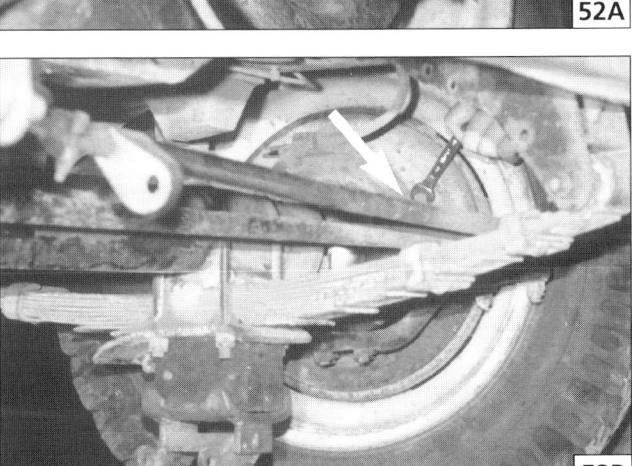

52B. Here's the rather awkward-to-get-at second front brake adjuster being tackled on a LWB model (arrowed).

Job 53. Top-up front axle oil.

You may find that with the amount of clearance under the front of the Land Rover that this Job can be carried out without raising the vehicle. If it is raised, however, ensure that it is level (raised front and rear) and observe all safety precautions.

53. You will need an axle drain plug key to remove the plug from the differential casing. The plug may be either a square headed or recessed type. Wire brush and wipe with a rag around the plug so that no dirt can drop in to the differential casing. With the plug removed, use a plastic container with a spout to inject the correct grade of oil (see Appendix 1) into the differential casing until it just starts to dribble out of the drain plug aperture. Refit the plug and wipe the differential casing.

Job 54. Grease front propshaft U/Js.

54. Lubricate the propshaft universal joints, if fitted with grease nipples, by adding 3 to 4 shots of grease from a grease gun to the nipples inside the U/Js and to the splines (arrowed).

Job 55. Check for oil leaks.

Check beneath the vehicle and especially around the oil filter and drain plug for leaks.

55A. Other common sources of leaks, usually due to failed oil seals are the areas around the transmission brake (hand brake) which will show up as drips on the transfer box casing around the drain plug and as a general wetness on the transmission brake drum.

55B. Also check the swivel pin housings for leaks around the housing oil seal.

If any leaks of this nature are found then seek SPECIALIST SERVICE from your Land Rover dealer unless you are competent to carry out major overhauls with the help of your manual.

Job 56. Check front brake pipes.

Check all front brake pipes for signs of chafing, leaks and corrosion. Unless the road wheels are removed, some of these pipes tend to be out of sight and out of mind, tucked away above the swivel joints and behind the brake back plates.

INSIDE INFORMATION i) bend each flexible hose back on itself, especially near the unions. This will show up perishing and cracking in the pipe. ii) have an assistant press hard on the brake pedal while you look out for bulges in the flexible hoses. If you see ANY signs of weakness or deterioration in any of the pipes, stop using the Land Rover until they have been replaced.

Job 57. Check clutch pipes.

Check clutch pipes for chafing, leaks and corrosion (or perishing of flexible pipe) and clutch slave cylinder for leaking fluid. This entails tracing the clutch pipe from the master cylinder across the bulkhead behind the engine - and on down to the slave cylinder, paying particular attention where there are pipe clips. Sometimes it is difficult to spot a failing clutch slave cylinder because the rubber boot is too efficient to let out escaping fluid. Peel back the boot and look for fluid leaks.

Job 58. Drain flywheel housing.

58. Remove the plug, if fitted, and drain the flywheel housing. It is advisable to fit (or refit) the plug if the Land Rover is to be used for wading in deep water.

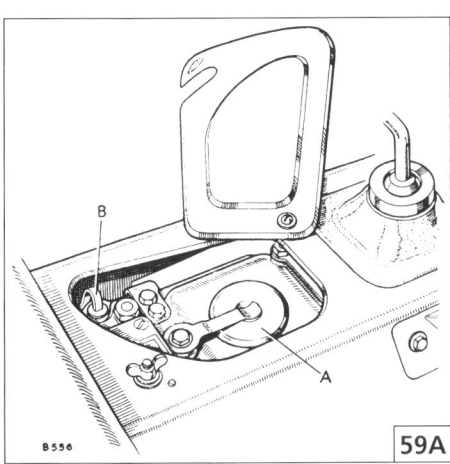

Job 59. Top-up gearbox and overdrive oil.

59A. On Series I models the gearbox can be topped-up from inside the vehicle after swinging aside the access plate on the gearbox cover. Withdraw the oil level dipstick (59A.B) and check that the level is up to the 'H' mark on the dipstick. If necessary, top-up with the oil specified in Appendix 1 through the filler plug (59A.A). (Illustration, courtesy Land Rover)

59B. On later models the dipstick is replaced by an oil level plug. The plug can be seen after removing the rubber grommet from the gearbox cover, but access to the plug is better from under the vehicle. With this arrangement, shown here, the gearbox should be filled through the filler plug until it runs out of the level plug orifice.

59C. The procedure is the same on V8 models but note the presence of a washer under the head of the filler/level plug which is accessed from beneath the vehicle. (Illustration, courtesy Land Rover)

59D. The V8 gearbox has an oil filter (59E.2) which must be removed, washed in white spirit, dried and replaced at every oil change. Once again, use a new washer beneath the plug (59E.1). (Illustration, courtesy Land Rover)

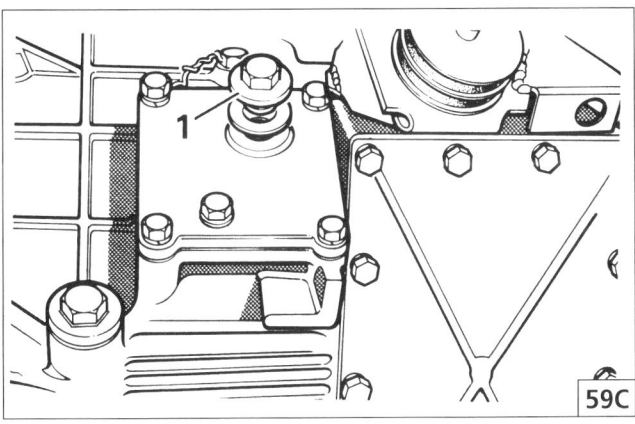

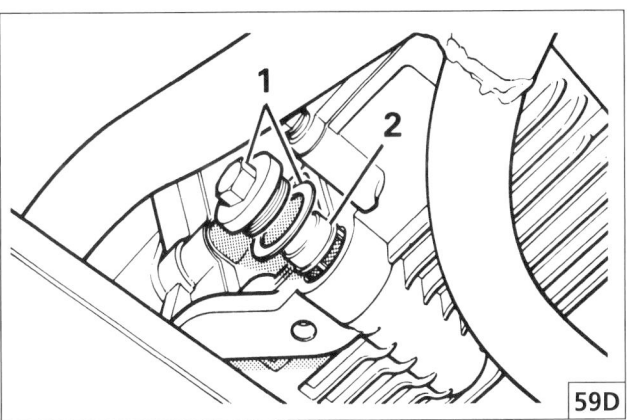

59E. VEHICLES FITTED WITH OVERDRIVE ONLY

This overdrive unit (being fitted to the back of a Series IIA gearbox) shows clearly where the level/top-up plug is situated (arrowed).

☐ Job 60. Top-up transfer box.

60A. The transfer box oil level is checked by unscrewing the level plug on the side of the casing. If oil doesn't run out when the plug is removed, topping-up is needed - but note that this isn't the topping-up plug! Leave out the level plug whilst topping-up is carried out.

60B. Remove the seat box centre panel, (or centre seat, if fitted) and add the oil specified in Appendix 1, through the filler plug until it runs out of the level plug. On all models except V8, the filler plug is 60B.A and the level plug is 60B.B. (Illustration, courtesy Land Rover)

60C. On V8 models, the filler plug (60C.3) and the level plug (60C.1) are also separate. (Illustration, courtesy Land Rover)

☐ Job 61. Adjust handbrake.

INSIDE THE VEHICLE, check the handbrake. It should be mounted securely, and it should stay in the 'on' position. The ratchet can sometimes wear, allowing the brake to slip 'off', and the release mechanism can sometimes seize inside the lever, which prevents the ratchet from holding. If undue movement of the handbrake itself is felt, it may be that the mountings are worn or damaged. If any of these faults are evident, seek advice from your Land Rover specialist.

You should also check the handbrake to see if it has to be pulled too far before it operates correctly. If the movement of the lever is excessive, adjustment is necessary.

It's not strictly necessary to raise the vehicle for this operation as the wheels don't need to be off the ground. However, the handbrake must be in the off position so make sure that the wheels are chocked both in front and behind before venturing underneath. If you need extra clearance, raise the vehicle as necessary and suitably support it.

SAFETY FIRST!
Don't work beneath a vehicle supported on axle stands with someone else sitting inside trying the hand brake. It's too risky that their movements will cause the vehicle to fall off the axle stands. Make sure that you are well clear of the raised vehicle when someone's inside it. Read carefully the information at the start of this chapter on lifting and supporting the vehicle.

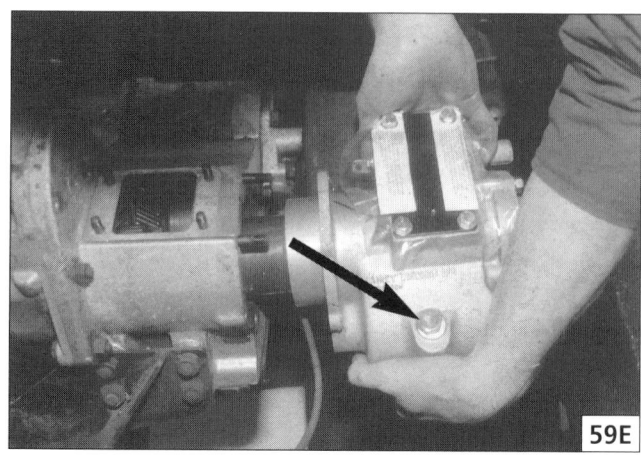

59E

60A

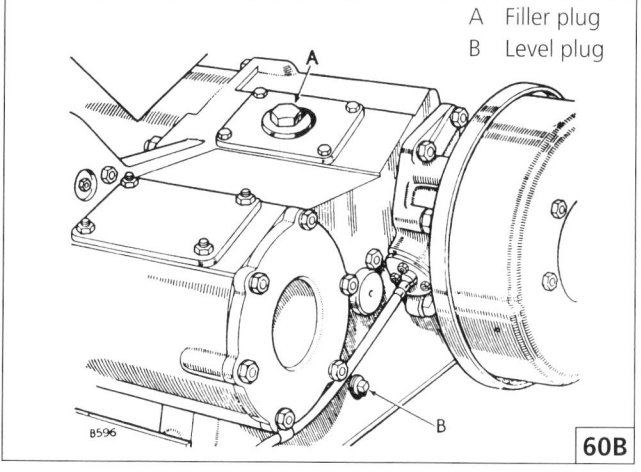

A Filler plug
B Level plug

60B

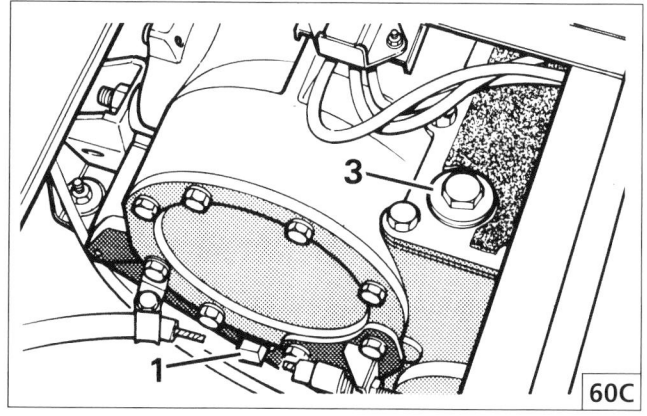

60C

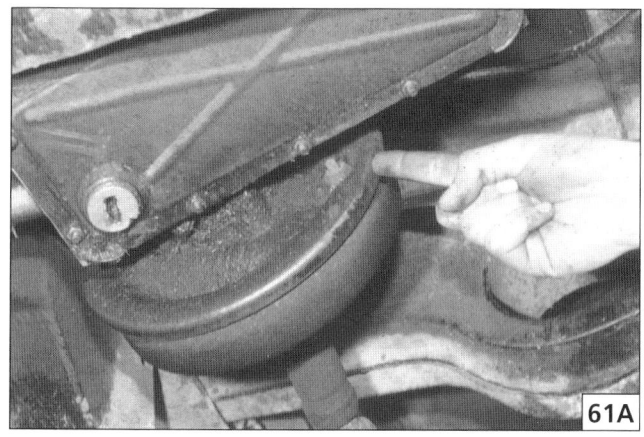

61A.

61A. The procedures for adjustment of the handbrake are the same for all models except the V8. So dealing with all except the V8s first, proceed as follows. Locate the handbrake adjuster which is on the front face of the transmission brake backplate. You will need a proper brake adjuster spanner as the adjuster is not very accessible and clearance is at a minimum.

Turn the adjuster clockwise until the transmission brake shoes are in full contact with the brake drum and the drum is locked. Now turn the adjuster anti-clockwise about two clicks until the drum is just free to rotate. Apply and release the handbrake to centralise the shoes and check the adjustment again.

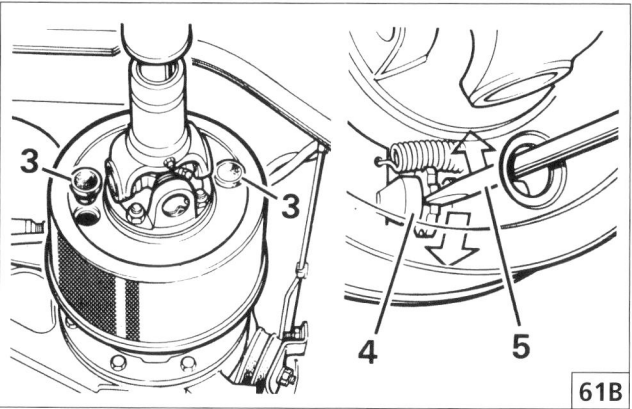

61B.

61B. On V8 models, the adjuster is inside the transmission brake drum and is accessible through two holes in the front of the drum. Remove the two rubber plugs (61B.3) from the brake drum then push the vehicle forward until the adjuster is visible through one of the holes. Using a screwdriver, engaged with the teeth of the brake adjuster wheel (61B.4) move the screwdriver up or down to rotate the adjuster until the brake shoes contact the drum and the drum is locked (61B.5). Now turn the adjuster about two clicks the other way until the drum is just free to rotate. Apply and release the handbrake to centralise the shoes and check the adjustment again. Refit the rubber plugs after adjustment. (Illustration, courtesy Land Rover)

You should also lubricate the release mechanism inside the handbrake itself to prevent the seizing mentioned earlier.

☐ Job 62. Adjust clutch pedal.

Clutch pedal adjustment is only necessary on Series I and II models. On all others the mechanism is set on assembly and should not require routine service adjustment.

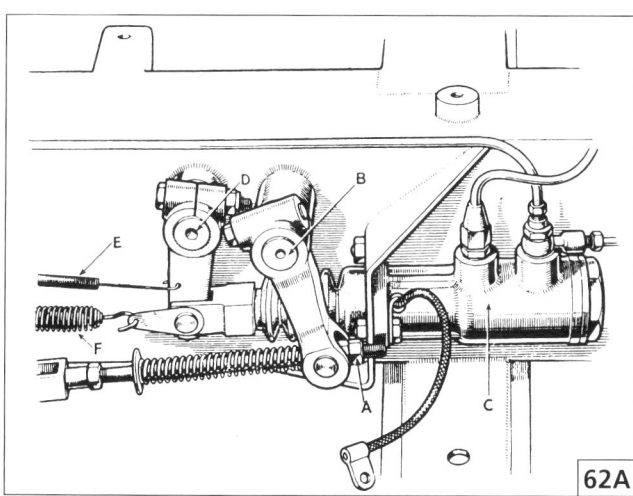

62A.

62A. On Series I models from 1948 to 1953, the clutch pedal adjustment is correct when there is approximately 0.75 in (20 mm) of free movement at the pedal before resistance is felt. If adjustment is necessary, turn the adjusting nut (62A.A) on the end of the linkage connecting rod anti-clockwise to increase the free movement, and clockwise to decrease it. The adjusting nut is machined on the face that contacts the pedal lever joint pin so that it locks in place every half a turn. Also shown in this illustration are the clutch and brake pedal shafts (62A.B and D), the brake master cylinder (62A.C) and the linkage springs (62A.E and F). (Illustration, courtesy Land Rover)

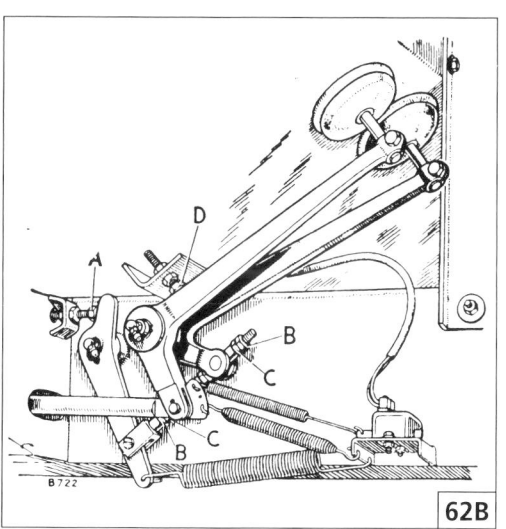

62B.

62B. On Series I models from 1954 to 1958 the adjustment is also correct when there is approximately 0.75 in (20 mm) free movement at the clutch pedal before firm resistance is felt. To increase or decrease the free movement, slacken the locknut and turn the stop bolt (62B.A) on the chassis member until the correct free play exists. Tighten the locknut. This adjustment will alter the position of the clutch pedal in relation to the brake pedal and this should now be reset. To do so, slacken the locknuts (62B.B) on the rod which connects the pedal to the clutch lever. Alter the pedal position as necessary by turning the adjusting nuts (62B.C) then tighten the locknuts when the pedal position is correct. Also shown in this illustration is the brake pedal stop bolt which does not require adjustment, and the two pedal shaft grease nipples which are the subject of the next Job. (Illustration, courtesy Land Rover)

62C. Series II Land Rovers use a hydraulic clutch arrangement with a different method of clutch adjustment. On these models the threaded push rod (62C.B) at the clutch slave cylinder can be (effectively) lengthened or shortened as required then locked by a locknut (62C.A). As with the earlier models the free movement at the pedal should be 0.75 in (20 mm) before resistance is felt. (Illustration, courtesy Land Rover)

☐ Job 63. Grease pedal shafts.

SERIES I VEHICLES

63. Grease nipples (arrowed) are fitted to the clutch and brake pedal shafts for periodic lubrication of the bushes and pivots (See 62B.). Clean around the end of each nipple and give them both a few strokes of the grease gun.

> *SAFETY FIRST!*
> **Lower the front and raise and support the rear after reading carefully the information at the start of this chapter on lifting and supporting the vehicle.**

☐ Job 64. Check rear brake pipes.

64A. Check all brake lines beneath the back end of the Land Rover for chafing, leaks and corrosion - once again, especially behind pipe clips where most corrosion takes place - and check all flexible pipes for chafing and perishing. Bend each one double to check for deterioration.

64B. Over the rear axle there should be a plate to which rubber-lined clips should be mounted. Check and replace, if necessary.

☐ Job 65. Top-up rear axle oil.

You may find that with the amount of clearance under the rear of the Land Rover that this Job can be carried out without raising the vehicle. If it is raised, however, ensure that it is level (raised front and rear) and observe all safety precautions.

Depending on the type of axle fitted, the filler plug will either be on the upper face of the differential side flange, or on the front face of the axle casing.

65. You will need an axle drain plug key to remove the filler plug. The plug may be either square or hexagon headed or of the recessed type. Wire brush and wipe with a rag around the plug so that no dirt can drop in to the differential casing. With the plug removed, use a plastic container with a spout to inject the correct grade of oil (see *Appendix 1*) until it just starts to dribble out of the drain plug aperture. Refit the plug and wipe the differential casing clean.

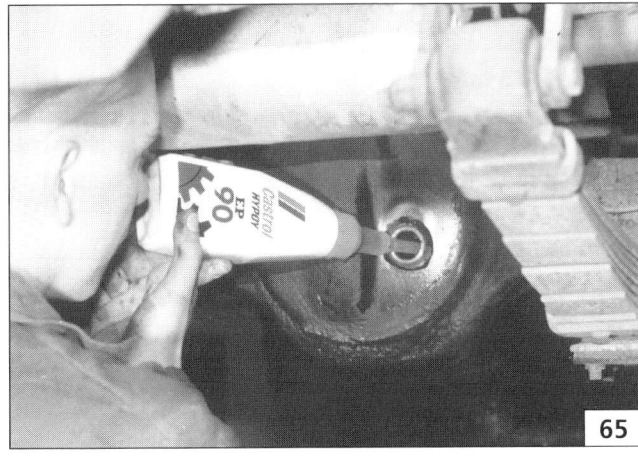

66

☐ Job 66. Grease rear propshaft U/Js.

66. Lubricate the propshaft universal joints by adding 3 to 4 shots of grease from a grease gun to the nipples inside the U/Js (if fitted).

☐ Job 67. Grease rear propshaft splines.

67. While you're doing the forward U/J, add a few shots of grease to the nipple that lubricates the propshaft sliding splines.

☐ Job 68. Adjust rear brakes.

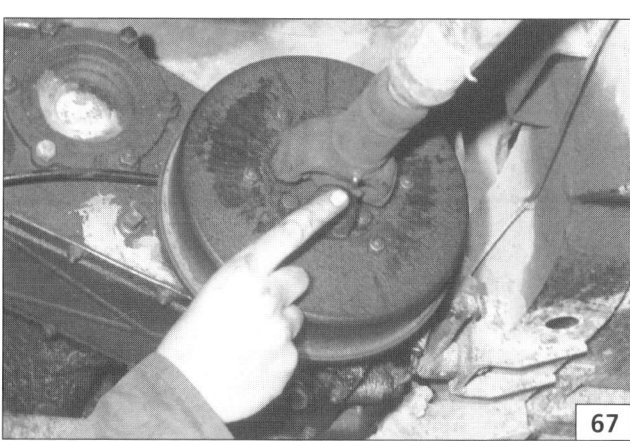

67

SAFETY FIRST! and SPECIALIST SERVICE:
Obviously, a vehicle's brakes are among its most important safety related items. Do not dismantle your Land Rover's brakes unless you are fully competent to do so. If you have not been trained in this work, but wish to carry out the work described here, we strongly recommend that you have a garage or qualified mechanic check your work before using the vehicle on the road. See also the section on BRAKES AND ASBESTOS in
Chapter 1, for further important information.

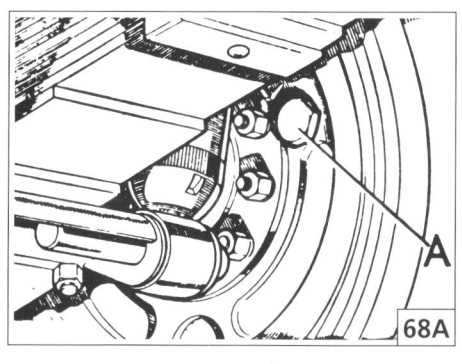

68A

68A. Rear brake adjustment is carried out by turning the hexagon (68A.A) or square shaped adjuster(s) located on the brake backplate. As a general rule, SWB Land Rovers have a single brake adjuster for each rear wheel. LWB Series I and II models also have a single adjuster for each rear wheel, while Series IIA, IIB, and III have two. There are exceptions on some models, so see how many you have before starting. If there are two adjusters, the second one will be diagonally opposite the first one. Before starting to check the brake adjustment, spray a little releasing fluid on to the back of the brake adjuster and brush and wipe off any loose dirt. Check first of all that the wheel can be rotated by hand when off the ground - it won't be all that easy because of the drag of the differential and gearbox but it will turn freely, bearing in mind all the mechanical stuff that is having to be rotated at the same time. (Illustration, courtesy Land Rover)

Try turning the brake adjuster in a clockwise direction (when looking at the brake back plate) until a little resistance is found. Now come out from underneath and try turning the road-wheel again. Continue turning the adjuster until the wheel is locked up and can't be turned by hand but DON'T force the adjuster. Once the wheel is locked, apply the footbrake firmly to centralise the brake shoes. Now turn the adjuster in an anti-clockwise direction until the road-wheel can just be rotated freely without any sense that the brakes are binding. If two adjusters are fitted, repeat the procedure on the second adjuster.

☐ Job 69. Change wheel positions.

Change the positions of the road wheels to equalise tyre wear. Land Rover's recommended swap pattern is as follows:

Recommended Swap Pattern
- Front right to rear right
- Rear right to spare
- Spare to front left
- Front left to rear left
- Rear left to front right

IMPORTANT: If your vehicle is fitted with uni-directional tyres, you will only be able to swap front and rears, maintaining the wheel positions on the same side of the vehicle. Tighten the wheel nuts securely then lower the vehicle to the ground.

3,000 mile Mechanical and Electrical - Road Test

☐ Job 70. Clean controls.

Clean the door handles, controls and steering wheel, which may well have become greasy from your hands while you were carrying out the rest of the service work on your Land Rover. Start up the engine while you are sitting in the driver's seat.

☐ Job 71. Check instrumentation.

Before pulling away, and with the engine running, check the correct function of all instruments and switches. Ensure that all warning light bulbs are working but that the lights are not remaining On when they should be Off. Check that instrument illumination is working.

> **SAFETY FIRST!**
> *If it is necessary to unscrew an instrument panel to change bulbs etc., start by disconnecting the battery. This will eliminate any risk of causing a short circuit and damaging wiring and electrical parts.*

71A. On early models with this type of instrument panel the (red) charging, (green) oil pressure and (amber) heater plug or choke warning light bulbs can be changed by unscrewing the lamp bezels from the front of the panel. To change the other warning light bulbs or instrument illumination bulbs the panel itself has to be unscrewed from the dashboard.

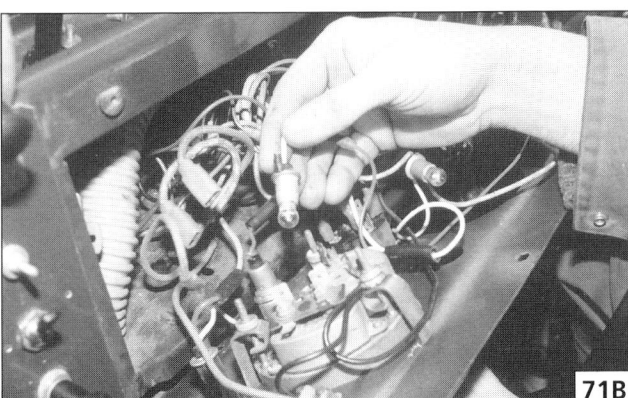

71B. Bulb holders are a friction fit: they pull out. Bulbs are a bayonet fit into the bulb holders.

71C. To change warning light bulbs in this type of panel, the single screw at each end of the panel should be undone. To enable the panel to be lifted sufficiently to allow access to the bulbs, the speedometer cable may need to be released from its securing clip (in engine compartment or behind dash depending on model).

☐ Job 72. Throttle pedal.

Check the throttle pedal for smooth operation. If the throttle does not operate smoothly, turn off the engine and check the linkage for wear or damage, and check the cable (where fitted) for a cracked or broken casing, kinks in the casing, or fraying at the cable ends, especially where the ends of the cable 'disappear' into the cable 'outer'. If you find any of these faults, repair or replace as necessary.

☐ Job 73. Hand brake function.

Check the function of hand brake as described under Job 61, but this time, add a further check. Park the vehicle on a steep slope and ensure that the handbrake 'holds' (gearbox in neutral). If it doesn't, you've got a big problem: either the mechanism has seized - usually the adjuster mechanism, inside the drum - or the brake shoes have become oiled - seek SPECIALIST SERVICE. Whatever you do, DON'T check the handbrake whilst the vehicle is on the move. The nature of the brake - on the transmission - is such that the transmission or drivetrain can thus be damaged.

☐ **Job 74. Brakes and steering.**

SAFETY FIRST!
Only carry out the following tests in daylight, in clear dry conditions when there are no other road users about and no pedestrians. Use your mirrors and make sure that there is no traffic following you when carrying out the following brake tests.

Only a proper brake tester at an MoT testing station will be able to check the operation of the brakes accurately enough for the MoT test, but you can rule out some of the most obvious braking problems in the following way. Drive along a clear stretch of road and, gripping the steering wheel fairly lightly between the thumb and fingers of each hand, brake gently from a speed of about 40 mph. Ideally, the vehicle should pull up in a dead straight line without pulling to one side or the other. If it pulls to the left (when being driven on the left-hand side of the road) or to the right (when being driven on the right-hand side of the road, such as in North America), it might be that there is no problem with your brakes, but that the camber on the road is causing the vehicle to pull over. If you can find a stretch of road with no camber whatsoever, you may be able to try the brake test again or failing that, find a one-way street where you can drive on the "wrong" side of the road and see if the pulling to one side happens in the opposite direction. If it does not, then you've got a problem with your brakes. Before assuming the worst, check your tyre pressures and try switching the wheels and tyres from front to rear. If the problem doesn't go away, seek SPECIALIST SERVICE.

The second test is to ensure that the self-centering effect of the steering works correctly. If the steering stiffens up over a period of time, you can easily get used to it so that you don't notice that it doesn't operate as it should. After going round a sharp bend, the steering should tend to move back to the straight-ahead position all by itself without having to be positively steered back again by the driver. This is because the swivel pins are set slightly ahead of the centre line of the wheels so that the front wheels behave rather like those on a supermarket trolley - or at least those few that work properly! If the swivel pins have become stiff internally or the steering box or relay box are lacking in lubricant, the steering will be stiff and no self-centering will be evident. Whichever the case, you've got a problem with the steering and should seek a little more of that SPECIALIST SERVICE, unless you're experienced enough to feel capable of diagnosing an rectifying these problems yourself, using your workshop manual.

Now, if you're ready to begin the road test proper, you can check the function of the brakes and the self-centering effect of the steering.

3,000 Mile Bodywork and Interior - Around the Vehicle

First carry out Jobs 17 and 23 to 26 as applicable

☐ **Job 75. Wiper blades and arms.**

Check the operation of the windscreen wipers and correct position of 'sweep'. The wiper arms push onto the splines but on early models are additionally held in place by a fixing nut. Fold back the arm, grasp in near the splines and pull off with a slight rocking movement. Put on a smear of grease before refitting to prevent seizing up.

☐ **Job 76. Check windscreen seals.**

Find and eliminate sources of water leaks before the situation becomes serious and rust begins to occur. Look at the windscreen seals and door seals and also look for - and hope you don't find rust in steel bulkheads. Leaks are best found with the inside of the Land Rover dry: have someone play a hose whilst you go leak hunting.

☐ **Job 77. Check windscreen.**

77. Check the windscreen for chips, cracks or other damage - see *Chapter 7, Getting Through the MoT* for what is and is not acceptable according to UK regulations.

☐ Job 78. Check mirrors.

78. Check your rear view mirrors, both inside and outside the car, for security, cracks and crazing. Also ensure that the interior rear view mirror is soundly fixed in place since they can come loose and when they do, the vibration can get so bad that you can't tell whether you're being followed by a long distance truck or one of the boys in blue!

INSIDE INFORMATION: Exterior mirrors often take a pounding from low-flying shrubbery: check mountings and renew if the spring-back mechanism has become sloppy.

3,000 Mile Bodywork - Under the Vehicle

First carry out Job 27

SAFETY FIRST!
Only raise the vehicle off the ground after reading carefully the information at the start of this chapter on lifting and supporting the vehicle.

☐ Job 79. Inspect underside.

79. When dry, scrape off mud and inspect the underside of the vehicle for rust and damage. Renew paint, underbody sealant

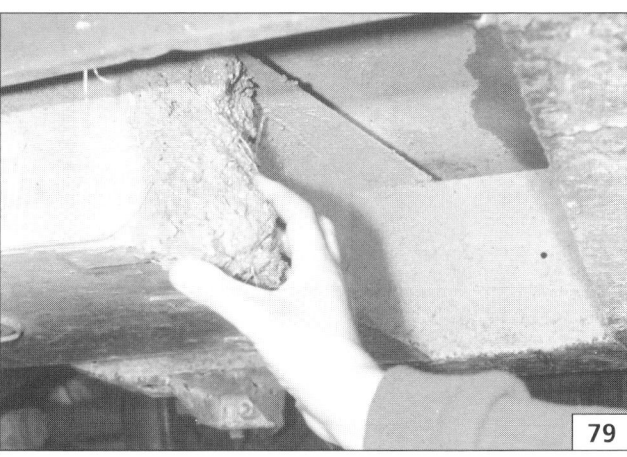

and wax coating locally as necessary. Look for loose underbody sealant in particular, especially that of the old-fashioned bitumen type. It goes brittle and comes loose, allowing water to get behind it and form a breeding ground for corrosion. Scrape off any such loose sealant and paint on wax coating in its place, when dry.

6,000 Miles - or Every Six Months, Whichever Comes First

6,000 Mile Mechanical and Electrical - The Engine Bay

First carry out Jobs 1 to 6, 18, 19 and 28 to 44 as applicable

☐ Job 80. Clean engine breather filters.

80A. Remove the breather filter on top of the rocker cover and additionally, remove the oil filler cap if it is the type incorporating a wire mesh filter - remove the retainer screw and keep the rubber 'O' ring safe - and clean them thoroughly in paraffin. Shake them dry and apply fresh engine oil to the wire mesh element. Shake off the surplus oil and refit the breathers to the engine.

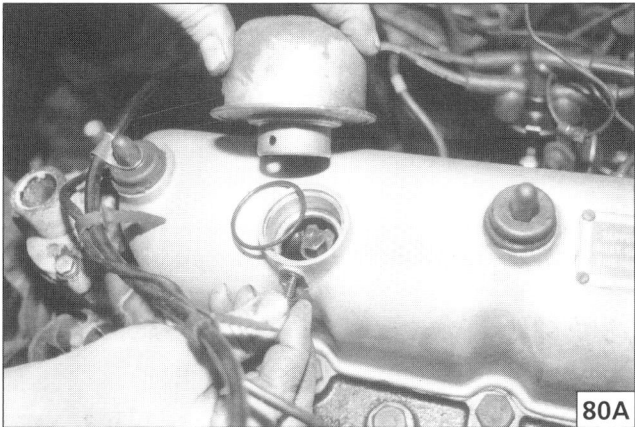

80B. On V8 engined models, remove the air cleaner (See Job 124) for access to the breather filter. Disconnect the rear breather hose (80B.2), slacken the retaining screw (80B.3) and withdraw the breather (80B.4) from the securing strap and front hose. Fit a new filter, reconnect the hoses and refit the air cleaner. (Illustration, courtesy Land Rover)

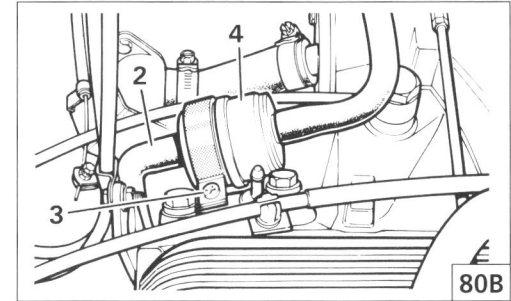

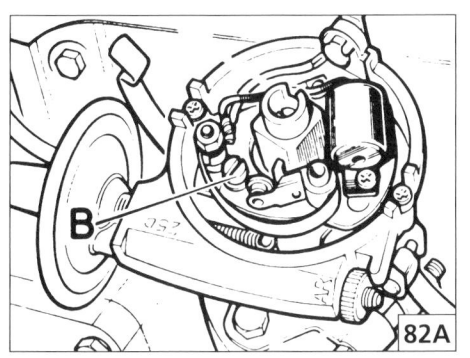

Job 81. Renew spark plugs.

OPTIONAL

Fit new spark plugs, with correct gaps. Some leave spark plugs in place for longer, but there is always the risk that the insulation will break down and lower the performance of the plug even though it may appear perfect in every other way. Never leave them in place for longer than 12,000 miles, even with regular cleaning and adjustment as described elsewhere in the schedule.

When fitting new spark plugs, ensure that the threads in the cylinder head are free enough for you to screw the plugs in as far as their seats - engine cold - by hand. If there are any obstructions, have your Land Rover dealer chase out the threads with a proper spark plug thread chasing tool. This is especially important with the V8 engine's aluminium heads. Take GREAT CARE not to fit spark plugs cross-threaded to these engines.

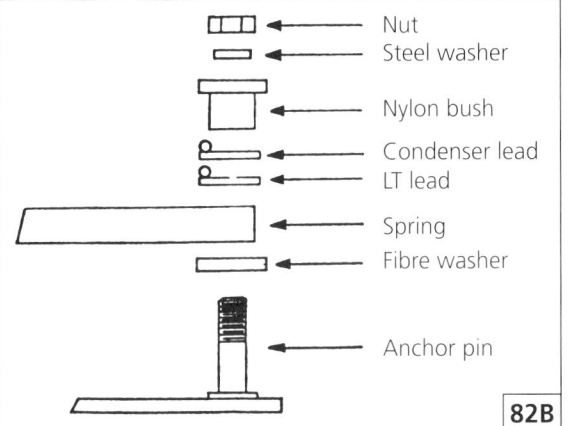

Nut	
Steel washer	
Nylon bush	
Condenser lead	
LT lead	
Spring	
Fibre washer	
Anchor pin	

Job 82. Renew CB points.

As contact breaker points are used they invariably deteriorate causing a steady and indiscernible drop off in performance. They're such inexpensive items that it is best to renew them at 6,000 miles although not necessarily at six months since it is purely use that causes them to deteriorate.

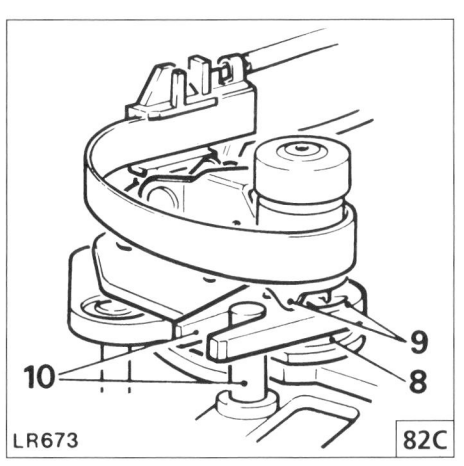

82A. With the distributor cap and rotor arm removed, this is the arrangement of components in the Lucas distributor that you are likely to encounter on all petrol engined Land Rovers up to the mid-70s. Unscrew the small terminal nut (and washer, if fitted) and lift off the upper nylon insulator followed by the two wires. Unscrew the points fixing screw (82A.B), taking great care not to drop the screw or the washer inside the distributor, and remove the points. They will either be a one-piece set in which case they can be lifted straight out, or they may be in two parts. If so, lift the moving point off the pivot post (noting the fibre washer underneath, if fitted) followed by the fixed point base.

Another inexpensive item and one that is well worth fitting every time points are renewed is the condenser. Note that the fixing screw that holds the condenser in place is even smaller and easier to lose than the one for fixing the points in place.

Position the new points assembly on the baseplate (making sure that the fibre washer goes under the moving point on the pivot post, if fitting the two-piece type points) and secure with the fixing screw. If you're fitting a new condenser, secure that in place now as well. (Illustration, courtesy Land Rover)

82B. The only tricky part about replacing the points on these distributors earlier is making sure you get the two wires and the nylon insulators in the right place. Follow the order shown here. Tighten the nut securely, but not so much as to deform the nylon insulator. Now, with the new points in place, adjust the points gap as described in Job. 37.

On later Lucas distributors the procedure is even simpler because the two electrical wires are joined together at a connector strap which engages with the hooked end of the moving point spring arm. Just slip the wires out of their location, undo the points fixing screw and remove the points. Make sure that the moving point spring arm sits squarely in its insulator when refitting. This is also the arrangement used on the V8 distributor.

82C. A further modification to the Lucas distributor introduced in the '70's was this sliding contact arrangement intended to reduce wear on the contact point faces. All you need to be aware of when replacing points, is that the fork arm engages over the peg (82C.10). Apart from that the procedure is as just described. (Illustration, courtesy Land Rover)

82D. The Ducellier distributor: To remove the points, first disconnect the low tension lead at its terminal and pull the condenser lead (82D.6) out of the connector block (82D.9). Then, with a screwdriver or long nose pliers, slide back the circlip (82D.5) and remove the washer (82D.8). Release the spring arm (82D.11) from the insulator and lift away the moving contact complete with wiring and connector block from the pivot post (82D.10). A single screw (82D.4) with its vulnerable washer retain the adjustable contact breaker plate to the base plate. Taking great care not to drop the screw and washer, lift the plate away. Once you see how it all comes apart, it's easy to put the new points back together again. Changing the condenser couldn't be easier either. A single screw holds it in its external position and the wire is a straightforward push connecter. Adjustment of the points gap is given in Job 37. (Illustration, courtesy Land Rover)

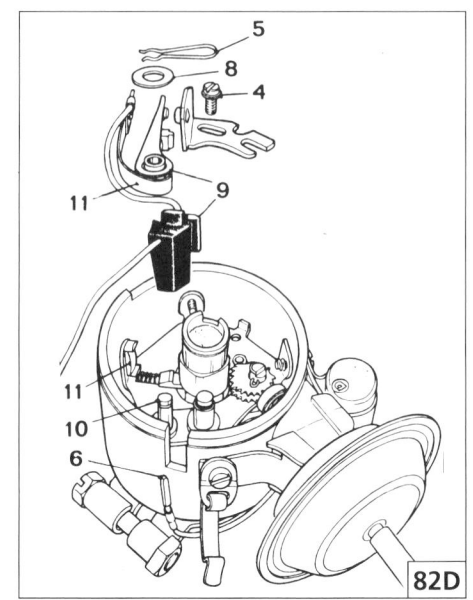

☐ Job 83. Adjust valve clearances.

NOT V8 MODELS

Note that the V8 engines have hydraulic tappets and no adjustment is necessary or possible. The following adjustments apply to 4- and 6-cylinder engines only.

Adjust the valve clearances with the engine cold. On petrol engine models it is best to remove the spark plugs when carrying out this work since the engine will have to be turned over several times. Fortunately, most Land Rovers have a starting handle which makes turning the engine over relatively easy but alternatively, (in the case of petrol engines) turn the engine by turning the fan by hand while pressing on the fan belt, gearbox in neutral (take care not to trap your hands in the pulleys).

INSIDE INFORMATION: Valve clearances are checked and adjusted when each valve is in the fully closed position. On the Land Rover the best way to do this is to turn the engine over until the valve being checked is fully open. Now turn the crankshaft/starting handle one complete turn, which will place the valve in the fully closed position on the heel of its respective camshaft lobe ready for checking and adjustment. The valve clearances vary according to engine type so check **Chapter 8, Facts and Figures** *for the correct clearances for your model before starting.*

Depending on which model of Land Rover you're working on, you will be dealing with a conventional overhead valve arrangement or a slightly less conventional Land Rover peculiarity, the overhead inlet valve and side exhaust valve arrangement.

83A. Starting with the overhead valve engines first, remove the rocker cover, secured by nuts or bolts that pass through grommets, and lift away. Again depending on model, you may need to remove the air cleaner ducting first for clearance.

83B. Begin with Number 1 valve at the front of the engine and check the clearance using a feeler gauge inserted between the valve stem and rocker arm. If the clearance is correct, the feeler gauge should be a tight sliding fit. If it isn't undo the locknut, which allows the centre screw to be moved in and out, changing the valve clearance. When it's right, tighten the locknut as the screw is held tight. You will probably find that the last turn of the locknut also tightens the screw further, no matter how hard you hold the screwdriver. Try edging the gap open a touch to allow for the fact but check with a feeler gauge when the locknut is tight

to ensure that the gap is correct. Now rotate the engine until the next valve is ready for checking and repeat the procedure until they are all adjusted. *Be sure to follow the INSIDE INFORMATION above on ensuring that each valve is in the fully closed position.*

83C. On 4-cylinder overhead inlet valve, side exhaust valve engines the procedure is similar to that previously described except that it will also be necessary to remove the tappet side covers for access to the exhaust valves. With the valve to be

checked fully closed, insert the feeler blade and adjust the clearance by means of the adjusting screw and retighten the locknut. Be sure to follow the INSIDE INFORMATION above on ensuring that each valve is in the fully closed position.

INSIDE INFORMATION: Some mechanics prefer to remove carburettor and manifold so that they can, at least, see what they are doing!

On 6-cylinder overhead inlet valve, side exhaust valve engines, the cover is held on by a line of four finger nuts. According to Land Rover, a different procedure is used for setting the valve to be adjusted in the fully closed position. Starting with the inlet valves on top of the engine first, turn the crankshaft until valve Number 6, counting from the front of the engine is fully open. In this position valve Number 1 will be fully closed and ready for checking and adjustment. When that's done, set valve Number 5 fully open and adjust valve Number 2, then it's 4 and 3 and so on, until they are all done. Apply the same procedure to the exhaust valves.

84

Job 84. Rocker cover gasket.

84. Fit a new gasket and grommets to the rocker cover and refit the cover. Using a little gasket sealer will help it stay in place on the rocker cover as it is fitted. Don't make the common mistake of over-tightening the cover - it *causes* leaks - just 'nip' the bolt or nuts down on to the cover.

Drive the car for several miles until it reaches its normal operating temperature. Check the rocker cover again for leaks.

Job 85. Cooling system.

SAFETY FIRST!
Only work on the cooling system when the engine - and thus the coolant - is cold.

Check the cooling and heating systems for leaks and all hoses for condition and tightness. Look at the ends of hoses for leaks and check the clamps for tightness; pinch and inspect the hoses to ensure that they are not starting to crack and deteriorate. If you don't want a hose to burst and let you down in the worst possible place, change any hoses that seem at all suspect.

Job 86. Coolant check.

Use a hydrometer to check the specific gravity of the coolant. If below the level recommended on the tester, top up with anti-freeze, until the correct specific gravity is obtained. Most have a system of coloured balls, some of which may float and some may not, to determine whether there is sufficient anti-freeze present.

V8 ENGINES
It is recommended that the proportion of anti-freeze to water should be around 50% and never more than 60%. These aluminium engines are more critical in this respect than cast-iron units.

INSIDE INFORMATION: Some owners think that there is little to be gained by using anti-freeze in their cast-iron block engine all the year round, particularly in those parts of the world where frost is not a problem. Wrong! Anti-freeze to a concentration of 25% not only gives protection against around -13 degrees Celsius (9 degrees Fahrenheit) of frost, it also helps to stop the radiator from clogging and so helps to keep the engine running cooler in hot weather. Owners also forget that there is aluminium in, or rather on, most engines and that it does corrode items such as the heater valves. Use anti-freeze and cut down on the common problems with heater valve corrosion, seizure and failure. A 50% mix, by the way, gives protection down to -36 degrees Celsius (-33 degrees Fahrenheit).

87

Job 87. Heater valve.

87. Talking of which (Job 86), check the heater control valve for correct operation and lubricate, with releasing fluid if seized; with thin oil if working. Ditto the control cable, adding oil or fluid to the ends before working the heater control open and shut a good few times.

Job 88. Check water pump.

Check the water pump for leaks - the first sign of failure - by looking for water leaks or stains around the spindle. Look especially along the engine just below the pump, where leaking will appear as a brown stain.

INSIDE INFORMATION: Grasp the fan blades and try to rock them forward and backward. Any excess movement is a sure sign that the water pump may soon be on the way out, even if it isn't leaking at the moment.

Job 89. Battery terminals.

SAFETY FIRST!
Refer to the information in Chapter 1, Safety First! for safe working practice in connection with working on the battery/ies.

Clean and grease the battery connections, using petroleum jelly or copper-impregnated grease. Check the terminal clamps and make sure they are tight.

Drive the vehicle out of doors.

INSIDE INFORMATION: The best way of cleaning old grease and corrosion from battery terminals is a kettle full of water that has just boiled. Pour it slowly over each terminal and you'll see a bright, shiny surface appear from underneath the fur. Make sure that the battery caps or cover are firmly in place first and pour more water down the sides of the battery and over the battery carrier so that nothing lodges on the metal battery carrier, causing corrosion.

If the battery terminals are badly furred, it is likely that some corrosion will have taken place inside the battery clamps. Indeed, it has been known for the clamps to be almost completely eaten away inside, while appearing sound from the outside. Disconnect the clamps, wash off any furring with hot water and clean both the inside of the clamps and the outside of the terminals with a medium grit sandpaper. Apply petroleum jelly or copper-impregnated grease to the bottom of the clamp but it's best to leave the electrical connection dry, and never apply ordinary grease to this area.

Job 90. Top-up carburettor dashpots.

Top up the Stromberg and SU carburettor dashpots with engine oil. Unscrew the dashpot cap and pull out the plunger. The dash-pot contains a damper which prevents the fuel flow needle in the carburettor from fluttering and allows more petrol to come through when you accelerate hard - performance and fuel economy will be better if the dash pots are not allowed to run dry. Use ordinary engine oil, nothing thicker. Very thin oil tends to disappear too quickly! Top up until the level is about 0.5 in (12 mm) from the top of the tube.

INSIDE INFORMATION: Some Stromberg and SU carburettors tend to consume oil very quickly for a variety of reasons, some to do with driving style, some to do with general wear. If your carburettors are like this, check the oil more frequently than every 6,000 miles.

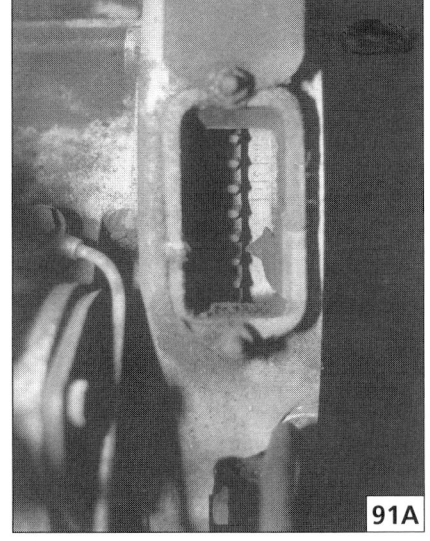

Job 91. Adjust ignition timing.

For correct operation of the ignition system it's necessary to make sure that the spark plugs are firing at just the right time, that is just before the piston on the firing stroke reaches the top of its travel. Note the position of the Number 1 spark plug HT lead on the distributor cap, then remove the cap. Turn the engine over in the correct direction of rotation (either by using the starting handle or pressing on the fan belt and turning the fan) until the distributor rotor arm is approaching the position of the Number 1 spark plug lead contact in the cap.

91A. Now locate the timing marks which consist of a pointer and scale either beneath a removable plate on the bellhousing and flywheel on early engines...

91B. ...or on the timing chain cover and crankshaft pulley on later engines. Turn the engine again, until the correct timing marks are aligned. Refer to *Chapter 8, Facts and Figures* for the correct static ignition timing setting for your car. With the engine in this position, the contact breaker points should just be opening. It's a bit tricky to determine the exact moment when the points open and the best way to do this is to connect a 12 volt test lamp between the low tension (thin wire) wiring connection on the distributor and a good earth (ground) - any unpainted metal part of the engine will do for the earth connection. Now, with the ignition switched on, the bulb will light when the points open. (Illustration, courtesy Land Rover)

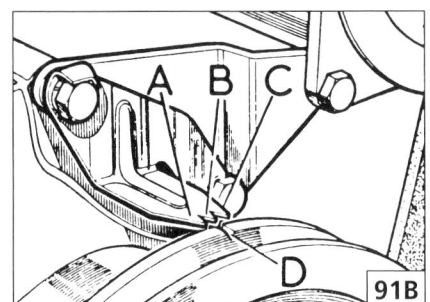

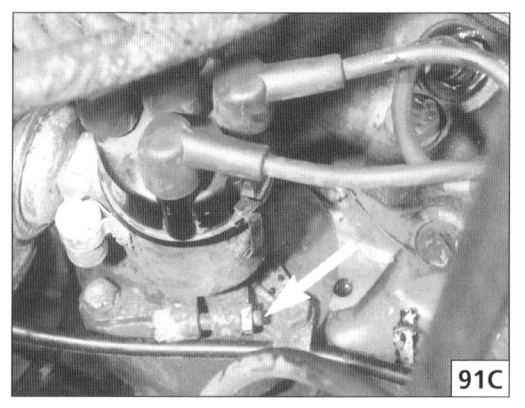

91C

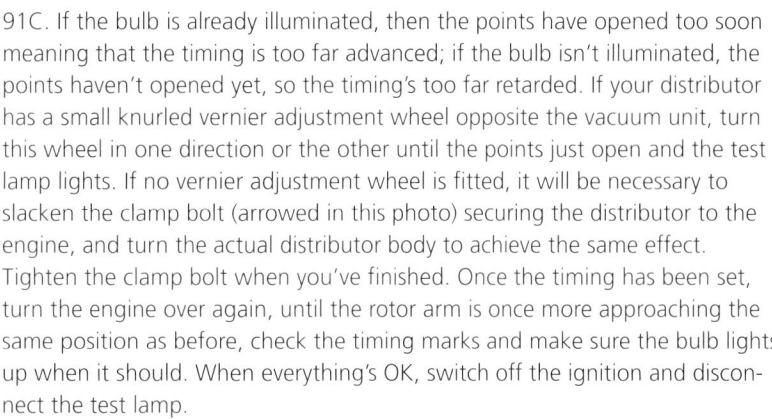

91C. If the bulb is already illuminated, then the points have opened too soon meaning that the timing is too far advanced; if the bulb isn't illuminated, the points haven't opened yet, so the timing's too far retarded. If your distributor has a small knurled vernier adjustment wheel opposite the vacuum unit, turn this wheel in one direction or the other until the points just open and the test lamp lights. If no vernier adjustment wheel is fitted, it will be necessary to slacken the clamp bolt (arrowed in this photo) securing the distributor to the engine, and turn the actual distributor body to achieve the same effect. Tighten the clamp bolt when you've finished. Once the timing has been set, turn the engine over again, until the rotor arm is once more approaching the same position as before, check the timing marks and make sure the bulb lights up when it should. When everything's OK, switch off the ignition and disconnect the test lamp.

91D

91D. The most accurate way of setting the ignition timing is dynamically using a stroboscopic timing light although once again it may be necessary to seek specialist advice as to the dynamic timing setting best for your engine as no figures are given by the manufacturer. Timing lights can be bought from motor accessory stores and then used as instructed or, SPECIALIST SERVICE: have your dealer or local garage check the ignition timing for you when you've finished the service.

This is what the various timing marks stand for.

EARLY TYPE (See 91A)

There is a line against which 'T.D.C.' is stamped. When this line is level with the pointer, the engine is at top dead centre. (One flywheel tooth equals about 4 degrees.) For 1948-51 models, set the line on the flywheel marked 'F.A. 15°' to the pointer before setting the distributor points. For 1952-53 models, use 'F.A. 8°'. For 1954-58, use 'F.A. 10°'.

SERIES IIA (see 91B)

The timing marks adjacent to the flywheel pulley, A, B and C represent 6 degrees before top dead centre (BTDC), 3 degrees BTDC and TDC, respectively. See *Chapter 8, Facts and Figures* for settings.

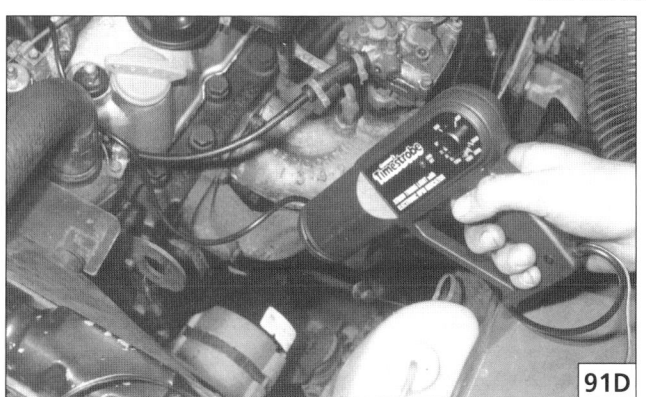

91E

91E. 6-CYLINDER MODELS.

The pointer (91E.A) should align with the relevant marks on the flywheel pulley - almost always '2° ATDC' with modern petrol. (Illustration, courtesy Land Rover)

91F. SERIES III

Some Series III vehicles have a single mark on the flywheel pulley and several pointers. The furthest 'clockwise' pointer equals 6 degrees After Top Dead Centre. Next on the 'left' equals TDC, next comes 3 degrees Before TDC and finally, on the 'left' is 6 degrees BTDC. (Illustration, courtesy Land Rover)

91F

91G. SERIES III

91G. Other Series III vehicles have a fixed pointer with fine lines on the pulley. The outer line represent 6 degrees Before Top Dead Centre (furthest on the 'left'/anti-clockwise) and 6 degrees After Top Dead Centre (furthest 'right'/clockwise). The centre line equals TDC and the other two 3 degrees BTDC and 3 degrees ATDC respectively. (Illustration, courtesy Land Rover)

V8 ENGINES

The timing mark is similar to 91G above. The static timing is 0° (TDC); 6° with engine running, at 650 revs/min. NB. Engine speed accuracy is of great importance!

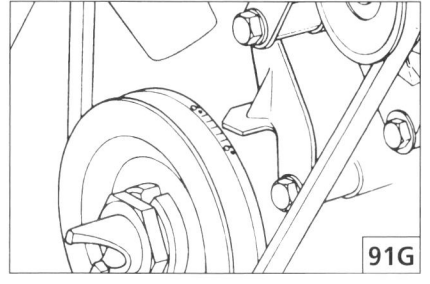

91G

☐ Job 92. Distributor advance.

On distributors fitted with a vacuum unit (not all of them were) this is a good time to see if the distributor vacuum advance is working properly. Trace the advance pipe running from the vacuum unit on the distributor to its connection on the carburettor or manifold. Disconnect the pipe at the carburettor or manifold and wipe clean the end. Carefully position it so that you can suck on the disconnected end, or if necessary, connect a length of small bore hose to make this easier. Suck on the pipe, while you watch the contact breaker points. If the vacuum unit is in good condition you'll feel resistance when you suck, and also see the distributor baseplate and points move slightly. If nothing happens, the rubber diaphragm inside the vacuum unit is likely to be punctured (a common occurrence) and a new vacuum unit will be needed. Refit the vacuum pipe and distributor cap after making this check.

☐ Job 93. Brake servo hose.

93.Check the condition and security of the brake servo vacuum hose and on later diesel models also check the condition of the vacuum reservoir tank, adjacent to the radiator, if one is fitted.

☐ Job 94. Exhaust emissions check.

SPECIALIST SERVICE: Have a properly equipped garage carry out an exhaust emissions check, especially for carbon monoxide (CO) and unburned hydrocarbons. This check is particularly important on later engines that have more sophisticated emission equipment fitted, designed to meet latest emission regulations.

6,000 Mile Mechanical and Electrical - Around the Vehicle

First carry out Jobs 7 to 16, 20 to 22, and 45 to 48 as applicable

☐ Job 95. Adjust headlamps.

SPECIALIST SERVICE: It is possible to adjust your own headlamps, but not with sufficient accuracy. Badly adjusted headlamps can be dangerous if they don't provide you, the driver, with a proper view of the road ahead, or they dazzle oncoming drivers and Land Rovers, with high-riding headlamps, can be particularly bad in this area. Older drivers and those with poor eyesight, can become disorientated when confronted with maladjusted head lights. Have the work carried out for you by a garage with beam measuring equipment. Any MoT testing station in the UK will be properly equipped.

☐ Job 96. Bonnet release.

96. Lubricate the bonnet release using silicone releasing fluid and check the operation and adjustment of the mechanism.

☐ Job 97. Locks and hinges.

97. Lubricate the door locks with silicone releasing fluid, using an extension tube to direct the spray. Check the operation of the door locks and adjust the striker plates if necessary.

6,000 Mile Mechanical and Electrical - Under the Vehicle

First carry out Jobs 49 to 69 as applicable

SAFETY FIRST!
Raise the front of the Land Rover off the ground after reading carefully the information at the start of this chapter on lifting and supporting the vehicle.

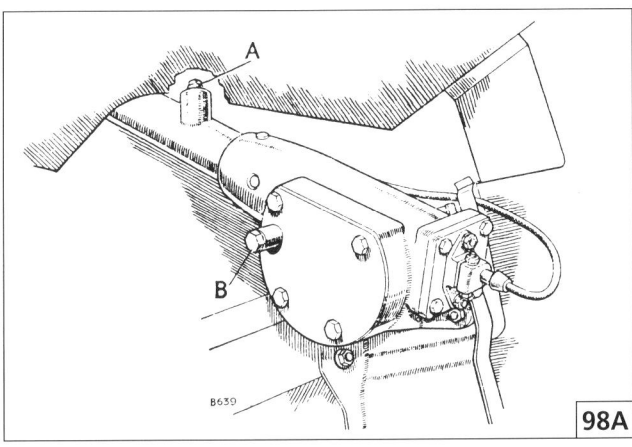

98A

□ Job 98. Lubricate steering box.

WORM & NUT STEERING BOXES

98A. Remove the level plug on the side of the unit, from beneath the wing (99A.B). If no oil dribbles out, top up with the correct grade through the filler plug (99A.A), reached from under the bonnet. (Illustration, courtesy Land Rover)

RECIRCULATING BALL STEERING BOXES

98B. The filler and level plug on all later models, seen here (arrowed) without air filter in place, is removed, and the oil level topped up to the level of the plug before being refitted.

□ Job 99. Check and adjust steering box.

99A. From under the front wheel arch, remove the cover over the steering unit by unscrewing the retaining nuts and bolts. Liberal amounts of penetrating oil may be needed here, especially if the cover has not been disturbed for some time. Check the steering unit for signs of oil leakage and check the tightness of the end plate and side cover plate securing bolts. Also check the tightness and security of the steering unit mounting bolts.

98B

WORM & NUT STEERING BOXES

99B. Early Series I models' adjuster screws, on the 'box itself (see 98A.B), are similar to those on later models (99C). End thrust on the steering column can be adjusted after first removing the steering wheel, dust shield and spring. Slacken the locknut (99B.B) and tighten the adjusting nut (99B.A) until the end-play just disappears. Check end-play by temporarily re-attaching the steering wheel and attempting to pull and push on the wheel. Also, jack the front of the vehicle off the ground and turn the steering from lock-to-lock several times to ensure that the steering is not tight or binding. (Illustration, courtesy Land Rover)

99A

RECIRCULATING BALL STEERING BOXES

99C. On later Series I and all other vehicles, excess free play at the steering wheel can be taken up, to a certain extent, by adjustment of the steering rocker shaft endplay. (The cover shown in 99A has now been removed.) To do this, set the road wheels in the straight ahead position and slacken the rocker shaft adjuster locknut on the side of the steering unit. Screw in the adjuster to eliminate any rocker shaft end play and tighten the locknut. Turn the steering wheel from full right to full left lock and check that this adjustment has not caused any stiffness or binding. If it has, back off the adjustment a little at a time until there is no stiffness or binding over the full extent of the steering range. Refit the steering box cover after adjustment.

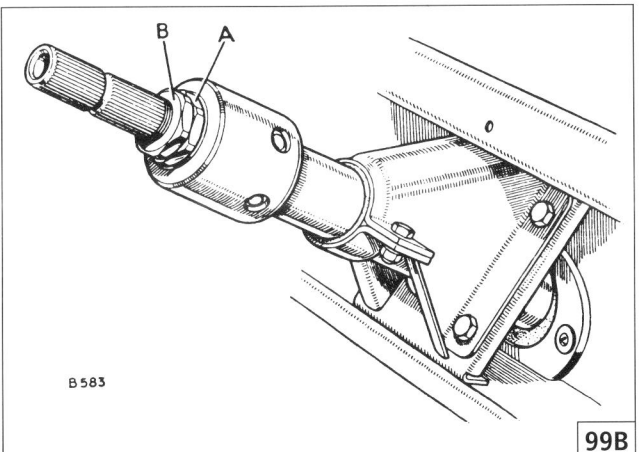

99B

99C

6,000 MILE SERVICE

☐ Job 100. Inspect front brakes.

*SAFETY FIRST! and SPECIALIST SERVICE: Obviously, a vehicle's brakes are among its most important safety related items. Do not dismantle your Land Rover's brakes unless you are fully competent to do so. If you have not been trained in this work, but wish to carry out the work described here, we strongly recommend that you have a garage or qualified mechanic check your work before using the vehicle on the road. See also the section on BRAKES AND ASBESTOS in **Chapter 1**, for further important information. Use only asbestos-free brake shoes.*

After fitting new brake shoes, it is recommended that you avoid heavy braking - except in an emergency - for the first 150-200 miles (250-300 km).

100A. First slacken off the brake adjuster(s) on the back plate to prevent the drum binding on the brake shoes as it is removed (See Job 52.). Now unscrew the two brake drum retaining screws.

100B. The brake drum will probably not slide straight off as it should. Hammer quite firmly around the outer edge of the brake drum but ONLY: i) with a soft faced mallet and ii) hitting the drum right on its edge, as shown. The brake drum can now be pulled and wriggled off its studs.

100C. However, there is a risk that the dust seal on the back of the drum might well break off the drum. To avoid this risk, note that there is a tapped thread in each brake drum. You can pull the drum off by screwing in a unified coarse bolt.

100D. If the brake shoes are worn down close to the rivets, or show any sign of oil or brake fluid contamination, replace them with new ones. If there is contamination, either from a leaking wheel cylinder or hub oil seal, this must be rectified before fitting new brake shoes. The various Land Rover brake shoe arrangements are quite simple and straightforward with few components to worry about. Look closely at the arrangement of the springs and identify which is the leading shoe and which is the trailing shoe and before you start, make a careful sketch of the correct location of all parts - and in particular, return springs.

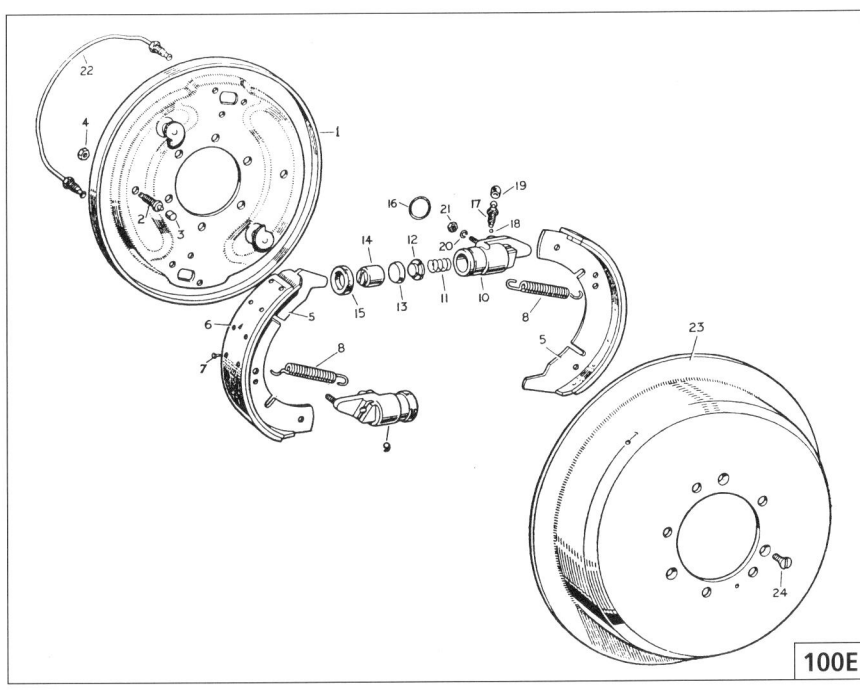

100E. There are many minor variants on Land Rover brakes, mainly to do with the number of wheel cylinders, adjusters and springs and the types of adjuster. Long Wheelbase Land Rovers have always had 11 in. brakes, unlike the Short Wheelbase's 10 in.. This is the Series I, II and III 107 in. and 109 in. 4-cylinder twin wheel cylinder layout. From June 1980, 88 in. Series III models were identically equipped. 6-cylinder and V8 109 in. models have a very similar set-up but with wider shoes, a different looking set of wheel cylinders and adjusters that have 'slipped' about 90 degrees around the back plate. These vehicles have the common 'snail cam' adjusters. (Illustration, courtesy Land Rover)

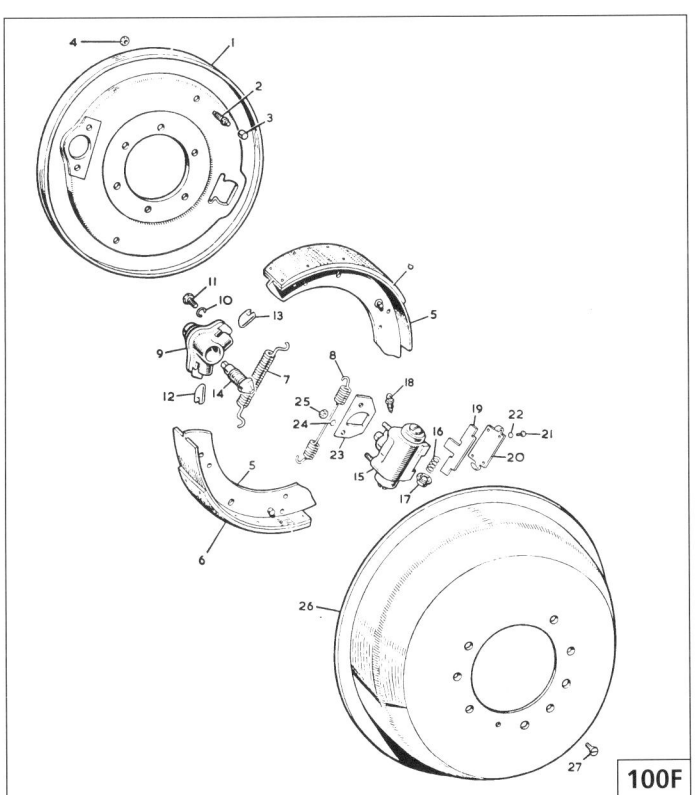

100F. This is the Long Wheelbase Series I and II rear brake with the less common taper-and-wedge adjusters, as also used on the park brake. (Illustration, courtesy Land Rover)

100G. INSIDE INFORMATION: Experienced Land Rover mechanics have seen many of these 10 in. brakes with a spring fitted between the peg and hole being pointed to here. This is a big mistake! If you do fit a spring here, you will have no "pedal" when you first apply the brakes and it will take a good three pumps on the brake pedal to restore any braking efficiency. A spring was never meant to be fitted here. The spring fitted as shown in this picture is however, correct. Do check with all types that the springs are in the correct location - most important!

100H. After removing the anchor plate (see 100R) try using a pair of mole grips to pull the rear, trailing shoe away from the bottom pivot, allowing it to pass to one side of the pivot and taking the pressure off the bottom spring.

100I. The bottom spring can be unhooked and the trailing shoe lifted away.

100J. With the bottom spring removed the leading shoe can be pulled away from the pivot and swung inwards sufficiently to take the tension off the top spring which can be disconnected leaving the front, leading shoe free to be removed.

100H

100K. Use string or wire to tie the wheel cylinder in the "closed" position, otherwise it will slowly pop itself open. Now use a proprietary brand of brake cleaner. Spray large quantities all over the back plate components. The cleaner will kill the dust and wash a good deal of it away, reducing the risk of brake squeal later on, and allowing the parts to work more efficiently. Wipe out any residue and be sure to throw away any rags you have used in a sealed plastic bag.

100L. Take this opportunity to loosen the snail cam brake adjuster (or adjusters), lubricating sparingly with brake grease.

100I

INSIDE INFORMATION: i) If it is at all worn, remove the adjuster and fit a new one. If it breaks while the brake shoes are fully adjusted up, you may have to resort to smashing the brake drum in order to remove it. ii) If the brake springs are bent, you will have great difficulty in replacing them later on and if the ends have begun to straighten out, they stand the risk of jumping off the brake shoes. In either case, replace them. With this model, the longer spring goes on the top and operates on the leading shoe while the shorter spring goes on the bottom, utilising the two outer holes on the bottom of each brake shoe, and ensures that both shoes locate properly on the bottom pivot. iii) You are strongly recommended to only use genuine Land Rover Parts brake components or those from a leading brake company. Before you reassemble, get it straight in your own mind which shoes are which.

100J

100K

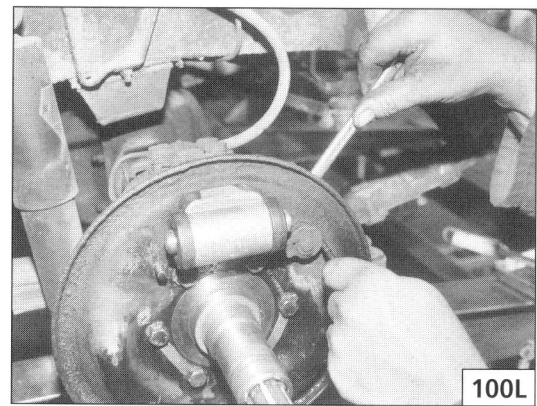

100L

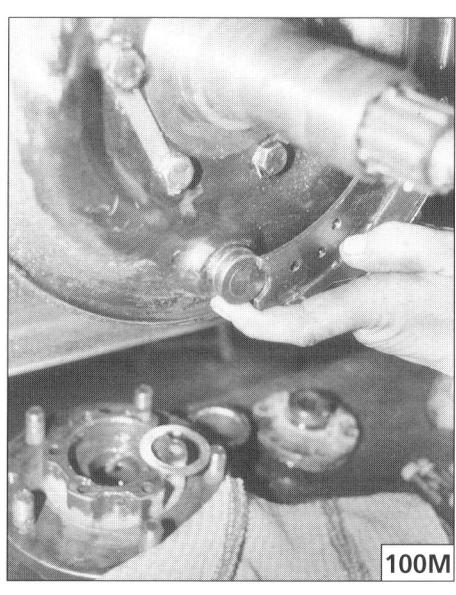

100M

100N

100M. Now reverse the procedure shown earlier, hooking the top spring in place and then locating the bottom of the brake shoe. Note that clean hands are required for this part of the work, to ensure that you don't get any oil or grease on the new brake shoes.

100O

100N. Then, the bottom spring is hooked into place on the outer hole of the shoe already fitted...

100O. ...and hooked into the outer hole of the complementary shoe.

100P. It's back to the self-grip wrench to pull against the force of the bottom spring and locate the bottom of the brake shoe on the pivot.

100Q. Hand pressure can now be used to locate the top of the shoe against the slot in the wheel cylinder. The tie that had been fitted to the wheel cylinder has already been removed, of course.

100P

100Q

100R. The anchor plate removed earlier is now refitted and the locking plate tabs bent over to secure the special set screws.

100S. Viewed from low down this shot illustrates the way in which it is rather more difficult to achieve all of this with the hub in place. (Brake shoes always have to be replaced when an oil seal hub leaks and it's best done - and easier to photograph! - when the hub is off the car). When the hub is still in place, it's just somewhat more fiddly to fit the return spring.

100R

100S

Note that with the exception of hydraulic parts, metal to metal contact points such as the tips of the shoes, the areas of the backplate where contacted by the shoe platforms, the brake adjusters, the wheel cylinder and the abutment slots should be lubricated sparingly with brake grease (not ordinary grease!).

☐ Job 101. Inspect front wheel cylinders.

101A. Peel back the rubber dust cover on each front brake wheel cylinder and examine for fluid leakage. Replace the wheel cylinder if any leakage or corrosion is found. Check that the wheel cylinder pistons aren't seized by having an assistant very carefully and slowly press down on the brake pedal while you watch the movement at the brake shoes. If either shoe doesn't move, the wheel cylinder piston is seized. Also check for evidence of contamination from oil, grease, or the wrong type of brake fluid. If any of these problems found: SPECIALIST SERVICE, consult a properly qualified garage. Brake fluid might need draining, flushing and renewing; brake wheel cylinders or seals might require replacement.

101A

101B. INSIDE INFORMATION: i) When you refit the brake drums, tap them around the perimeter with a soft-faced mallet as you tighten up the two drum retaining screws.

101B

101C. INSIDE INFORMATION: ii) This is what can happen if you don't! This wheel stud shows how a wheel came loose and rubbed on the studs after a brake drum was fitted but not properly bedded down.

Now adjust the brakes correctly as shown in Job 52. Apply the brakes firmly using the foot pedal to centralise the shoes, before backing off the adjuster(s) so that the wheel will just turn freely.

101C

102

Job 102. Front hub/swivel assemblies.

102. Grasp the road wheel at the top and bottom and try to rock it in and out. You should be able to feel movement if there is any excess wear in the hub/swivel assemblies. Use a lever to lift and lower the road wheel and look for movement in the hub which will confirm that wear has taken place. If any serious movement is detected, it could mean an MoT failure. Correcting this problem is definitely a SPECIALIST SERVICE operation.

103A

Job 103. Check steering balljoints.

You will, of course, grease the ball joints (when grease nipples are fitted) as part of each 3,000 mile service. Now, at 6,000 miles, you should take the extra time required to thoroughly check each one for wear, as shown, and for split rubber gaiters: in both cases, immediate replacement is required.

103A. Check for play in the track rod end ball joints on all the Land Rover steering linkages.

103B

103B. There's one at the relay unit, two at the left-hand front wheel and one at the right-hand front wheel.

103C

103C. The easiest way to do this is to grasp the steering linkage arm and try to move it up and down. Alternatively, have an assistant grip the track rod end ball joint, wrapping the hand around the ball-joint, and as you move the steering wheel back and forth or do the same with the road wheel, your helper will 'sense' any play in the joints. SPECIALIST SERVICE: Should play be present, have the job looked at by your Land Rover specialist.

☐ Job 104. Front shock absorbers.

104A. Check for fluid leaks from the front shock absorbers. If they are seeping, it will show from under the top shroud. Look for any signs of corrosion or damage all around the shock absorber body.

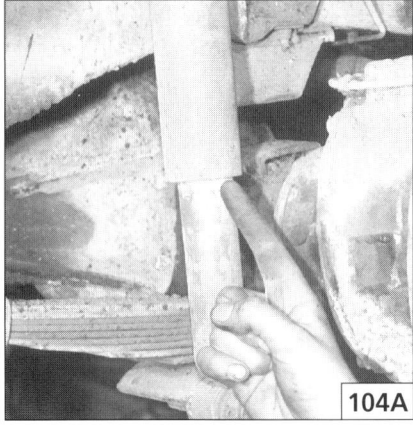

104B. Also check the condition of the shock absorber bushes (arrowed) by twisting the shock absorber from side to side. If they appear soft, spreading - or non-existent! - fit new ones. Faulty or leaking shock absorbers must be replaced, always in pairs (both front or both rear).

☐ Job 105. Oil front springs.

Spray or brush oil - or better still, wax underbody treatment - over the edges of the leaf springs. This allows the leaves to slide against each other as they should, improving the ride and cutting out squeaks, but keep oil off the rubber bushes.

☐ Job 106. Lubricate hand brake linkage.

Lubricate the exposed linkages of the handbrake mechanism and at the same time check that all the levers move freely and that all split pins, washers and other fasteners are in place and in sound condition.

SAFETY FIRST!
Lower the front of the Land Rover, then raise the rear after reading carefully the information at the start of this chapter on lifting and supporting the vehicle.

☐ Job 107. Inspect rear brakes.

Land Rover front and rear brakes are very similar - on some models, identical - and all the information contained in Job 100 is equally applicable here.

☐ Job 108. Inspect rear wheel cylinders.

This Job is also very much the same as for the front wheel cylinders and reference should be made to Job 101.

☐ Job 109. Check exhaust system.

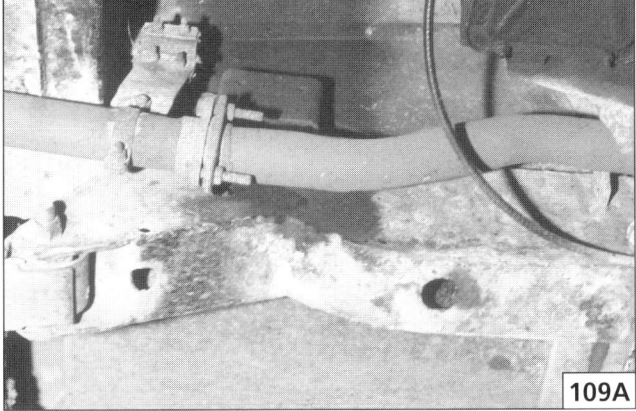

109A. Check the condition and security of the entire exhaust system looking carefully for any signs of corrosion on the pipes and silencers, or leakage at the joints. Replace gaskets if necessary.

INSIDE INFORMATION: Consider using stainless steel nuts and bolts on the clamps - you'll probably have to saw the old ones off because of rust.

109B. Also check the condition of the mountings. Most Land Rovers use a fabric strap type mounting which is prone to deterioration after a period of time. Check these carefully.

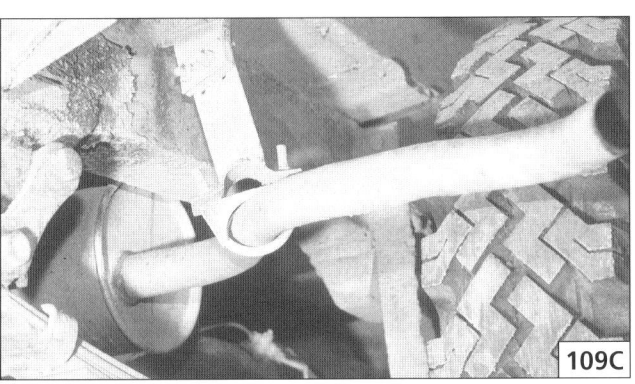

109C. Temporary mountings usually need replacing with the real McCoy, although this ugly looking make-do is effective.

Job 110. Rear shock absorbers.

110A. Check for fluid leaks from the rear shock absorbers just as was done for the front. Again, fluid seepage will show from under the top shroud. Look for any signs of corrosion or damage all around the shock absorber body.

110B. Check the condition of the shock absorber bushes by twisting the shock absorber from side to side. Fit new bushes if any problems are found, or renew the shock absorbers in pairs if faulty.

Job 111. Oil rear springs.

111. Give the rear springs the oil spray or underbody wax treatment to lubricate the leaves and eliminate squeaks. This photo shows a prime candidate for treatment. It also looks sagged - seek SPECIALIST SERVICE advice, especially if you suspect a broken leaf.

Lower the vehicle to the ground.

6,000 Mile Bodywork and Interior - Around the Vehicle

First carry out Jobs 17, 23 to 26, and 75 to 78 as applicable

Job 112. Seats and seat belts.

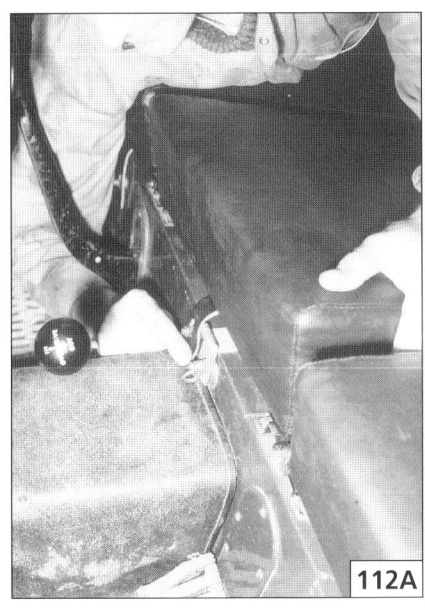

112A. Check the condition and security of seats and seat belts. Make sure that your seats are as secure as Land-Rover seats can be and in particular, that seat bases locate as they should. Examine the seat belt buckles and make sure that they lock satisfactorily and can be unlocked when there is some load on the belt.

112B. Pull hard on each length of belt webbing near where each section is fitted to the vehicle to ensure that it feels strong and firmly anchored, and check the webbing to ensure that it is neither frayed nor otherwise damaged.

☐ Job 113. Inertia reel mechanisms.

113. Check inertia reel belts. With most types, you can test by tugging, if you pull hard and quickly on the belt the reel should lock; with others the lock may only work under braking. Carry out a careful road test, in the daylight, under dry road conditions and with no other traffic or pedestrians about.

6,000 mile Bodywork - Under the Vehicle

First carry out Jobs 27 and 79

SAFETY FIRST!
Only raise the Land Rover off the ground after reading carefully the information at the start of this chapter on lifting and supporting the vehicle.

☐ Job 114. Rustproof underbody.

Renew the wax treatment to wheel arches and underbody areas. Refer to *Chapter 5, Rustproofing*, for full details.

112B

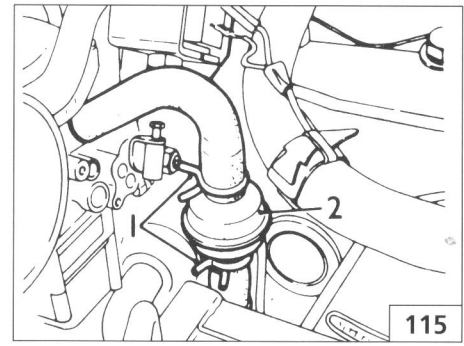

113

12,000 Miles - or Every Twelve Months, Whichever Comes First

12,000 Mile Mechanical and Electrical - Emission Control Equipment

The first emission control equipment was fitted to 6-cylinder models and there are numerous variations fitted to all later Land Rovers, particularly on V8 models.

SPECIALIST SERVICE: Very many emission control components are not serviceable without the correct specialist equipment such as a vacuum gauge, pressure gauge, exhaust gas analyser, distributor advance tester, carburettor piston loading tool, and an engine oscilloscope, depending upon model of car. Without describing every type of emission control system in detail, the following Job numbers list the components that can be tested or serviced at home. All should be carried out at the 12,000 miles/twelve months service interval. Have the rest of the system checked over by your properly equipped Land Rover Dealer.

CERTAIN 6-CYLINDER MODELS ONLY - fitted with a Crankcase Emission Valve System with Air Pump. Please note that this system will only work properly if the engine is generally kept in a proper state of tune.

☐ Job 115. Renew crankcase breather flame trap.

6-CYLINDER AND V8 MODELS ONLY
115. Release the hose clips and remove the crankcase breather flame trap. On 6-cylinder engines the flame trap (115.2) is adjacent to the carburettor on the side of the engine. On the V8 it's above the left-hand rocker cover. It should be replaced with a new one. (Illustration, courtesy Land Rover)

115

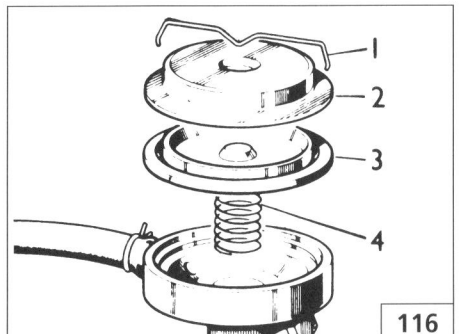

116

Job 116. Crankcase breather valve.

EARLY 4-CYLINDER AND ALL 6-CYLINDER MODELS ONLY

116. Take off the spring clip (116.1) and remove the cover plate (116.2), diaphragm (116.3), metering valve and valve spring (116.4). Clean the metal parts with methylated spirit but don't use this to clean the diaphragm; just give it a wipe over with a cloth. (Illustration, courtesy Land Rover)

INSIDE INFORMATION: i) If there are stuck-on deposits, try boiling the metal parts in an old saucepan first. If any parts are damaged, or if the diaphragm looks perished, replace it. Reassemble, taking care that the metering valve fits correctly in its guides and that the diaphragm seats correctly. ii) If the breather pipes have become blocked, it is certain that the breather connections on the engine block will also be congested. Give all the components of the system a good inspection and replace any that appear suspect.

Job 117. Check air injection system.

SPECIFIC EXPORT 6-CYL. MODELS ONLY

Where fitted, check the condition and security of all the air injection system pipes and hoses. Check that the bolts securing the outlet adaptor to the air pump are tight and check all the air injection pipe unions at the exhaust manifold.

Job 118. Replace air pump belt.

SPECIFIC EXPORT 6-CYL. MODELS ONLY

Change the air pump drive belt if it shows any signs of deterioration. When correctly tensioned, the belt should deflect by about 0.25 in. (6.3 mm) half way along the longest part of the belt between the pulleys (See Job 40).

Job 119. Test check valve.

SPECIFIC EXPORT 6-CYL. MODELS ONLY

Air injection systems fitted with an air pump have a check valve on the inlet side. Check it by removing, then trying to blow through from one end and then the other. The valve should not allow air to pass back to the air pump. If it does so, discard and replace.

Job 120. Emission system.

SPECIFIC EXPORT 6-CYL. MODELS ONLY

SPECIALIST SERVICE: Have a specialist run a check over the emission control and evaporative loss control systems for leaks and correct operation of all the valves and components that cannot be checked without specialist equipment.

12,000 Mile Mechanical and Electrical - The Engine Bay

First carry out Jobs 1 to 6, 18, 19, 28 to 44 and 80 to 94 as applicable

Job 121. Cabin heater and hoses.

Check the condition and security of all heater hoses and pipes and check for any sign of leakage from the vicinity of the heater itself.

121

INSIDE INFORMATION: When you have to replace hoses, don't bother trying to take them off in the conventional way. If the hose clamps unscrew, fine - but they probably won't. And if the hose pulls off the stub, fine - but it's probably been firmly glued on by the heat. So, use a junior hacksaw to cut through the hose, just away from the stub. Cut carefully through the clamp, pulling it away with pliers and/or gloved hands - it will be sharp! Then cut carefully through the hose at a 45 degree angle to the end of the stub TAKING GREAT CARE ALL THE WHILE NOT TO CUT INTO THE STUB! When you've gone through, peel the hose remnant off the stub and away - you could save hours, prevent bleeding knuckles and reduce the risk of damaging the heater core through too much pulling.

☐ Job 122. Check injectors.

DIESEL MODELS ONLY

   SPECIALIST SERVICE: Have the diesel injectors tested by an injection specialist for correct operating pressure and injection spray pattern. But beware! Some non-specialist garages may claim to be able to carry out this work but you are recommended to use a recognised diesel specialist or Land Rover Dealer for this work.

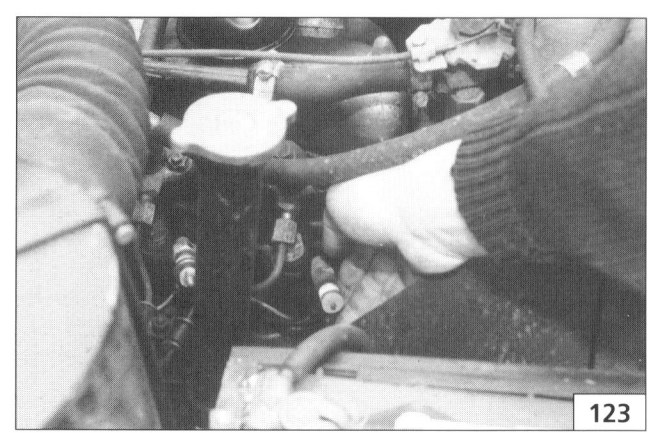

☐ Job 123. Diesel heater plug wiring.

DIESEL MODELS ONLY

123. Check the heater plug wiring for fraying, chafing or any signs of deterioration. Check that the wiring connections at the heater plugs are secure.

SAFETY FIRST!

Do not attempt any form of diesel injector testing yourself. The injectors operate under extremely high pressure and injury may result from the injected fuel penetrating your skin.

☐ Job 124. Renew air cleaner element.

V8 MODELS ONLY

On V8 engines a renewable paper air cleaner element is used instead of the oil bath air cleaner fitted to all other engines. There are two types of air cleaner assembly that may be encountered, one with an air intake temperature control system and one without.

124A. On vehicles without an air temperature control system, unscrew the end cover retaining bolt and lift off the strap and end cover (124A.1). Replace the element (124A.2) and refit the end cover, strap and retaining bolt. (Illustration, courtesy Land Rover)

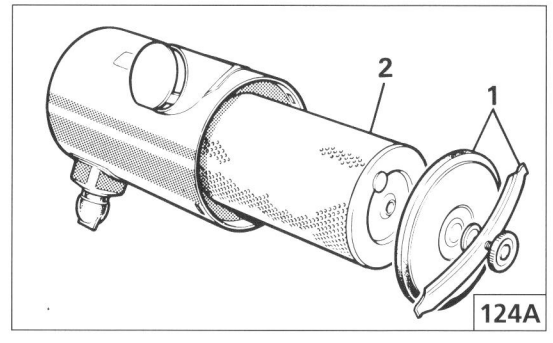

124.B Where an air temperature control system is fitted to the air cleaner assembly, it is necessary to remove the complete air cleaner to allow access to the filter elements. Release the vacuum hoses from the clips (124B.1 and 2) on top of the air cleaner and detach the hoses from their engine connections. Slacken the hose clip and detach the warm air intake (124B.3). Slacken the clips and detach the two side intake elbows (124B.5). Lift the air cleaner (124B.4) and ease it forward off its mountings then detach the non-return valve hose (124B.8) and the engine breather hose. Lift the complete assembly off the engine. (Illustration, courtesy Land Rover)

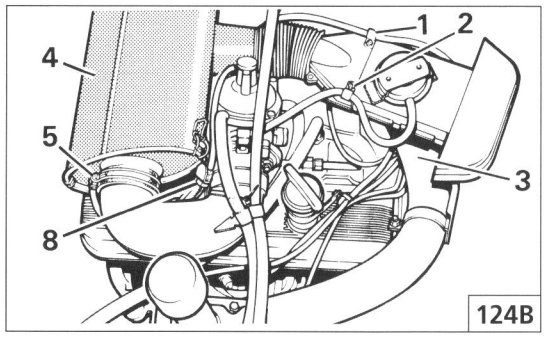

124C. There are two filter elements inside the casing, one at each end. Spring back the holding clips (124C.9) and ease off the two end cap assemblies (124C.11). Remove the element retaining screw and washer and take off the securing plate (124C.10) from each end cap. Lift away the elements (124C.13) and recover the seals (124C.12). Fit new elements and reassemble the air cleaner components.(Illustration, courtesy Land Rover)

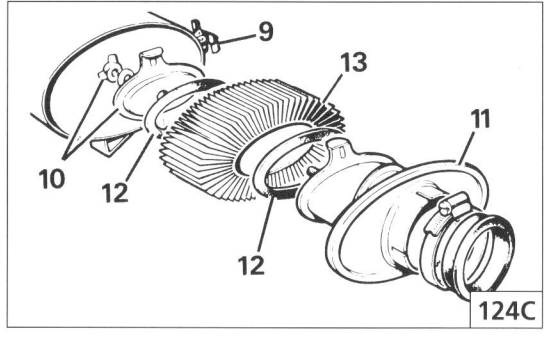

SPARK PLUG CONDITIONS

You can learn a lot about the condition of an engine from looking at the spark plugs. The following information and photographs, reproduced here with grateful thanks to NGK, show you what to look out for.

1. Good Condition

If the firing end of a spark plug is brown or light grey, the condition can be judged to be good and the spark plug is functioning at its best.

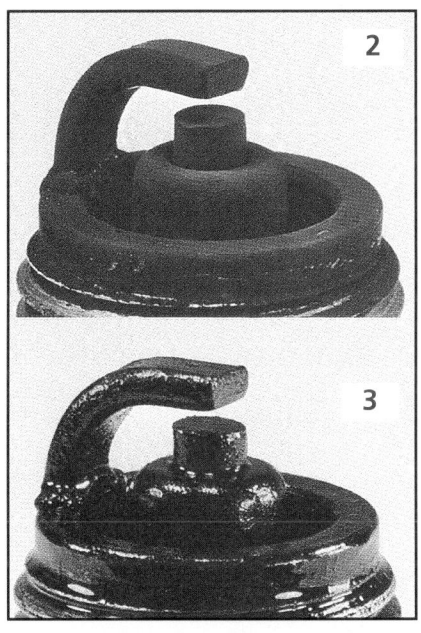

2. Carbon Fouling

Black, dry, sooty deposits, which will eventually cause misfiring and can be caused by an over-rich fuel mixture. Check all carburettor settings, choke operation and air filter cleanliness. Clean plugs vigorously with a brass bristled wire brush.

3. Oil Fouling

Oily, wet-looking deposits. This is particularly prone to causing poor starting and even misfiring. Caused by a severely worn engine but do not confuse with wet plugs removed from the engine when it won't start. If the "wetness" evaporates away, it's not oil fouling.

4. Overheating

When having been overheated, the insulator tip can become glazed or glossy, and deposits which have accumulated on the insulator tip may have melted. Sometimes these deposits have blistered on the insulator's tip.

5. Normal Wear

A worn spark plug not only wastes fuel but also strains the whole ignition system because the expanded gap requires higher voltage. As a result, a worn spark plug will result in damage to the engine itself, and will also increase air pollution. The normal rate of gap growth is usually around 'half-a-thou.' or 0.0006 in. every 5,000 miles (0.01 mm. every 5,000 km.).

6. Abnormal Wear

Abnormal electrode erosion is caused by the effects of corrosion, oxidation, reaction with lead, all resulting in abnormal gap growth.

7. Breakage

Insulator damage is self-evident and can be caused by rapid heating or cooling of the plug whilst out of the car or by clumsy use of gap setting tools. Burned away electrodes are indicative of an ignition system that is grossly out of adjustment. Do not use the car until this has been put right.

☐ **Job 125. Cylinder compressions.**

PETROL MODELS ONLY
The following procedure is applicable to petrol engine models only. Diesel engines have much higher compression pressures and require the use of dedicated diesel compression test equipment. On diesels, treat this Job as a SPECIALIST SERVICE operation.

> *SAFETY FIRST!*
> **Take off the HT lead that runs from the coil to the distributor at the coil end so that there is no risk of sparks or an electric shock. Carry out this work out of doors, and make sure that the transmission is in neutral.**

125

Ensure that the engine oil is up to the recommended level and that the engine is at running temperature. Remove the spark plugs but take care, because they will be extremely hot!

125. Screw the tester or hold it against the first spark plug port. Have an assistant hold the throttle fully open while the engine is spun over on the starter motor and make a note of the maximum reading on the gauge. Repeat the operation on each cylinder. If the engine is in good condition, there should not be a variation of more than five to six p.s.i. (or at the very most ten p.s.i.) between each cylinder.

INSIDE INFORMATION: i) Low similar readings on two adjacent cylinders suggests a faulty head gasket between the two cylinders. ii) If one cylinder shows a higher reading than the others, check the spark plug from that cylinder for oil or excessive carbon. Worn or broken piston rings could allow oil to be forced passed the rings to create a better seal - ironically, an indication that the engine is very heavily worn. iii) If you suspect worn or broken rings, pour a teaspoon full of engine oil through the spark plug hole and carry out the check again. If there is a temporary increase in the p.s.i. reading, suspect the piston rings. If there is no increase, then the valves in the cylinder head are probably badly burnt.

☐ **Job 126. Lubricate dynamo.**

Earlier Land Rovers are fitted with dynamos and many have a lubrication hole in the opposite end to the pulley. Lubricate the dynamo bearings through the oil hole in the rear end housing with a few drops of oil. Take care not to over-oil or to get oil inside the body of the dynamo.

> *SAFETY FIRST!*
> **Disconnect the battery and read the precautions given in Chapter 1, Safety First! before doing any work on the fuel system.**

☐ **Job 127. Clean fuel sediment bowl.**
The fuel pump sediment bowl arrangement described below is fitted to 4-cylinder petrol engines and early diesel engines. The procedures for cleaning are the same for both types.

127. The fuel sediment bowl is not easy to get at, tucked away as it is down at the rear right-hand side of the engine. To clean the bowl and filter, slacken the thumb screw at the base of the bowl, and as you hold the bowl, swing the strap to one side. Lift away the bowl and withdraw the mesh filter.

Clean the parts thoroughly and refit, but make sure that the sealing ring in the pump housing is in good condition first. Operate the hand priming lever a few times to refill the bowl with fuel.

On diesel models the fuel system must now be bled as described in Job 131.

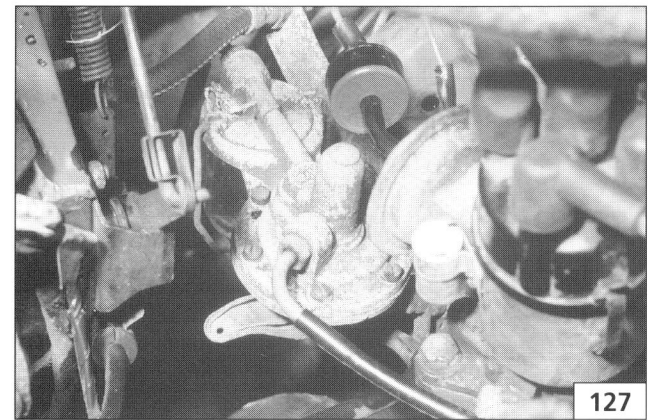
127

☐ Job 128. Renew bulkhead fuel filter.

6-CYLINDER PETROL MODELS ONLY

SAFETY FIRST!
*Disconnect the battery and read the precautions given in **Chapter 1, Safety First!** before doing any work on the fuel system.*

128. To renew the fuel filter element, Unscrew the retaining bolt (128.C) at the base of the filter while supporting the filter element holder (128.B). Withdraw the filter assembly, lift out and discard the element (128.A) and thoroughly clean out the holder. Renew the seals, if necessary, including the seal on the retaining bolt and refit the components. (Illustration, courtesy Land Rover)

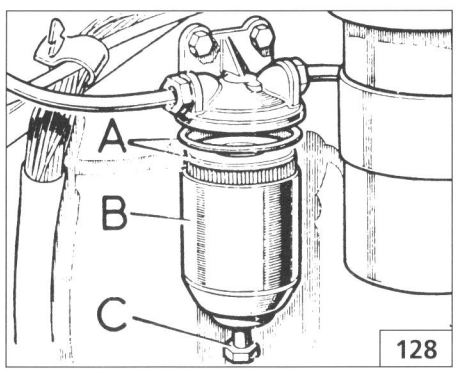

☐ Job 129. Clean fuel sedimenter.

DIESEL MODELS ONLY

The sedimenter (where fitted) is attached to the right-hand chassis rail. Refer to Job 18 for further details of the component parts.

To clean the element, first disconnect the fuel inlet pipe and raise it above fuel tank level to prevent the tank from draining. Hold the sedimenter body and unscrew the retaining bolt at the top. Remove the body and element. Clean the parts thoroughly, fit new seals and reassemble the sedimenter.

Reconnect the fuel hose, then slacken the drain plug at the base of the sedimenter. Tighten the drain plug when pure diesel fuel, free from air bubbles, emerges. Take care to catch spilled diesel in a suitable container; don't contaminate the ground. Wipe the surrounding area clean and dry.

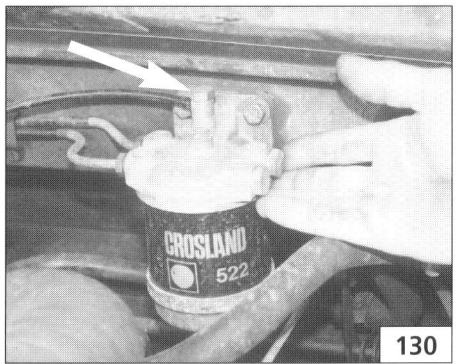

☐ Job 130. Renew fuel filter element.

DIESEL MODELS ONLY

On early models the fuel filter elements are mounted on the engine and on the bulkhead. They are easily identifiable by the one piece container which encloses the paper element inside.

130. Later models have bulkhead mounted filters either singly or in a pair. They can be identified by the semi-exposed element retained by a lower housing body.

To renew the element on early models, slacken the plug at the base of the container and catch the fuel in a suitable bowl. Disconnect the bleed back pipe on top of the housing then, while supporting the container, unscrew the centre nut also on top of the housing. Lift away the assembly and collect the large seal under the lip of the housing and the small seals from the filter element. Clean the container thoroughly, fit new seals and element and reassemble. Bleed the fuel system as described in Job 131.

To renew the element on later models, support the lower housing body and unscrew the retaining bolt on the upper housing. Lift away the element and lower housing body and collect the seals. Thoroughly clean the lower housing body then, using a new element and new seals, reassemble the filter components. Bleed the fuel system as described in the next Job.

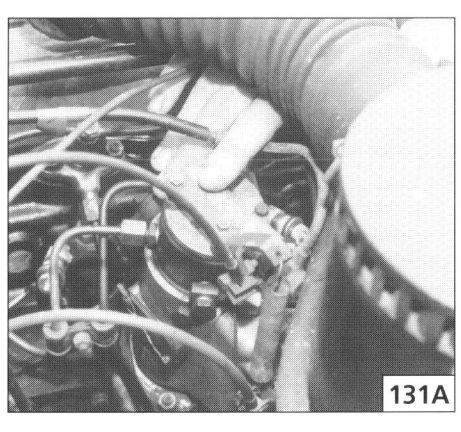

☐ Job 131. Bleed fuel system.

DIESEL MODELS ONLY

Whenever a filter has been changed on diesel models, it will be necessary to bleed the system to remove any trapped air. DO NOT attempt to start the engine before doing so.

Slacken the air vent screw, (130, arrowed) which can be found on top of whichever filter has just been renewed or disturbed. Some vehicles have a bulkhead mounted twin installation - in which case, first one vent screw then the other should be bled - but all units are similar except that the air vent screw may be near the front of the upper housing.

131A. Operate the hand priming lever on the fuel pump a few times until fuel can be seen flowing from the bleed pipe or air vent screw. Now tighten the bleed pipe or vent screw.

Operate the hand priming lever a few times more to disperse any remaining air and see if the engine will start. If only the filters have been disturbed, it should. If however, other parts of the system have been disturbed, or if you are ever unfortunate enough to run out of fuel, these additional steps will be necessary.

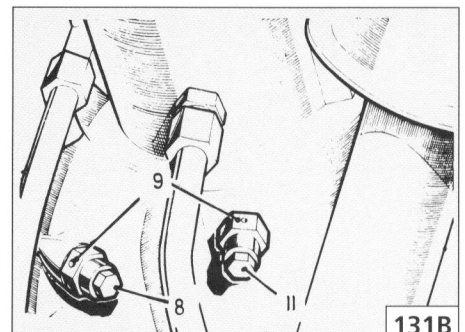

131B. If the engine doesn't start the first time, repeat the above procedure again then slacken the air vent screw on the fuel distributor pump body (131B.8). Operate the hand priming lever (131A) until fuel without any trace of air bubbles emerges from the bleed hole (131B.9). Now tighten the air vent screw.

Slacken the additional air vent screw in the fuel distributor control cover (131B.11), and operate the hand priming lever until air-free fuel emerges from the bleed hole. Tighten the air vent screw. The engine should now start and run smoothly. (Illustration, courtesy Land Rover)

12,000 Mile Mechanical and Electrical - Around the Vehicle

First carry out Jobs 7 to 16, 20 to 22, 45 to 48 and 95 to 97 as applicable

☐ **Job 132. Toolkit and jack.**

Inspect the toolkit, wipe the tools with an oily rag to stop them rusting and lubricate the jack, checking that it works smoothly.

☐ **Job 133. Test shock absorbers.**

'Bounce' test each corner of the Land Rover in turn in order to check the efficiency of the shock absorbers. If the vehicle 'bounces' at all, the shock absorbers have had it. They should be replaced in pairs as an axle set. Efficient shock absorbers can make an enormous difference to your vehicle's safety and handling.

INSIDE INFORMATION: In practice, a Land Rovers springs are so strong and stiff that you will be hard pressed to discern anything from this conventional MoT test, although you can try by jumping up and down on the outer ends of the front bumpers. Do check each shock absorber for leaks, body corrosion or deterioration in the rubber bushes.

12,000 Mile Mechanical and Electrical - Under the Vehicle

First carry out Jobs 49 to 69 and 98 to 111 as applicable

SAFETY FIRST!
Raise the front of the Land Rover off the ground after reading carefully the information at the start of this chapter on lifting and supporting the vehicle.

☐ **Job 134. Renew transfer box oil.**

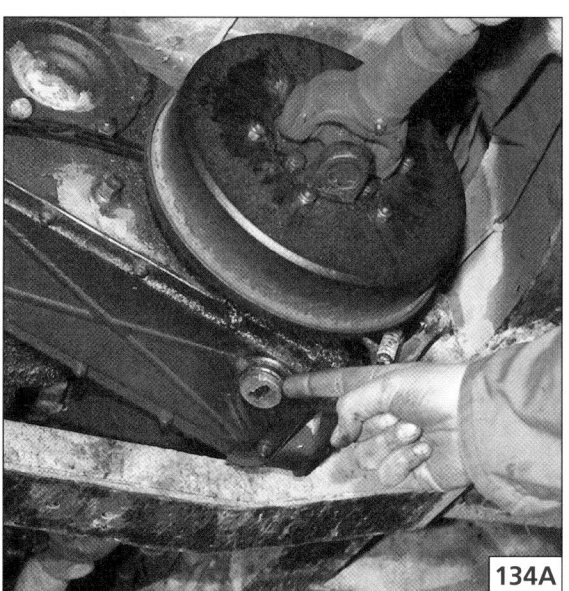

This Job should be done immediately after a short drive so that the oil is warm enough to flow freely but not so hot as to scald you.

134A. The drain plug is shown here for all models except V8. You will need a special flat removal tool to remove the drain plug, or a very wide bladed screwdriver. Check the condition of the sealing washer (where fitted) before replacing the plug.

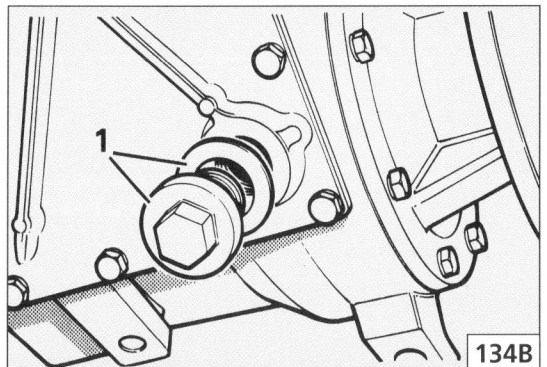
134B

134B. Here's the drain plug and sealing washer (132B.1) on V8 models which requires a conventional spanner or socket for removal. (Illustration, courtesy Land Rover)

Refill the transfer box as described in Job 60.

INSIDE INFORMATION: In winter, the thick oil will be time-consuming to squeeze out. Stand the bottle (sealed) in hot water for several minutes before using.

☐ Job 135. Renew gearbox oil and overdrive oil (if fitted).

As for Job 134, this Job also should be done immediately after a short drive so that the oil is warm enough to flow freely.

135A. The drain plug for all models except V8 is shown here; refilling is described in Job 59.

135A

135B. On V8 models there is a small filter behind the drain plug. Remove the drain plug and washer (135B.1) and clean this filter (135B.2) while the oil is draining. (Illustration, courtesy Land Rover)

VEHICLES WITH OVERDRIVE ONLY
Drain the oil from the overdrive unit - remove the drain plug, then refill with fresh oil remembering to use a new drain plug washer.

☐ Job 136. Renew front axle oil.

136. Drain the front axle oil and refill with fresh oil as described in Job 53.

☐ Job 137. Front axle breather.

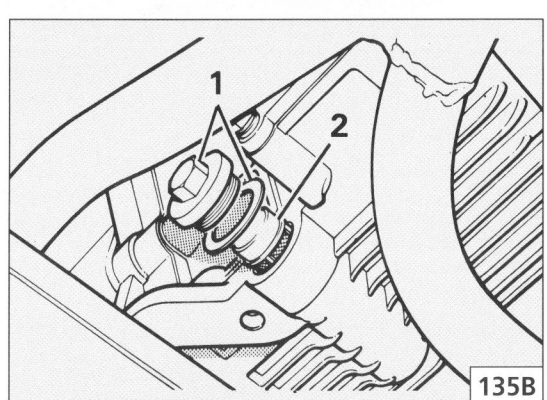
135B

137. Clean around the breather located on the upper side of the axle assembly and unscrew the breather from its taper seat.

Soak the assembly in a suitable solvent, such as white spirit, paraffin or diesel fuel for a few minutes and give it a good clean with a soft wire brush. If you shake the breather, you will be able to hear the ball valve inside rattling around indicating that it's free and not seized. If you don't hear anything, the breather should be renewed.

136

137

12,000 MILE SERVICE

Job 138. Front suspension security.

138A. Check the tightness of the front spring U-bolt nuts, making sure that the correct locknuts are fitted, and that the U-bolts themselves are not damaged or distorted.

138B. Check the leaf springs for broken leaves and for the condition of the retaining straps. Also check the condition and tightness of the shackle nuts and bolts. It's a good idea to check the spring eye bushes by levering between the spring and chassis with a stout bar. Any wear here means new bushes and that's a pig of a job to do. Definitely a SPECIALIST SERVICE operation.

138A

SAFETY FIRST!
NEVER try burning out old bushes. The hot rubber can explode, the spring temper could be lost and there are terrible potential health hazards - see
'Fluoroelastomers' in Chapter 1 - Safety First!

138B

Job 139. Check front propshaft U/Js.

139. Check for wear in the propeller shaft universal joints by moving the shaft up and down with a lever and looking for movement in the joint. Also check the tightness of the flange retaining bolts: you'll be surprised how often you find them loose!

INSIDE INFORMATION: It's sometimes difficult to detect wear in a U/J when it's in place on the vehicle, just by moving the propshaft. But if you see signs of rust or red coloured dirt and grit around the U/J, you can bet it's worn out. That red coloured dirt indicates that the joint is absolutely dry of lubricant and when you take it apart, all the needle bearings inside will fall out in a heap of rust on the floor - honest!

139

Job 140. Service freewheeling hubs.

VEHICLES FITTED WITH FREEWHEELING HUBS ONLY
It pays to strip down, clean and grease freewheeling hubs since they are in a most exposed position. Genuine Land Rover approved units have service kits (140.7) available. Replacement bearings (140.10) are available, when necessary. The Spirolox ring (140.2) is applicable to 109 in. models only.

SAFETY FIRST!
Lower the front of the Land Rover and raise the rear after reading carefully the information at the start of this chapter on lifting and supporting the vehicle.

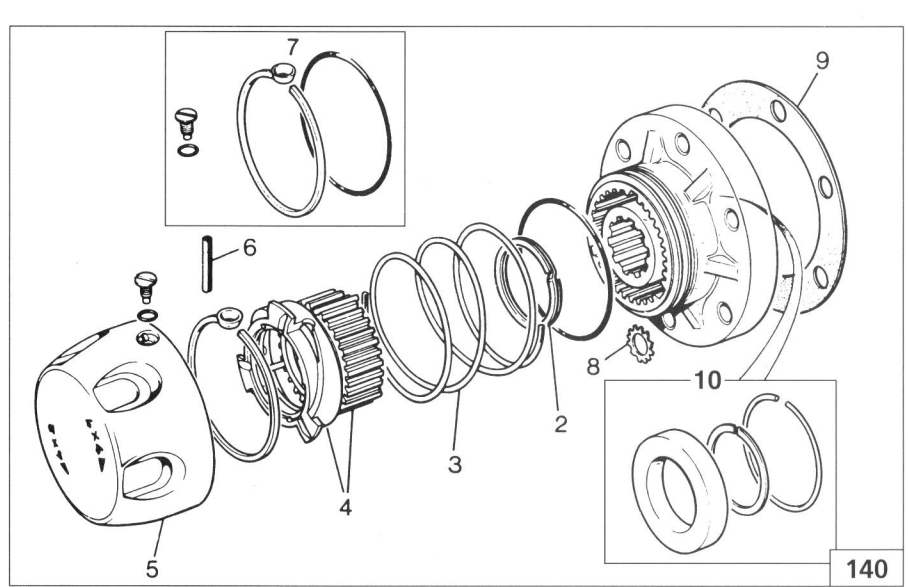
140

Job 141. Renew rear axle oil.

141. Drain the rear axle oil and refill with fresh oil as described in Job 65.

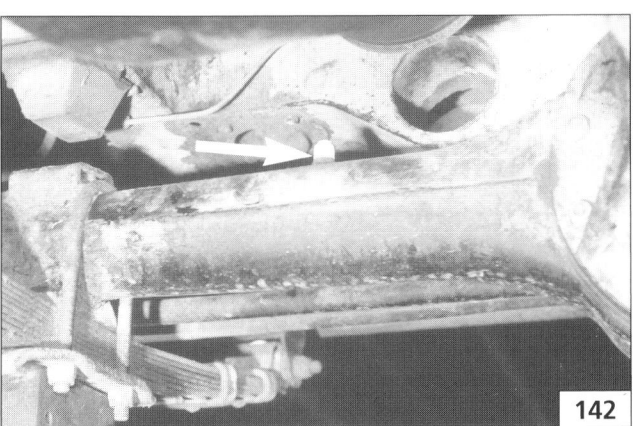

Job 142. Rear axle breather.

142. Here's the location of the rear axle breather (arrowed) which needs the same treatment as for the one at the front described in Job 137.

Job 143. Rear suspension security.

143. Check the rear springs, U-bolts and shackles as described in Job 138.

SAFETY FIRST!
Take care not to pull the vehicle off axle stands when pulling hard on mounting fixings. Have an assistant keep an eye on things as you work: better still, do this when the wheels are on the ground.

Job 144. Check rear propshaft U/Js.

144. Check the condition of the rear propshaft U/Js (seen here from above, vehicle body removed) and the tightness of the flange bolts noting the comments in Job 139.

12,000 Mile Bodywork - Around the Vehicle

☐ **Job 145. Check/lubricate door hinges.**

SERIES II & IIA ONLY
Check the door hinges for wear. See if there is any play in them when you attempt to move them up and down with the door open, grasping them at the opening/door handle end.

145. Remove the securing nut from the bottom of the hinge after pushing back the tab washer and remove the spring. When removed from both hinges, the door, complete with hinge pin, can be lifted away. Watch out for the brass cones! If play was present when you checked, fit new cones. Otherwise, grease and replace.

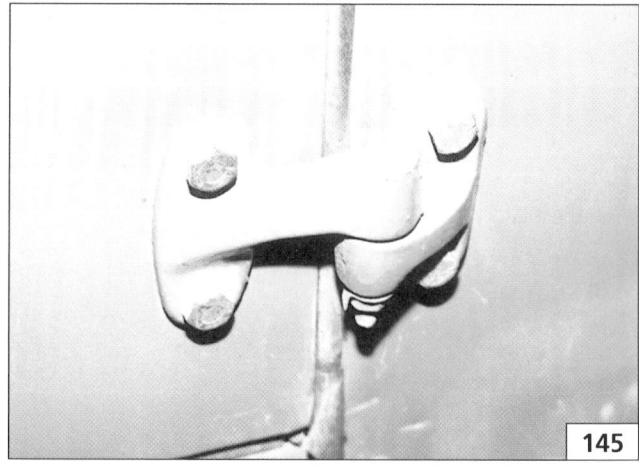
145

12,000 Mile Bodywork - Under the Vehicle

First carry out Jobs 27, 79 and 114 as applicable

Job 146. Tighten wing and body bolts.
Check the tightness of all fasteners securing the body to the chassis and also (visually) the fasteners holding the wing and other body panels to each other. Replace any missing nuts and bolts.

146

Job 147. Top-up rustproofing.
Renew the wax rust treatment to the underside of the vehicle. See *Chapter 5, Rustproofing* for full details.

24,000 Miles - or Every Twenty Four Months, Whichever Comes First

24,000 Miles, Mechanical and Electrical - The Engine Bay

☐ **Job 148. Engine mountings.**

Check the condition of the engine mountings inspecting carefully for swollen or deteriorated rubber caused by oil leaks. Check the tightness of the mountings at the same time.

☐ **Job 149. Refill cooling system.**

SAFETY FIRST!
Only work on the cooling system when the engine is cold. If you try to drain a hot engine, the water inside can boil up as the pressure is removed, releasing spurting, scalding steam and water.

Every two years, the coolant should be drained from the cooling system and discarded and then refilled with fresh. This is to ensure that the anti-corrosion properties of the coolant are retained and you should also take the opportunity to flush out the cooling system, getting rid of any debris that may have built up in there. Before draining down the cooling system, turn the heater tap fully open and remove the radiator cap. On the V8, remove the expansion tank cap and the plug from the top of the radiator.

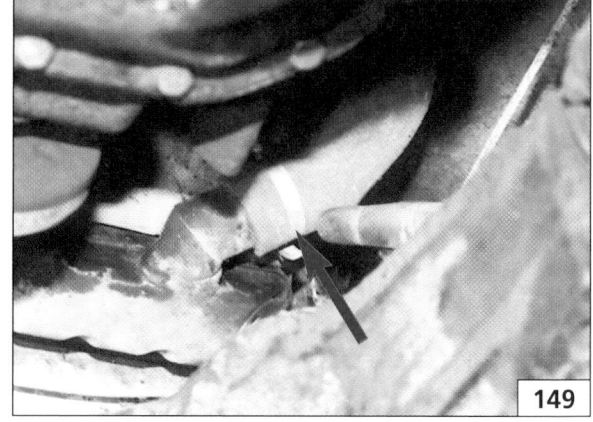
149

149. On Series I, 4-cylinder models there is a drain tap on the rear right-hand side of the cylinder block, on later 4-cylinder petrol and diesel models it's on the left-hand side of the block next to the engine dipstick, and on 6-cylinder models it's on the right-hand side, next to the engine breather. On later models, drain plugs may be fitted in place of the taps. On V8 models two cylinder block drain plugs are fitted, one on each side of the cylinder block. Radiator drain taps or plugs are in a variety of places but their location should be obvious on inspection. In some instances, there may not be a drain plug. In this case the only way of draining down the radiator is by removing the bottom hose. Here is its location on a typical replacement radiator with no drain plug (arrowed).

Before refilling the system, flush it through. Disconnect the top and bottom hoses, and with the radiator cap or filler plug refitted, put a garden hose into the radiator bottom hose and plug the gap between the garden hose and the larger bore of the bottom hose with a rag. Turn on the tap and run the water until no more sediment comes out of the top hose. Try turning the heater tap on and off so that the flow through the heater surges through it. If you suspect the heater of being badly clogged, disconnect the two heater hoses and flush the heater radiator separately. Now take the garden hose and insert it into the bottom stub of the radiator and flush that out in the same way.

Mix water and anti-freeze in a 50/50 solution. After reconnecting the hoses and closing all drain taps, refill with the prepared coolant - in the case of the V8, top up the engine until full, then top up the expansion tank until it is half full. Replace plugs and caps and run the engine until the top of the radiator begins to feel warm. *INSIDE INFORMATION: Fill the system slowly and squeeze the bottom hose a few times during filling to expel any trapped air.*

SAFETY FIRST!
Whilst carrying out the following, keep your hands away from the cooling fan and belts.

150

Stop the engine and slowly remove the radiator cap or expansion tank cap and top up once again. For vehicles fitted with an overflow bottle, refill it to just above the level of the overflow hose. Now run the engine, up to full operating temperature, revving the engine rapidly on several occasions so that the water pump pushes the water quickly round the system and removes any air locks. Wait for the water to cool down fully and then check the levels once again. Take care to check the water levels after the first time you use the vehicle on the road, allowing the water to cool down fully before taking off the pressure cap.

☐ Job 150. Radiator pressure cap.

Renew the radiator pressure cap - the spring weakens over time and the rubber seal perishes which reduces the pressure in the system which, in turn, allows the coolant to boil at a lower temperature.

☐ Job 151. Renew drive belts.

Renew the dynamo or alternator drivebelt (fanbelt).

24,000 Mile Mechanical and Electrical - Under the Vehicle

151

SAFETY FIRST!
Raise the Land Rover off the ground as necessary after reading carefully the information at the start of this chapter on lifting and supporting the car.

☐ Job 152. Engine flushing oil.

With newer engines, ones that have had the benefit of regular oil changes, this operation probably won't be necessary. After draining the engine oil in the normal way, leave the oil filter in place and refill the sump with engine flushing oil. Follow the instructions which come with the oil but in general, run the engine for a little while to allow the flushing oil to clean out the engine's oil passages. Drain off the flushing oil and then carry out the remainder of Job 28, Drain Engine Oil.

Job 153. Change brake fluid.

SAFETY FIRST! and SPECIALIST SERVICE: Obviously, a vehicle's brakes are among its most important safety related items. Do not work on the brakes unless you are fully competent to do so. If you have not been trained in this work, but wish to carry out the work described here, we strongly recommend that you have a garage or qualified mechanic check your work before using the car on the road. See also the section on BRAKES AND ASBESTOS in Chapter 1, for further important information. If this work is carried out in an unskilled manner, the car's braking system could fail totally. If the work is not carried out at all, the system could also fail. Brake fluid deteriorates over a period of time - it absorbs moisture from the air and then, under heavy braking, the water can turn to vapour, creating a vapour lock in the braking system and leaving the car without brakes. The brake fluid renewal procedures vary considerably especially with later models. Do not attempt to carry out this work without a workshop manual and a thorough understanding of what is involved. It may be best to invest in the cost of having this work carried out by a qualified Land Rover specialist.

Job 154. Check brake drums.

First read the **SAFETY FIRST!** and **SPECIALIST SERVICE** note at the beginning of the previous Job.

Examine the thickness and depth of wear of the brake drums. If excessively scored or worn thin or if *any* sign of cracking is found, replace them. If you don't have sufficient experience to know whether the drums are excessively worn or not, take professional advice from a fully trained mechanic.

INSIDE INFORMATION: Tap the drum, suspended on a piece of string or a hook, to see if it rings true. If it produces a flat note, the drum is cracked and must be replaced; don't use the car until you have done so.

Job 155. Brake back plates.

First read the **SAFETY FIRST!** and **SPECIALIST SERVICE** note at the beginning of Job 153.

Strip and clean the rear brake back plates using brake cleaner (to reduce risk of brake squeal and seizure) and clean out and lubricate the brake adjuster.

Job 156. Grease front propeller shaft splines.

Undo the retaining nuts and disconnect the propshaft universal joint flange at the transmission end. Unscrew the blanking plug from the propshaft sliding portion and fit a grease nipple in its place. You may find that there is already a grease nipple there if a previous owner decided to leave it.

Compress the sliding portion so as not to overfill with grease then apply a few strokes of the grease gun to the grease nipple. Move the sliding portion in and out a few times to distribute the grease, refit the blanking plug and reconnect the universal joint flange.

Job 157. Drain swivel pin housings.

157. Unscrew the drain plug at the base of the swivel pin housings (arrowed) and allow the oil to drain. Refill with fresh oil. Where the vehicle is used under arduous conditions, Land Rover advise owners to carry out this Job at more frequent intervals.

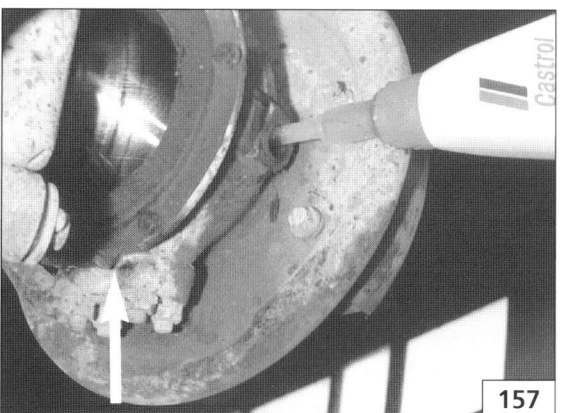

24,000 mile Bodywork and Interior - Around the car

Job 158. Lamp seals.

Remove the side lamp/indicator lenses, particularly the fronts, and ensure that the seals are effective. If water has been getting in to the lamps, remove the bulbs and smear a little petroleum jelly inside the bulb holder to help prevent rust. Renew the seal.

36,000 Miles - or Every Thirty Six Months, Whichever Comes First

Carry out all of the Jobs listed under the earlier service headings before carrying out these additional tasks.

36,000 Mile Mechanical and Electrical - The Engine Bay

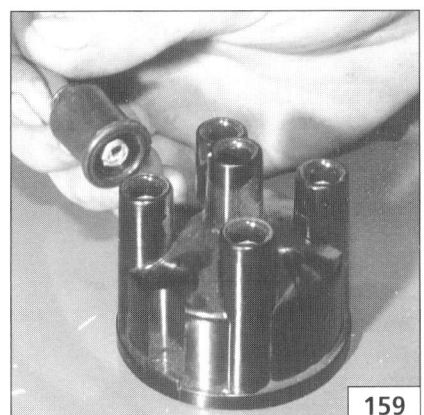

159

☐ **Job 159. Overhaul ignition.**

159. Replace the distributor cap, high tension leads and condenser. Faulty leads and cap may look perfect but can be major contributors to poor starting in damp weather. Replace them before they start to go wrong and let you down! Take great care not to confuse the order in which the leads are fitted. Make a diagram of the distributor cap and write down the correct lead positions. You can now match the new to the old.

☐ **Job 160. Clean float chambers.**

If your Land Rover is fitted with one of the simpler carburettors, there will be no problem in carrying out this work for yourself. Otherwise, SPECIALIST SERVICE: Have your Land Rover specialist dismantle and clean the carburettor(s) to remove the accumulation of sediment from the float chambers, before it starts to clog the jets.

☐ **Job 161. Renew brake servo filter.**

SPECIALIST SERVICE: Where appropriate, have the brake servo filter replaced by your Land Rover specialist.

36,000 Mile Mechanical and Electrical - Under the Vehicle

SAFETY FIRST!
Raise the Land Rover off the ground as necessary after reading carefully the information at the start of this chapter on lifting and supporting the vehicle.

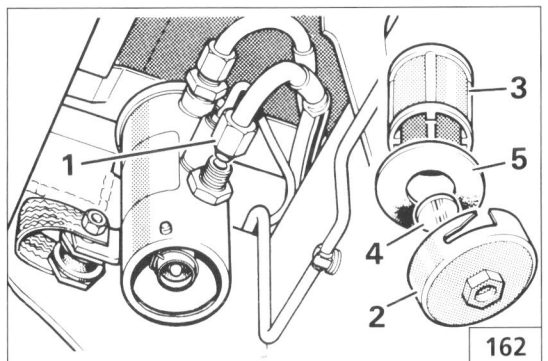

162

☐ **Job 162. Clean electric fuel pump filter.**

6 CYLINDER & V8 MODELS ONLY

SAFETY FIRST!
*Disconnect the battery and read the precautions given in **Chapter 1, Safety First!** before doing any work on the fuel system.*

When an electric fuel pump is fitted, rather than the engine-mounted mechanical pump, it is located on the right-hand chassis member between the transmission and the rear axle.

162. Disconnect the fuel inlet pipe (162.1) from the pump and plug over its end to stop the fuel tank draining. If for reasons of access you wish to remove the pump to clean the filter, disconnect the remaining fuel pipe, and the electrical connections then unbolt and remove the pump. Release the end cover (162.2) then take out the filter (162.3) and seal (162.4) and the magnet (162.4). Clean all the parts thoroughly then reassemble using a new seal if necessary. (Illustration, courtesy Land Rover)

☐ **Job 163. Braking system seals.**

SPECIALIST SERVICE: have your Land Rover specialist renew the rubber seals in the brake master cylinder, wheel cylinders and where applicable, the servo unit.

YOU HAVE NOW COMPLETED ALL OF THE SERVICE JOBS LISTED IN THIS SERVICE GUIDE, THE 'LONGEST' INTERVAL BETWEEN ANY JOBS BEING 3 YEARS OR 36,000 MILES. WHEN YOU HAVE FILLED IN EACH OF THE SERVICE INTERVALS SHOWN HERE, YOU MAY PURCHASE CONTINUATION SHEETS TO ENABLE YOU TO CONTINUE AND COMPLETE YOUR SERVICE HISTORY FOR AS LONG AS YOU OWN THE CAR.

PLEASE CONTACT PORTER PUBLISHING AT:

The Storehouse, Little Hereford Street, Bromyard, Hereford, HR7 4DE, England. Tel: 01885 488800.

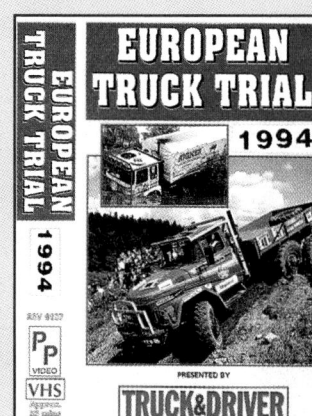

CHAPTER 4
REPAIRING BODYWORK BLEMISHES

However well you look after your car, there will always be the risk of car park accident damage - or even worse! The smallest paint chips are best touched up with paint purchased from your local auto. accessory shop. If your colour of paint is not available, some auto. accessory shops offer a mixing scheme or you could look for a local paint factor in Yellow Pages. Take your car along to the paint factor and have them match the colour and mix the smallest quantity of cellulose paint that they will supply you with.

Larger body blemishes will need the use of body filler and aluminium and galvanised bodywork demands the use of special filler since ordinary fillers won't adhere and will eventually break away. Always use filler with a reputable name, such as GalvX, produced by the makers of David's Isopon and that's what we used to carry out this repair.

SAFETY FIRST! Always wear plastic gloves when working with any make of filler, before it has set. Always wear a face mask when sanding filler and wear goggles when using a power sander.

4.1 The aluminium panels on a Land Rover dent quite easily and we have used a panel taken off a Land Rover to demonstrate how to carry out a small dent repair.

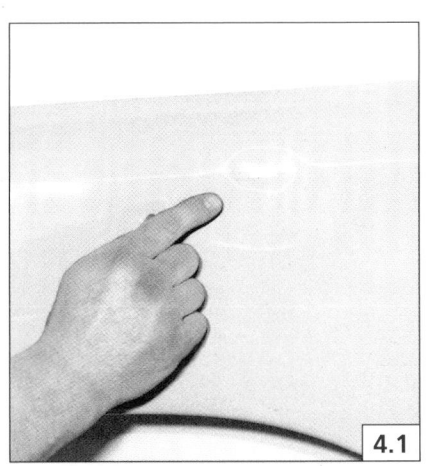

4.1

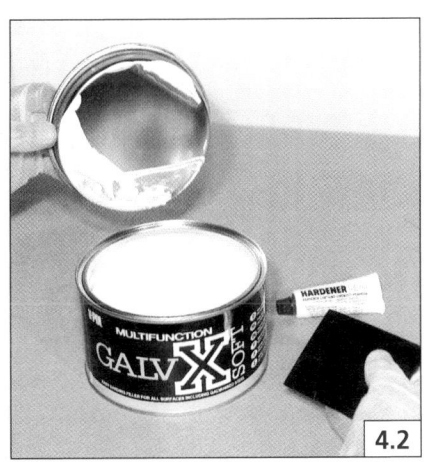

4.2

4.2 As we said earlier, we used a filler which is specially formulated to adhere to aluminium and galvanised body panels. You may not be able to get hold of it from specialist motorist stores but if you look up paint factors in your Yellow Pages you will be able to ring around and find one that stocks it. This filler is also particularly fine - excellent for 'stopping' minor blemishes - and sands very easily.

4.3

4.3 The makers of GalvX recommend that you remove the paint from the repair area and for a distance of 1 in. (25 mm) all the way around the damaged area. The repair area should be left clean and dry and free of dust. If you can, get hold of some professional spirit wipe in order to wipe the panel down and remove all contaminants that could cause paint problems. If not, wipe over the area with white spirit (mineral spirit) and then wash off with washing-up liquid in water - not car wash detergent. *Take care not to power sand deeply into the aluminium!*

4.4 Mask off the area around the repair. You can, as we did, take off the masking tape and paper before spraying the finish coat, so that the overspray blends in to the surrounding paint after it has been polished with cutting compound, available from any high street motor accessory store.

4.4

4.5 Use a piece of plastic on which to mix the filler and hardener, following the instructions on the can.

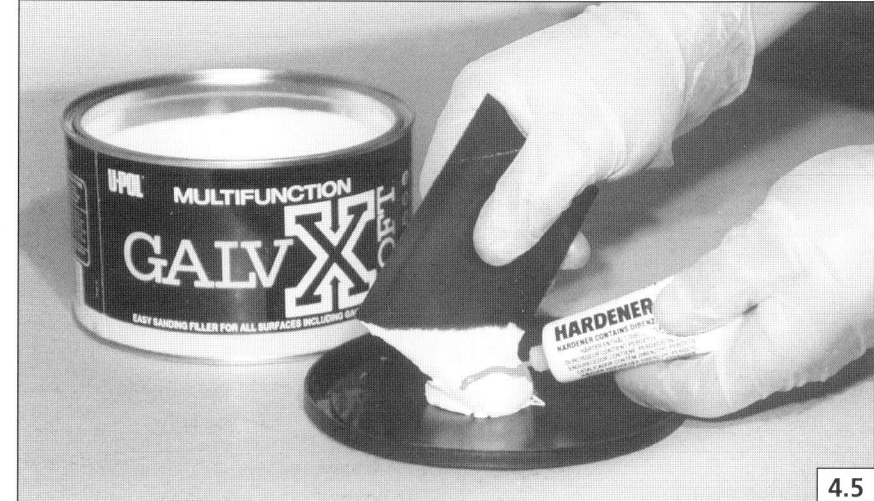

4.5

4.6 Mix the filler and hardener thoroughly until the colour is consistent and no traces of hardener can be discerned. It's best to use a piece of plastic or metal rather than cardboard because otherwise, the filler will pick up fibres from the surface of the card.

4.6

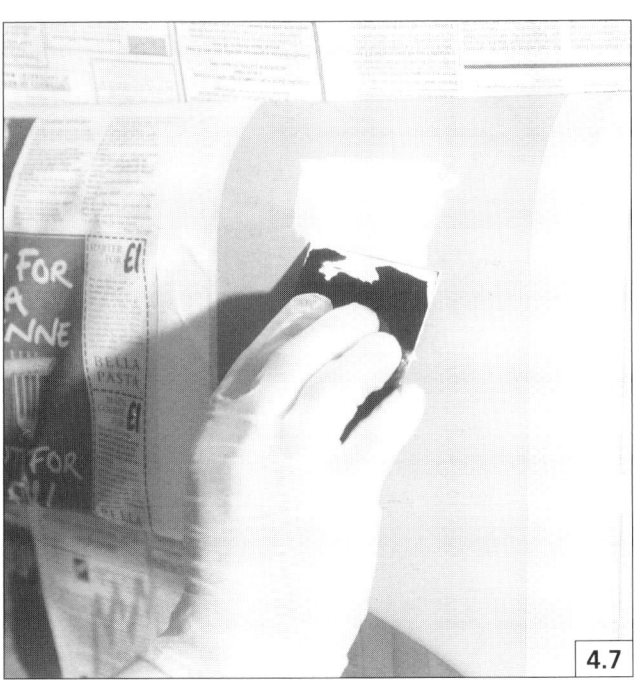

4.7 You can now spread the filler evenly over the repair.

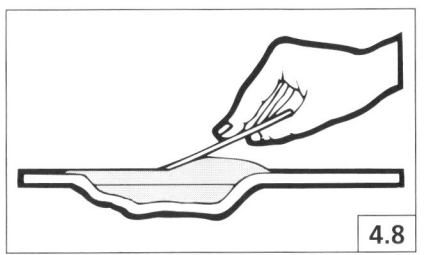

4.8 If the dent is particularly deep, apply the paste in two or more layers, allowing the filler to harden before adding the next layer. The final layer should be just proud of the level required, but do not overfill as this wastes paste and will require more time to sand down. (Illustration, courtesy David's Isopon)

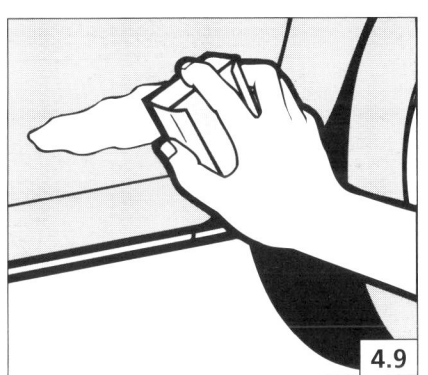

4.9 It is essential when sanding down that you wrap the sanding paper around a flat block. Sand diagonally in alternate directions until the filler is level with the surrounding panel but take care not to go deeply into the edges of the paint around the repair. There will invariably be small pin holes even if the right amount of filler was applied first time. Use a tiny amount of filler scraped very thin over the whole repair, filling in deep scratches and pin holes and then sanding off with a fine grade of sand paper - preferably dry paper rather than wet-or-dry because you don't want to get water on to the bare filler - until all of the coarser scratches from the earlier sanding have been removed. (Illustration, courtesy David's Isopon)

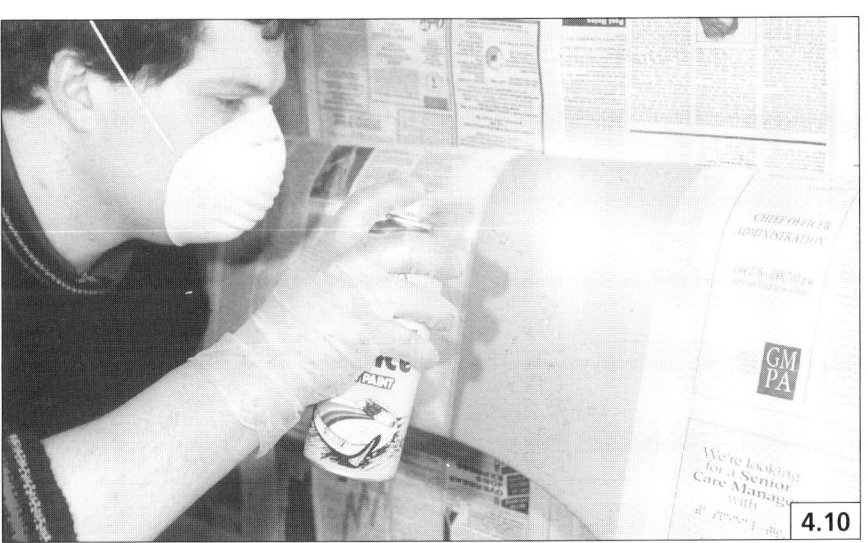

4.10 You can now use an aerosol primer to spray over the whole area of the repair but not right up to the edges of the masking tape...

4.11 ...and you can now use wet-or-dry paper to sand the primer paint since the Isopon is now protected from the water by the paint. Again, use a sanding block.

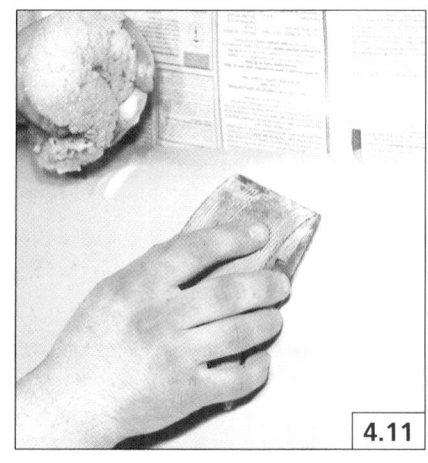
4.11

SAFETY FIRST! Always wear an efficient mask when spraying aerosol paint and only work in a well-ventilated area, well away from any source of ignition, since spray paint vapour, even that given off by an aerosol, is highly flammable. Ensure that you have doors and windows open to the outside when using aerosol paint but in cooler weather, close them when the vapour has dispersed, otherwise the surface of the paint will "bloom" - take on a milky appearance. In fact, you may find it difficult to obtain a satisfactory finish in cold and damp weather.

4.12 Before starting to spray, ensure that the nozzle is clear. Note that the can must be held with the index finger well back on the aerosol button. If you let your finger overhang the front of the button, a paint drip can form and throw itself on to the work area as a paint blob. This is most annoying and means that you will have to let the paint dry, sand it down and start again. One of the secrets of getting a decent coat of paint which doesn't run badly is to put a very light coat of spray paint on to the panel first, followed by several more coats, allowing time between each coat for the bulk of the solvent to evaporate. Alternate coats should go horizontally, followed by vertical coats as shown on the inset diagram.

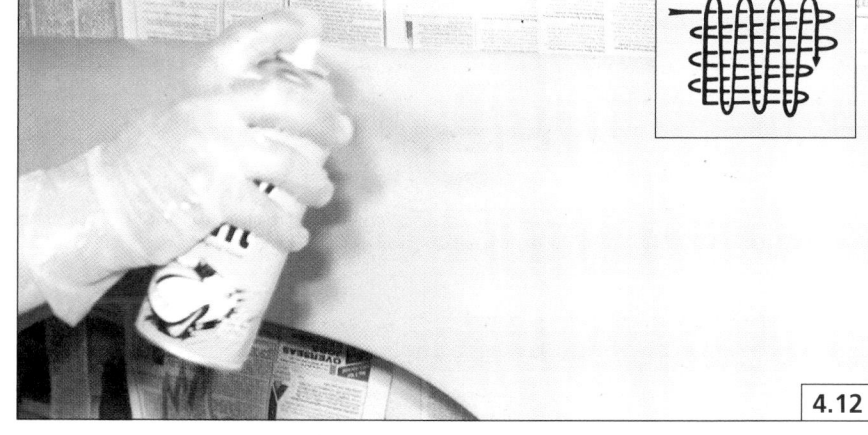
4.12

4.13 If carried out with great care and skill, this type of repair can be virtually invisible. After allowing about a week for the paint to dry, you will be able to polish it with a light cutting compound, blending the edges of the repair into the surrounding paintwork.

Do note that if your repairs don't work out first time and you have to apply more paint on top of the fresh paint that you have already used, allow a week to elapse otherwise there is a strong risk of pickling or other reactions to take place. Also note that a prime cause of paint failure is the existence of silicone on the surface of the old paint before you start work. These come from most types of polish and are not all that easy to remove. Thoroughly wipe the panel down with white spirit before starting work and wash off with warm water and washing-up liquid to remove any further traces of the polish and the white spirit - but don't use the sponge or bucket that you normally use for washing the car otherwise you will simply introduce more silicones onto the surface!

4.13

4.14 We are grateful to W. David & Son, the makers of GalvX and Isopon for their assistance with this section of the book and to CarPlan for their supply of the aerosol paints featured here. Both Isopon, one of the best general filler pastes on the market and CarPlan aerosol paints are widely available through high street motorists' stores.

4.14

CHAPTER 5 - RUSTPROOFING

When mechanical components deteriorate, they can cost you a lot of money to replace. But when your Land Rover's bodywork deteriorates it can cost you the vehicle, if the deterioration goes beyond the point where it is economic to repair. Some owners seem to think that because the bodywork is aluminium and the chassis is one of the toughest around, rusting can't be a problem, but that just isn't true. Although Land Rovers are designed to be around for decades rather than years, even the thick steel of the Solihull vehicle's chassis is capable of rusting away. Second, when aluminium corrodes, it's even more difficult than steel to repair, and where aluminium is in contact with steel, it corrodes in double-quick time. Therefore, time and money spent on maintaining your Land Rover's bodywork will save you even more money in the long run than that spent on its mechanical components. You may have noticed several places in *Chapter 3, Service Intervals Step-by-Step* maintaining the vehicle's underbody treatment is called for - this is how it's done. Please remember that different models of Land Rover have 'access' holes (they weren't put there for that, of course) in different places, so it isn't possible to be specific about which chassis and bodies have to be drilled and which can use existing holes.

Do take note of the fact that in Britain, the Automobile Association has carried out research into rust-proofing materials and has found that inadequately applied materials do more harm than good. A car's body panels are forever in the process of rusting unless there is a barrier in place to keep out the air and moisture which are necessary to help the rusting process along. However, if that barrier is inefficiently applied, the rusting process concentrates itself on the areas where the rustproofing is missing, which speeds up the corrosion and makes it even worse in the unprotected areas than it would otherwise have been. So take great care that you apply the rustproofing materials as thoroughly as possible. It's not a question of quantity; more a question of quality of application - reaching every part of the car with a type of rustproofing fluid that "creeps" into each of the seams, into any rust that may have already formed on the surface and using an applicator that applies the fluid in a mist rather than in streams or blobs which unfortunately is all that some of the hand applicators we have seen seem to do.

Also, you should note that the best time to apply rustproofing materials to your car is in the summer when the warmer weather will allow the materials to flow better inside the hidden areas of the car's bodywork and, just as importantly, the underside of the car and the insides of the box sections will be completely dried out. In spite of what anyone says, you are better off applying rust preventative materials when the car is dry than when it is wet.

SAFETY FIRST! Wear gloves, a face mask and goggles when applying rustproofing materials. Keep such materials away from your eyes but if you do get any into your eyes, wash out with copious amount of cold water and, if necessary, seek medical advice. All rustproofing materials are flammable and should be kept well away from all sources of ignition, especially when applying them. All such materials are volatile and in vaporised form are more likely to catch fire or explode. Do bear in mind that, if any welding has to be carried out on the car within a few months of rustproofing materials being injected into it, you must inform those who are carrying out the welding because of the fire risk. Cover all brake components with plastic bags so that none of the rustproofing material can get on to the brake friction materials and keep away from the clutch bellhousing and from exhaust manifold and exhaust system.

Always carry out this work out of doors since the vapour can be dangerous in a confined space.

INSIDE INFORMATION: i) All electric motors should be covered up with plastic bags so that none of the rustproofing fluids get into the motors - although this isn't too much of a problem with Land Rovers! ii) Ensure that all drain channels are clear, so that any excess rustproofing fluid can drain out. Then check once again that they are clear after you have finished carrying out the work, to ensure that the newly applied fluid has not caused them to be clogged up, otherwise water will get trapped in there, negating much of the good work you have carried out.

☐ Job 1. Clean Underbody

1. You will need to clean off the underside of the vehicle before commencing work, scraping off any thick deposits of mud and also removing any loose paint or underseal beneath the car. You could use a power washer - but you'll have to leave the car for about a week in warm dry weather so that it dries out properly underneath. Some garages have car washing equipment on the forecourt that enables you to wash underneath the wheel arches where, of course, most of the heavy mud resides.

All of the better rustproofing materials manufacturers make two types: one which is "thinner" and which is for applying to box sections and another one which is tougher and is for applying to the undersides of wheel arches and anywhere that is susceptible to blasting from debris thrown up by the wheels.

☐ Job 2. Equipment

2.Gather together all the materials and equipment you will need to carry out the work. Bear in mind the safety equipment you will need - referred to in Safety First! - see above. You will also need lifting equipment and axle stands - see *Chapter 1, Safety First!* for information on raising and supporting a car above the ground and also the Introduction to *Chapter 3, Service Intervals Step-by-Step,* for the correct procedures to follow when raising your car with a trolley jack. You will need copious amounts of newspaper to spread on the floor because quite a lot of the fluid will run out of the car and you may need to park your car over newspaper for a couple of days after carrying out this treatment. Do remember that the vapour given off will continue for several days and you would be best parking the car out of doors for about a week after carrying out the work shown here. Probably the best known makes of rust preventative fluid in the UK are Waxoyl and Dinitrol. The latter product came out top in a survey carried out by Practical Classics magazine and they also have the advantage that they produce an inexpensive application gun which does a proper job of atomising the fluid and putting a thorough misting inside each enclosed box section. If you don't own a compressor, you will have to hire one in order to power the Dinitrol applicator but the results will be better than can be obtained with any hand operated applicator. (Illustration, courtesy Frost Auto Restoration Techniques)

AROUND THE CAR

☐ Job 3. Doors

3. Where door trims are fitted, remove them to gain proper access. In most cases, you will be able to insert your injection tube into door hinge holes or other openings left in the door's construction. As with every part of the vehicle, you push the wand in as far as it will go, drawing it out slowly as the rustproofer is sprayed from the end, until all of the enclosed area is treated. The Series I door has the simplest structure...

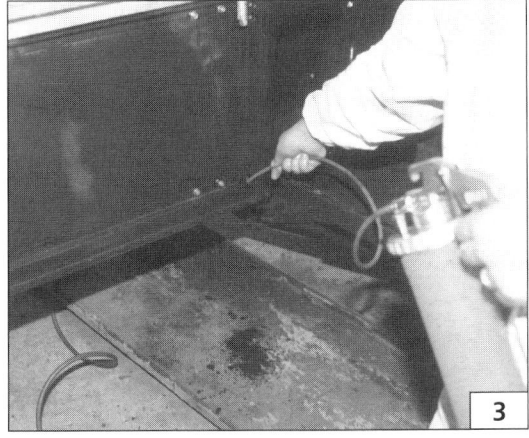

☐ Job 4. Series II & III door tops

4. ...while in the case of later vehicles, the rust-prone door tops will need careful attention. Drill the insides to gain satisfactory access.

5

Job 5. Tailgate and Rear Body

5. Tailgates don't normally rust away, but if you want to be sure, you will have to drill the ribs, perhaps from the inside. Nearby, however, are the rear body mountings and the rear body itself, where it butts up against the rear crossmember. These areas are notorious for going filigree and repay careful attention.

Job 6. Drilling Holes

6. Show vehicles, such as John Fletcher's Series I pictured here, and working vehicles, have different priorities. In the former case, you won't want to drill holes in the bodywork, even where access can't be obtained. Dinitrol 3654 has the ability to creep no less than 20mm into seams and here, it's being applied to seams, brackets and bolts. After a while, you can wipe off the residue, leaving the Dinitrol to do its stuff inside the seams. You must recognise that the protection offered cannot be as effective when the Dinitrol is applied in this way. You'll need plenty of rags which, because they will be highly flammable, need to be disposed of safely.

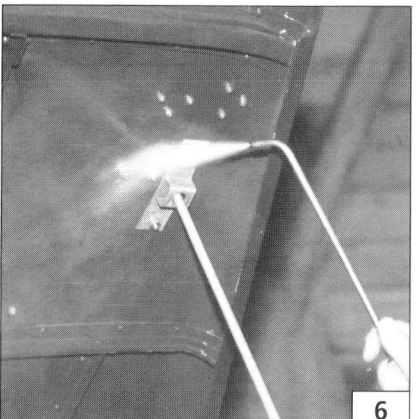

6

Job 7. Mounting Points

7. Mounting bolts will remain tight but become protected against corrosion if treated. Some types of rustproofing fluids, it is claimed, may cause rubber bushes to swell and deteriorate, but Dinitrol has the effect of keeping them supple.

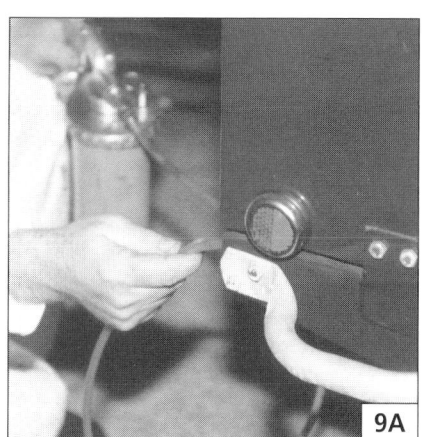

7

Job 8. Door Hinge Posts

8. These are vertical box sections located behind the front wings and you can gain access with your injector at the base of each post. Be thorough since they are prone to corrosion especially behind and around the bottom hinge.

BENEATH THE CAR

Job 9. Rear Crossmember

This part of the Land Rover is reached partly from beneath the car and partly from behind. Treat this area well because it is a major corrosion spot and its replacement is a moderately major undertaking.

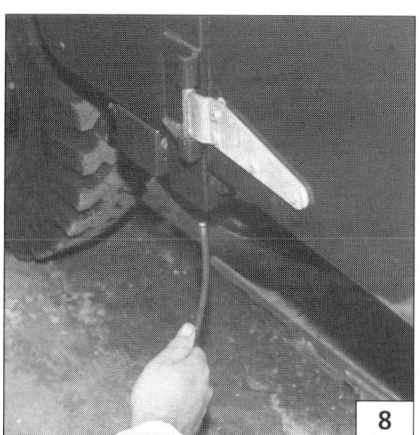

8

9A

9A. In the case of Series I vehicles, there is open access at the ends and from the front (inside) of the crossmember.

9B. There are often small access holes to be found on vehicles from Series II-on, but you may well have to drill suitable access holes: well worth doing in this area!

9B

INSIDE INFORMATION: i) Some car manufacturers coat the engine bay and the engine with protective clear (or yellow) wax when it is new. The wax is then washed off with a steam cleaner or with degreaser every two or three years and fresh wax applied. This makes the engine look dingy but protects metal surfaces against corrosion, screws against seizure and helps to keep rubber supple. Provided that you kept the wax off manifolds and any other very hot areas and away from any electrical or brake components and out of the brake master cylinder - covering each item individually with taped-on plastic bags should do it - you could preserve the components in your engine bay in the same way. Check that the makers of whichever rustproofing fluid you select don't recommend against using their product for this purpose. ii) Always buy any blanking grommets you may want to use - a dozen or so are usually enough - before you drill any holes in the car's underbody. Grommets are often only available in a limited range of sizes and you will find it easier to match a drill to a given size of grommet than the other way around.

10

☐ Job 10. Front and Rear Wheel Arches

Apply thinner, 'creeping' fluid to all seams and places where aluminium body comes into contact with steel chassis or bulkhead. Then give a coating of the heavier fluid across the whole of the inside each of the wheel arches. If you use only one of the other, you won't have the benefit of protection inside the seams, or the thinner fluid will wash out of the seams if you don't apply the heavier stuff over the top.. Also, under the front wings, pay special attention to the head light backs which are also rather good at corroding!

☐ Job 11. Chassis Rails and Outriggers

11A. Some crossmembers have access holes aplenty; others will have to be drilled. Even more important, seen to the right of this shot, are the outriggers. They tend to trap dirt (and should be cleaned off regularly to help further to prevent corrosion) and must be treated inside and out, paying particular attention to chassis-body mountings, once again.

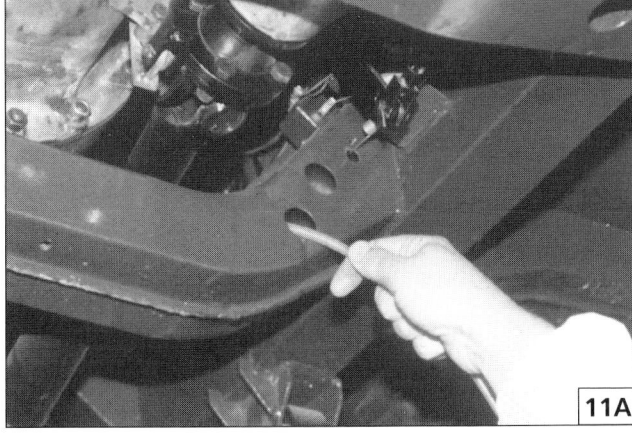

11A

11B. Another crossmember; another helpful hole. But be careful not to confuse box-section holes with drain holes for the floor above! Pay especially careful attention to the areas around the fuel tank - a great mud trap - and around the battery, where acid fumes can help corrosion along considerably.

☐ Job 12. Detective Work

12. Be prepared to spend some time working out exactly what does what and what goes where in terms of chassis and body sections. In view of what was said earlier about encouraging corrosion in any areas you miss, it is important not to miss any! This gusseted box section at the rear left of the Series I chassis could easily be missed if you weren't vigilant.

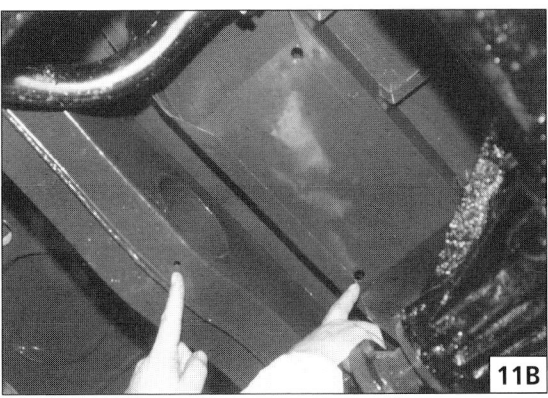

11B

12

Thanks are due to Beryl Miller M.D. of Dinol GB Ltd and Roger McNickle who supplied the Dinitrol used here and kindly and efficiently carried out all of the work featured in this section, and to John Fletcher of Clifton on Teme who kindly made his Land Rovers available to us.

CHAPTER 6 - FAULT FINDING

This Chapter aims to help you to overcome the main faults that can affect the mobility or safety of your car. It also helps you to overcome the problem that has affected most mechanics - amateur and professional - at one time or another... Blind Spot Syndrome!

It goes like this: the car refuses to start one damp Sunday morning. You decide that there must be no fuel getting through. By the time you've stripped the fuel pump, carburettor, fuel lines and "unblocked" the fuel tank, it's time for bed. And the next day, the local garage finds that your main HT lead has dropped out of the coil! Something like that has happened to most of us!

Don't leap to assumptions: if your engine won't start or runs badly, if electrical components fail, follow the logical sequence of checks listed here and detailed overleaf, eliminating each "check" (by testing, not by "hunch") before moving on to the next. Remember that the great majority of failures are caused by electrical or ignition faults: only a minor proportion of engine failures come from the fuel system, follow the sequences shown here - and you'll have better success in finding that fault. Before carrying out any of the work described in this Chapter please read carefully *Chapter 1 Safety First!*

ENGINE WON'T START.

1. Starter motor doesn't turn.

2. Starter motor turns slowly.

3. Starter motor noisy or harsh.

4. Starter motor turns engine but car will not start. See 'Ignition System' box.

5. Is battery okay?

6. Can engine be rotated by hand?

7. Check battery connections for cleanliness/tightness.

8. Test battery with voltmeter.

9. Have battery 'drop' test carried out by specialist.

10. If engine cannot be rotated by hand, check for mechanical seizure of power unit, or pinion gear jammed in mesh with flywheel - 'rock' car backwards and forwards until free, or apply spanner to square drive at front end of starter motor.

11. If engine can be rotated by hand, check for loose electrical

connections at starter, faulty solenoid, or defective starter motor.

12. Battery low on charge or defective - re-charge and have 'drop' test carried out by specialist.

13. Internal fault within starter motor - e.g. worn brushes.

14. Drive teeth on ring gear or starter pinion worn/broken.

15. Main drive spring broken.

16. Starter motor securing bolts loose.

IGNITION SYSTEM.

17. Check for spark at plug (remove plug and prop it with threads resting on bare metal of cylinder block). Do not touch plug or lead while operating starter.

18. If no spark present at plug, check for spark at contact breaker points when 'flicked' open (ignition 'on'). Double-check to ensure that points are clean and correctly gapped, and try again.

19. If spark present at contact breaker points, check for spark at central high tension lead from coil.

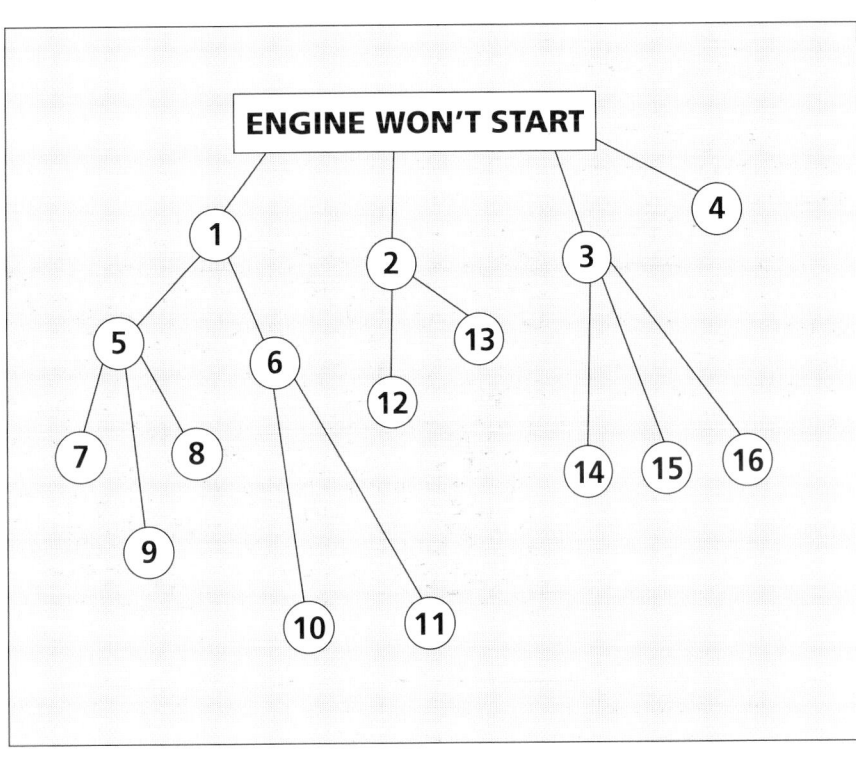

20. If spark present at central high tension lead from coil, check distributor cap and rotor arm; replace if cracked or contacts badly worn.

21. If distributor cap and rotor arm are okay, check high tension leads and connections - replace leads if they are old, carbon core type suppressed variety.

22. If high tension leads are sound but dirty or damp, clean/dry them.

23. If high tension leads okay, check/clean/dry/re-gap sparking plugs.

24. Damp conditions? Apply water dispellant spray to ignition system.

25. If no spark present at contact breaker points, examine connections of low tension leads between ignition switch and coil, and from coil to contact breaker (including short low-tension lead within distributor).

26. If low tension circuit connections okay, examine wiring.

27. If low tension wiring is sound, is condenser okay? If in doubt, fit new condenser.

28. If condenser is okay, check for spark at central high tension lead from coil.

29. If no spark present at central high tension lead from coil, check for poor high tension lead connections.

30. If high tension lead connections okay, is coil okay? If in doubt, fit new coil.

31. If spark present at plug, is it powerful or weak? If weak, see '27'.

32. If spark is healthy, check ignition timing.

33. If ignition timing is okay, see 'Fuel System' box. (see 36).

FUEL SYSTEM.

34. Check briefly for fuel at feed pipe to carb. (Disconnect pipe and turn ignition 'on', ensuring pipe is aimed away from hot engine and exhaust components and into a suitable container). If no fuel present at feed pipe, is petrol tank empty? (Rock car and listen for 'sloshing' in tank, as well as looking at gauge).

35. If tank is empty, replenish!

36. If there is petrol in the tank but none issues from the feed pipe from pump to carburettor, check that the small vent hole in the fuel filler cap is not blocked and causing a vacuum.

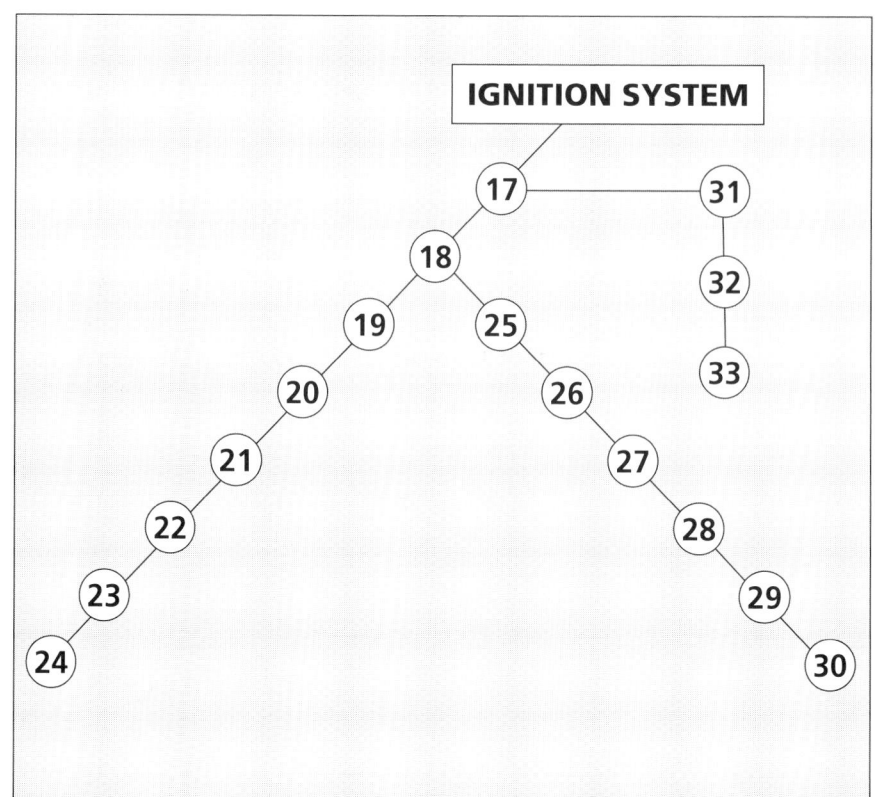

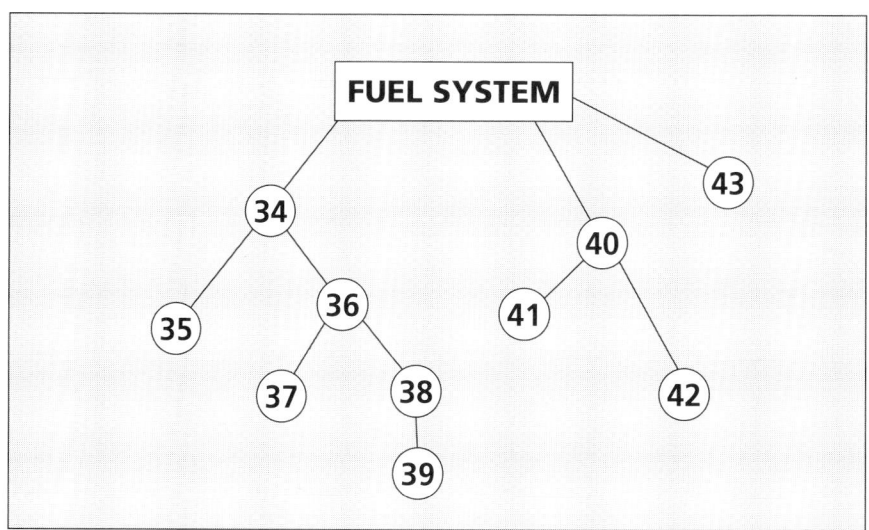

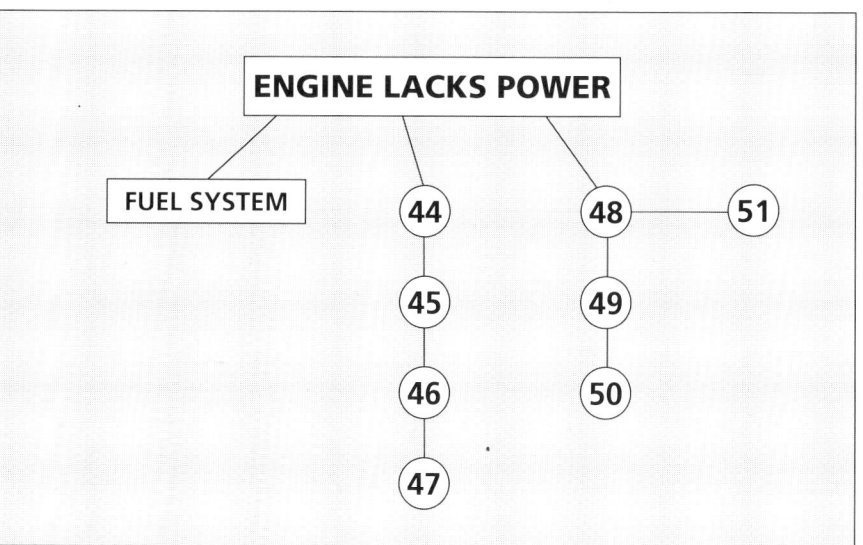

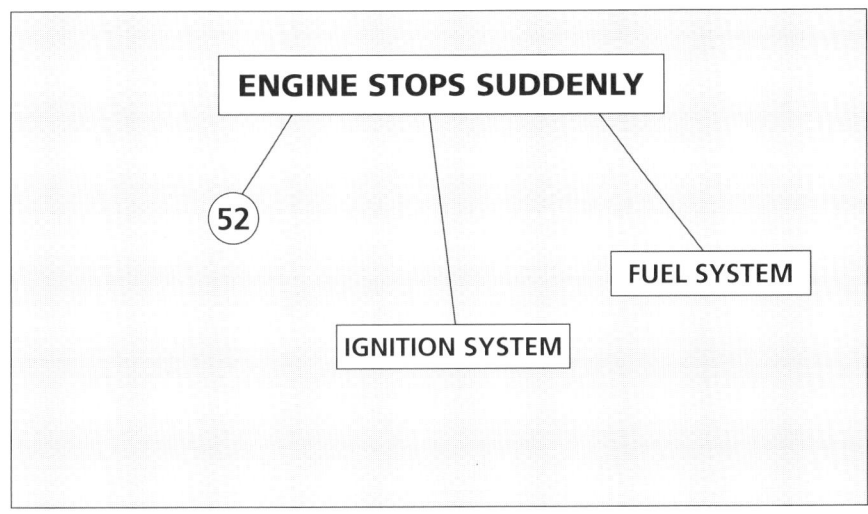

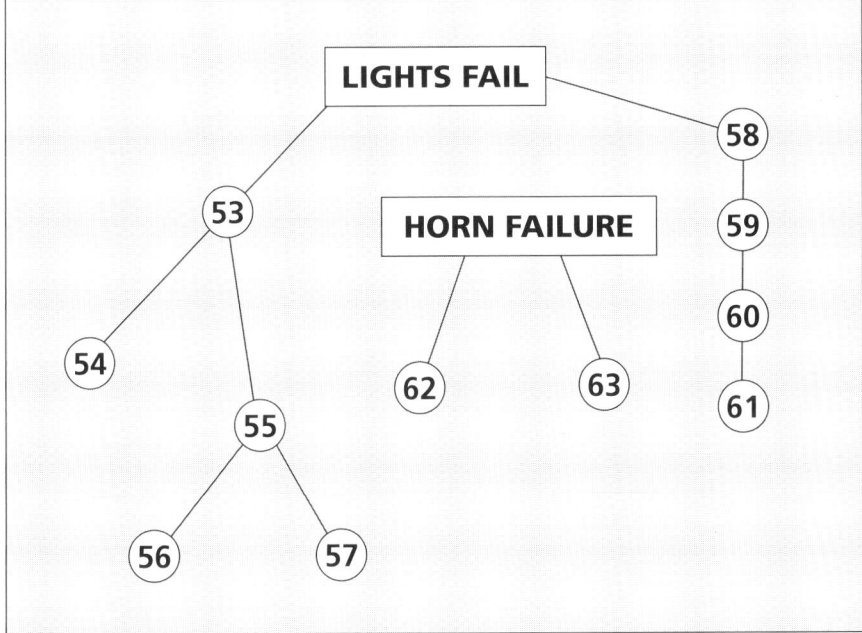

'shut'. Other possibilities include float needle valve(s) sticking 'open' or leaking, float punctured, carburettor incorrectly adjusted or air filter totally blocked. Clean plugs before replacing.

42. If the spark plugs are dry, check whether the float needle valve is jammed 'shut'.

43. Check for severe air leak at inlet manifold gasket or carburettor gasket. Incorrectly set valve clearances.

ENGINE LACKS POWER.

44. Engine overheating. Check oil temperature gauge (where fitted). Low oil pressure light may come on.

45. Thermostat not opening/closing at the correct temperatures or the cooling air flaps not operating because they've seized. Replace or free-off as necessary.

46. If thermostat/air flaps okay, check oil level. BEWARE - DIPSTICK AND OIL MAY BE VERY HOT.

47. If oil level okay, check for slipping fan belt, cylinder head gasket 'blown', partial mechanical seizure of engine, blocked or damaged exhaust system.

48. If engine temperature is normal, check cylinder compressions.

49. If cylinder compression readings low, add a couple of teaspoons of engine oil to each cylinder in turn, and repeat test. If readings don't improve, suspect burnt valves/seats.

50. If compression readings improve after adding oil as described, suspect worn cylinder bores, pistons and rings.

51. If compression readings are normal, check for mechanical problems, for example, binding brakes, slipping clutch, partially seized transmission, etc.

ENGINE STOPS SUDDENLY.

52. Check for sudden ingress of water/snow onto ignition components, in adverse weather conditions. Sudden failure is almost always because of an ignition fault. Check for simple wiring and connection breakdowns.

LIGHTS FAIL.

53. Sudden failure - check fuses.

54. If all lamps affected, check switch and main wiring feeds.

37. Check for a defective fuel pump. With outlet pipe disconnected AND AIMED AWAY FROM PUMP AND HOT EXHAUST COMPONENTS, ETC. as well as your eyes and clothes, and into a suitable container, turn the engine over and fuel should issue from pump outlet.

38. If pump is okay, check for blocked fuel filter or pipe, or major leak in pipe between tank and pump, or between pump and carb.

39. If the filter is clean and the pump operates, suspect blocked carburettor jet(s) or damaged/sticking float, or incorrectly adjusted carburettor.

40. If fuel is present at carburettor feed pipe, remove spark plugs and check whether wet with unburnt fuel.

41. If the spark plugs are fuel-soaked, check that the automatic choke is operating as it should and is not jammed

FUEL SYSTEM - SAFETY FIRST!
*Before working on the fuel system, read **Chapter 1, Safety First!** Take special care to 1) only work out of doors, 2) wear suitable gloves and goggles and keep fuel out of eyes and away from skin: it is known to be carcinogenic, 3) if fuel does come into contact with skin, wash off straight away 4) if fuel gets into your eyes, wash out with copious amounts of clean, cold water. Seek medical advice if necessary, 5) when draining fuel or testing for fuel flow, drain or pump into a sufficiently large container, minimising splashes, 6) don't smoke, work near flames or sparks or work when the engine or exhaust are hot.*

55. If not all lamps are affected, check bulbs on lamps concerned.

56. If bulbs appear to be okay, check bulb holder(s), local wiring and connections.

57. If bulb(s) blown, replace!

58. Intermittent operation, flickering or poor light output - check earth (ground) connections(s).

59. If earth(s) okay, check switch.

60. If switch okay, check wiring and connections.

HORN FAILURE.

61. If horn does not operate, check fuse, all connections (particularly earths/grounds) and cables. Remove horn connections and check/clean. Use 12v/6v test lamp to ascertain power getting to horn. On 6v cars, start engine - battery sometimes not charged enough to sound horn.

62. If horn will not stop(!), disconnect the horn and check for earthing of horn button or cable between button and horn unit and the wiring and contacts in the horn switch and steering column tube. The horn wire can often short itself out at the lower end of the steering tube - check!

FUEL GAUGE PROBLEMS.

63. Gauge reads 'empty' - check for fuel in tank.

64. If no fuel present, replenish!

65. If fuel is present in tank, check for earthing and wiring from tank to gauge, and for wiring disconnections. On many models, gauge is mechanical - check cable is sound from gauge to tank and that it is not trapped.

66. Gauge permanently reads 'full', regardless of tank contents. Check wiring and connections as in '66'.

67. If wiring and connections all okay, sender unit/fuel gauge defective.

68. With wiring disconnected, check for continuity between fuel gauge terminals. Do NOT test gauge by short-circuiting to earth. Replace unit if faulty.

69. If gauge is okay, disconnect wiring from tank sender unit and check for continuity between terminal and case. Replace sender unit if faulty.

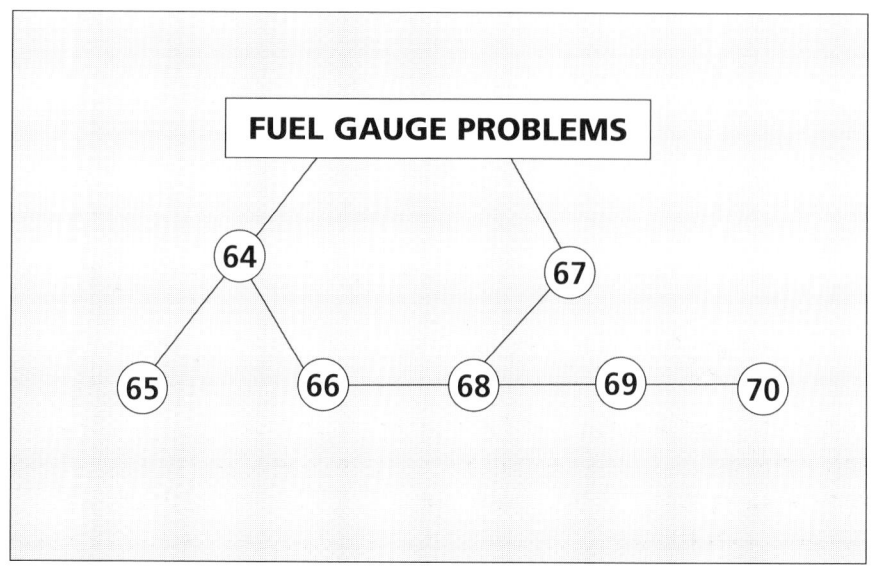

SUPPLEMENTARY INFORMATION - DIESEL ENGINES

The following fault finding chart covers in detail only those parts of the system that can be checked at home. If a simple solution is not found, it will be necessary to call on the services of a Land Rover specialist or diesel injection specialist.

1. *No fuel.* If the tank is allowed to run dry, the system will have to be bled as described in Chapter 3.

2. *Fuel blockages* from the tank to the pump can be checked at home. It is most important that any checks on the fuel system from the pump to the engine are carried out by a specialist. The high pressure means that a blockage is unlikely but also means that there is a safety hazard involved in working on this part of the system.

3. *Air in fuel system.* Bleed as described in Chapter 3.

4. *Glow plugs (cold engine).* These only fail after a very high mileage and usually one at a time. The usual symptom is an engine which starts, misfires and smokes badly until warmed up. Proper checking is usually SPECIALIST SERVICE.

5. *Slow cranking speed* can be caused by bad electrical connections or a flat battery.

6. *Worn bores* will affect a diesel engine more severely than a petrol engine so a worn out engine is less likely to start or run properly.

7. *Stop control faulty.* Check that the solenoid in the stop control "clicks" when the solenoid is switched on or off, in which case you can assume it is working. If a manually-controlled valve is fitted, check that the valve at the pump operates when the knob is moved. Otherwise, this is also SPECIALIST SERVICE.

8. *Injection pump faulty.* SPECIALIST SERVICE

9. *Injector faulty.* SPECIALIST SERVICE

10. *Injector feed pipe leaking.* SPECIALIST SERVICE

	1	2	3	4	5	6	7	8	9	10
Engine will not start	✓	✓	✓	✓	✓	✓	✓	✓		
Engine will not stop							✓			
Engine misfires	✓					✓		✓	✓	✓
Excessive (black) smoke from exhaust								✓	✓	

CHAPTER 7
GETTING THROUGH THE MOT

This Chapter is for owners in Britain whose Land Rovers need to pass the annual, compulsory 'MoT' test. The Test was first established in 1961 by the then Ministry of Transport and it attempts to ensure that vehicles using British roads reach minimum standards of safety. Approximately 40 per cent of vehicles submitted for the test fail it, but many of these failures could be avoided by knowing what the vehicle might 'fall down' on, and by taking appropriate remedial action before the test 'proper' is carried out. It is also worth noting that a vehicle can be submitted for a test up to a month before the current certificate expires - if the vehicle passes, the new certificate will be valid until one year from the date of expiry of the old one, provided that the old certificate is produced at the time of the test.

It is true that the scope of the test has been considerably enlarged in the past few years, with the result that it is correspondingly more difficult to be sure that your Land Rover will reach the required standards. In truth, however, a careful examination of the relevant areas, perhaps a month or so before the current certificate expires, will highlight components which require attention, and enable any obvious faults to be rectified before you take the vehicle for its test.

In view of the numbers of additions to the test in recent years it is MOST IMPORTANT that UK owners check for themselves that legislation has not changed yet again, since this book was written. Also, non-UK owners should obtain information on the legal requirements in their own territory - and act accordingly.

If the Land Rover is muddy or particularly dirty (especially underneath) it would be worth giving it a thorough clean a day or two before carrying out the inspection so that it has ample time to dry. Do the same before the real MoT test. An examiner can refuse to test a vehicle which is particularly dirty underneath. On the other hand a clean vehicle makes a better impression and it will help the examiner to see what he is supposed to be examining. Generally, this will work in the owners favour. For example, if a component or an area of underbody or chassis is particularly difficult to examine due to a build-up of oily dirt etc., and if the examiner is in doubt about its condition, he is entitled to fail that component or whatever because it was not possible for him to conclude that it reached the required standard. Had it been clean, it might well have been tested, and passed!

MoT testers do not dismantle assemblies during the test but you may wish to do so during your pre-test check-up for a better view of certain wearing parts, such as the brake shoes for example. See Chapter 3, Service Intervals Step-by-Step for information on how to check the brakes.

SAFETY FIRST!
*The MoT tester will follow a set procedure and we will cover the ground in a similar way, starting inside the Land Rover, then continuing outside, under the bonnet, underneath etc. When preparing to go underneath, do ensure that it is jacked on firm level ground and then supported on axle stands or ramps which are adequate for the task. Wheels which remain on the ground should have chocks in front of and behind them, and while the rear wheels remain on the ground, the hand brake should be firmly ON. For most repair and replacement jobs underneath these normal precautions will suffice. However, the vehicle needs to be even more stable than usual when carrying out these checks. There must be no risk of it toppling off its stands while suspension and steering components are being pushed and pulled in order to test them. Read carefully **Chapter 1, Safety First! and the introduction to Chapter 3** for further important information on raising and supporting the vehicle above the ground.*

This chapter provides a procedure for checking your Land Rovers condition prior to its official MoT Test. The same procedure could be equally useful to U.K. and non-U.K. owners alike when examining vehicles prior to purchase (or sale for that matter). However, it must be emphasised that the official MoT Certificate should not be regarded as any guarantee of the condition of a vehicle. All it proves is that the vehicle reached the required standards, in the opinion of a particular examiner, at the time and date that it was tested.

PASS THE MoT!

The aim of this chapter is to explain what is actually tested on a Series I, II or III Land Rover and (if it is not obvious) how the test is done. This should enable you to identify and eliminate problems before they undermine the safety or diminish the performance of your vehicle and long before they cause the expense and inconvenience of a test failure.

TOOL BOX

Dismantling apart, few tools are needed for testing. A light hammer is useful for tapping panels underneath the vehicle when looking for rust. If this produces a bright metallic noise, then the area being tapped is sound. If the noise produced is dull, the area contains rust or filler. When tapping chassis sections, listen also for the sound of debris (that is, rust flakes) on the inside of the panel. Use a screwdriver to prod weak areas. This may produce holes, of course, but if the rust is that far advanced you really ought to know about it. A strong lever (such as a tyre lever) is useful for applying the required force to spring bushes etc. when assessing whether there is any wear in them.

You will need an assistant to operate controls and to turn the steering wheel while you inspect components under the vehicle.

Two more brief explanations are required before we start our informal test. First, the age of the vehicle determines exactly which lights, seat belts and other items it should have. Frequently in the next few pages you will come across the phrase "Vehicles first used ..." followed by a date. A vehicle's "first used date" is either its date of first registration, or the date six months after it was manufactured, whichever was earlier. Or, if it was originally used without being registered (such as a vehicle which has been imported to the U.K. or an ex-H.M. Forces vehicle etc.) the "first used date" is the date of manufacture.

Secondly, strictly speaking, for a vehicle to pass the MoT test, there must not be excessive rust, serious distortion or any fractures affecting certain prescribed areas of the chassis or bodywork. These prescribed areas are load-bearing parts of the chassis or bodywork within 30 cm (12 in.) of anchorages or mounting points associated with testable items such as seat belts, brake pedal assemblies, master cylinders, servos, suspension and steering components and also body mountings. Not that very much of a Land Rovers bodywork rusts anyway, as most of it is aluminium (which corrodes instead), but the bulkhead is made of steel and the lower part of the bulkhead does rust and does include the bulkhead to chassis mountings - which are important load-bearing areas. Most of the other critical load-bearing areas and mounting points are on the chassis itself and will not be affected by rust in the body even if that rust is very much closer than the prescribed 30 cm (12 in.) - so in these instances the rust will not cause a failure of the test.

The following notes are necessarily abbreviated, and are for assistance only. They are not a definitive guide to all the MoT regulations. It is also worth mentioning that the varying degrees of discretion of individual MoT testers can mean that there are variations between the standards as applied. However, the following points should help to make you aware of the aspects which will be examined. Now, if you have your clipboard, checklist and pencil handy, let's make a start...

THE 'EASY' BITS

Checking these items is straightforward and should not take more than a few minutes - it could avoid an embarrassingly simple failure...

LIGHTS:

Within the scope of the test are headlamps, side and tail lights, brake lamps, direction indicators, and number plate lamps (plus rear fog lamps on all vehicles first used on or after 1 April, 1980, and any earlier vehicles subsequently so equipped, and also hazard warning lamps if fitted). All must operate without flickering and must be clean and not significantly damaged. The switches should all work properly. Pairs of lamps should give approximately the same intensity of light output, and operation of one set of lights should not affect the working of another - such trouble is usually due to bad earthing.

Indicators should flash at between 60 and 120 times per minute (rev the engine to encourage them, if a little slow, although the examiner might not let you get away with it!) Otherwise, renew the (inexpensive) flasher unit and check all wiring and earth connections. When Land Rovers were originally fitted with semaphore indicators, they are legally acceptable, provided that they work properly, light up when 'out' and close down efficiently, with an operative interior warning light. In modern traffic conditions, however, they are unsafe and we recommend strongly the use of supplementary flashing indicators.

Interior 'reminder' lamps, such as for indicators, rear fog lamps and hazard warning lamps should all operate in unison with their respective exterior lamps.

Head lamp aim must be correct - in particular, the lights should not dazzle other road users. An approximate guide can be obtained by shining the lights against a vertical wall, but final adjustment may be necessary by reference to the beam checking machine at the MoT station - if necessary, you may have to ask the examiner to adjust the lights so that they comply.
Reflectors must be unbroken, clean, and not obscured - for example, by stickers.

WHEELS AND TYRES

Check the wheels for loose nuts, cracks, and damaged rims. Missing wheel nuts or studs are also failure points, naturally enough!

There is no excuse for running on illegal tyres. The legal requirement is that there must be at least 1.6 mm. of tread depth remaining, over the 'central' three-quarters of the width of the tyre all the way around. From this it can be deduced that there is no legal requirement to have 1.6 mm. (1/16 in.) of tread on the 'shoulders' of the tyre, but in practice the tread should be visible in order to secure a test pass. In any case, for optimum safety - especially 'wet grip' - you would be well advised to change tyres when they wear down to around 3 mm. (1/8 in.) or so depth of remaining tread.

Visible 'tread wear indicator bars', found approximately every nine inches around the tread of the tyre, are highlighted when the tread reaches the critical 1.6 mm. point.

Tyres should not show signs of cuts or bulges, rubbing on the bodywork or running gear, and the valves should be in sound condition, and correctly aligned.

Cross-ply and radial tyre types must not be mixed on the same axle, and if pairs of cross-ply and radial tyres are fitted, the radials must be on the rear axle.

WINDSCREEN

The screen must not be damaged (by cracks, chips, etc.) or obscured so that the driver does not have a clear view of the road. Permissible size of damage points depends on where they occur. Within an area 290 mm. (nearly 12 in.) wide, centred on the centre of the steering wheel and up to the top of the area swept by the windscreen wiper, any damage must be confined within a circle less than 10 mm. (approx. 0.4 in.) in diameter. This is increased to 40 mm. (just over 1.5 in.) for damage within the rest of the screen area swept by the wipers.

WASHERS AND WIPERS

The wipers must clear an area big enough to give the driver a clear view forwards and to the side of the vehicle. The wiper blades must be securely attached and sound, with no cracks or 'missing' sections. The wiper switch should also work properly. The screen washers must supply the screen with sufficient liquid to keep it clean, in conjunction with the use of the wipers.

MIRRORS

If your Land Rover was first used before 1 August, 1978, it needs to have one rear view mirror only. Later vehicles must have at least two, one of which must be on the driver's side. The mirrors must be visible from the driver's seat, and not damaged or obscured so that the view to the rear is affected. Therefore cracks, chips and discolouration can mean failure.

HORN

The horn must emit a uniform note which is loud enough to give adequate warning of approach, and the switch must operate correctly. Multi-tone horns playing 'in sequence' are not permitted, but two tones sounding together are fine.

SEAT SECURITY

The seats must be securely mounted, and the frames should be sound.

NUMBER (REGISTRATION) PLATES

Both front and rear number plates must be present, and in good condition, with no breaks or missing numbers or letters. The plates must not be obscured, and the digits must not be re-positioned to form names, for instance.

VEHICLE IDENTIFICATION NUMBERS (VIN)

Land Rovers first used on or after 1 August, 1980 are obliged to have a clearly displayed VIN - Vehicle Identification Number (or old-fashioned 'chassis number' for older vehicles), which is plainly legible. See *Chapter 2, Buying Spares* for the correct location on your Land-Rover.

EXHAUST SYSTEM

The entire system must be present, properly mounted, free of leaks and it should not be noisy - which can happen when the internal baffles fail. 'Proper' repairs by welding, or exhaust cement, or bandage are acceptable, as long as no gas leaks are evident. Then again, common sense (if not the MoT) dictates that exhaust bandage should be a very short-term emergency measure only. For safety's sake, fit a new exhaust if yours is reduced to this!

SEAT BELTS

Belts are not needed on Land-Rovers first used before 1 January, 1965. On vehicles after this date - and earlier examples, if subsequently fitted with seat belts - the belts must be in good condition (i.e. not frayed or otherwise damaged), and the buckles and catches should also operate correctly. Inertia reel types, where fitted, should retract properly.
Belt mountings must be secure, with no structural damage or corrosion within 30 cm. (12 in.) of them.

MORE DETAILS

You've checked the easy bits - now it's time for the detail! Some of the 'easy bits' referred to above are included here, but this is intended as a more complete check list to give your Land Rover the best possible chance of gaining a First Class Honours, MoT Pass!

INSIDE THE VEHICLE

☐ 1. The steering wheel should be examined for cracks and for damage which might interfere with its use, or injure the driver's hands. It should also be pushed and pulled along the column axis, and also up and down, at 90 degrees to it. This will highlight any deficiencies in the wheel and upper column mounting/bearing, and also any excessive end float, and movement between the column shaft and the wheel. Rotate the steering wheel in both directions to test for free play at the wheel rim - this shouldn't exceed approximately 13 mm. (1.5 in.), assuming a 380 mm. (15 in.) diameter steering wheel.

☐ 2. Check that the switches for headlamps, sidelights, direction indicators, hazard warning lights, wipers, washers and horn, appear to be in good working order and check that the tell-tale lights are working where applicable.

☐ 3. Make sure that the windscreen wipers operate effectively with blades that are secure and in good condition. The windscreen washer (when required) should provide sufficient liquid to clear the screen in conjunction with the wipers.

☐ 4. Check for windscreen damage, especially in the area swept by the wipers. From the MoT tester's point of view, Zone A is part of this area, 290 mm (11.5 in.) wide and centred on the centre of the steering wheel. Damage to the screen within this area should be capable of fitting into a 10 mm (approx. 0.5 in.) diameter circle and the cumulative effect of more minor damage should not seriously restrict the driver's view. Windscreen stickers or other obstructions should not encroach more than 10 mm (approx 0.5 in.) into this area. In the remainder of the swept area the maximum diameter of damage or degree of encroachment by obstructions is 40 mm (approx. 1.6 in.) and there is no ruling regarding cumulative damage. Specialist windscreen companies can often repair a cracked screen for a lot less than the cost of replacement.

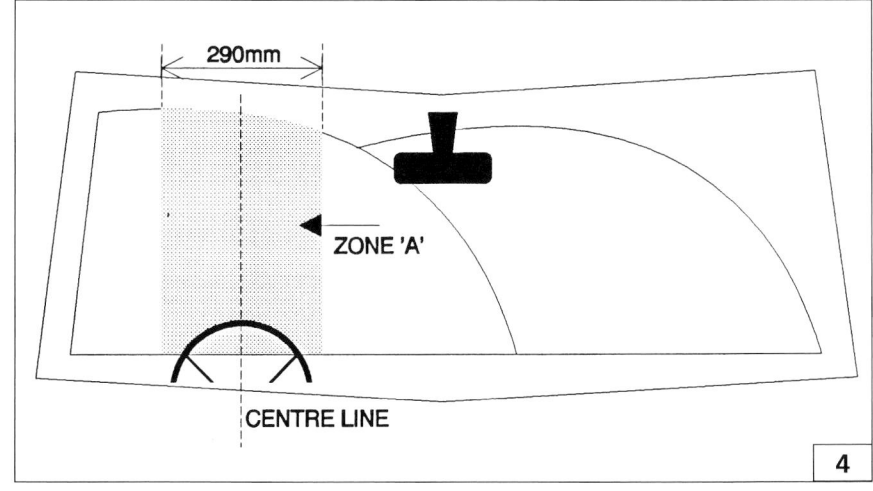

☐ 5. The horn control should be present, secure and readily accessible to the driver, and the horn(s) should be loud enough to be heard by other road users. Gongs, bells and sirens are not permitted (except as part of an anti-theft device) and two (or more) tone horns (which alternate between two or more notes) are not permitted at all. On vehicles first used after 1 August 1973, the horn should produce a constant, continuous or uniform note which is neither harsh nor grating.

☐ 6. There must be one exterior mirror on the driver's side of the vehicle and either an exterior mirror fitted to the passenger's side or an interior mirror. The required mirrors should be secure and in good condition.

☐ 7. Check that the hand brake operates effectively without coming to the end of its working travel. The lever and its mechanism must be complete, securely mounted, unobstructed in its travel and in a sufficiently good condition to remain firmly in the "On" position even when knocked from side to side. The 30 cm rule (regarding damage to body/chassis areas) applies in the vicinity of the hand brake lever mounting.

☐ 8. The foot brake pedal assembly should be complete, unobstructed, and in a good working condition, including the pedal rubber (which should not have been worn smooth). There should be no excessive movement of the pedal at right angles to its normal direction (indicating a badly worn pedal bearing or pivot). When fully depressed, the pedal should not be at the end of its travel. The pedal should not feel spongy (indicating air in the hydraulic system), nor should it tend to creep downwards while held under pressure (which indicates a faulty master cylinder). However, if the pedal is depressed and held in this position while the engine is started, it should dip slightly as the engine starts. This indicates that the vacuum servo unit (if fitted) is working properly.

☐ 9. Seats must be secure on their mountings and seat backs must be capable of being locked in the upright position. The normal Land Rover set-up is acceptable, if hardly an ideal demonstration of this requirement.

☐ 10. On Land Rovers first used on or after 1 January 1965, but before 1 April 1987, the driver's seat and front passenger's seat furthest from the drivers seat need belts. These can be simple diagonal belts on vehicles first used before 1 April, 1981, rather than the three-point belts (lap and diagonal belts for adults with at least three anchorage points - the type which we prefer) required by later vehicles. On these vehicles there is no legal requirement for the middle passenger seat to have a belt. Examine seat belt webbing and fittings to make sure that all are in good condition and that anchorages are firmly attached to the vehicle's structure. Locking mechanisms should be capable of remaining locked, and of being released if required, when under load. Flexible buckle stalks (if fitted) should be free of corrosion, broken cable strands or other weaknesses.

☐ 11. Check that on retracting seat belts the webbing winds into the retracting unit automatically, albeit with some manual assistance to start with.

☐ 12. Note the point raised earlier regarding corrosion around seat belt anchorage points. The MoT tester will not carry out any dismantling here, but he will examine all the anchorage points both from inside and outside the vehicle, where applicable.

☐ 13. Before getting out of the vehicle, make sure that ALL doors can be opened from the inside.

OUTSIDE THE VEHICLE

☐ 14. Before closing the driver's door check the condition of the lower part of the door hinge post and adjoining areas of the bulkhead. Any rust or other damage which weakens the panelwork in this area is likely to be within 12 in. (30 cm) of the bulkhead to chassis mounting (which is under the bottom of the hinge post) and therefore, strictly, a reason for failing the test. Remember to check the same area on the passengers side of the vehicle.

Now check all of the lights, front and rear, (and the number plate lights) while your assistant operates the light switches.

☐ 15. As we said earlier, you can carry out a rough and ready check on head lamp alignment for yourself, although it will certainly not be as accurate as having it done for you at the MoT testing station. Drive your Land Rover near to a wall, as shown. Check that your tyres are correctly inflated and the vehicle is on level ground.

Draw on the wall, with chalk:
  a horizontal line about 2 metres long, and at same height as centre of head lamp lens.
  two vertical lines about 1 metre long, each forming a cross with the horizontal line and the same distance apart as the head lamp centres.
  another vertical line to form a cross on the horizontal line, midway between the others.

Now position your car so that:
  it faces the wall squarely, and its centre line is in line with centre line marked on the wall.
  the steering is straight.
  head light lenses are 5.0 metres (16 ft) from the wall.

Switch on the headlamps' 'main' and 'dipped' beams in turn, and measure their centre points. You will be able to judge any major discrepancies in intensity and aim prior to having the beams properly set by a garage with beam measuring equipment.

Headlamps should be complete, clean, securely mounted, in good working order and not adversely affected by the operation of another lamp, and these basic requirements affect all the lamps listed below. Headlamps must dip as a pair from a single switch. Their aim must be correctly adjusted and they should not be affected (even to the extent of flickering) when lightly tapped by hand. Each head lamp should match its partner in terms of size, colour and intensity of light, and can be white or yellow.

☐ 16. Side lights should show white light to the front and red light to the rear. Lenses should not be broken, cracked or incomplete. Note that the original 'D' lights may fail because they have insufficient lens area. Modern 'repro.' 'D' lights, without a centre bar, get over the problem, if necessary.

☐ 17. Vehicles first used before 1 April 1986 do not have to have a hazard warning device, but if one is fitted, it must be tested, and it must operate with the ignition switch either on or off. The lights should flash 60-120 times per minute, and indicators must operate independently of any other lights.

distance between headlamp centres

height of headlamps above floor

2m long horizontal line

floor

Drawing on wall

wall

3.8m

15

☐ 18. Check your stop lights. Pre-1971 vehicles need only one, but when two are fitted, both are tested, so you will not get away with one that works and one that doesn't! Stop lamps should produce a steady red light when the foot brake is applied.

☐ 19. There must be two red rear reflectors - always fitted by the manufacturers, of course! - which are clean, and securely and symmetrically fitted.

☐ 20. Vehicles first used on or after 1 April 1980 must have one rear fog lamp fitted to the centre or offside of the vehicle and, so far as fog lamps are concerned, the MoT tester is interested in this lamp on these vehicles only. It must comply with the basic requirements (listed under headlamps) and emit a steady red light. Its tell-tale lamp, inside the car, must work to inform the driver that it is switched on.

☐ 21. There must be registration number plates at the front and rear of the Land Rover and both must be clean, secure, complete and unobscured. Letters and figures must be correctly formed and correctly spaced and not likely to be misread due to an uncovered securing bolt or whatever. The year letter counts as a figure. The space between letters and figures must be at least twice that between adjacent letters or figures.

☐ 22. Number plate lamps must be present, working, and not flickering when tapped by hand, just as for other lamps. Where more than one lamp or bulb was fitted as original equipment, all must be working.

The MoT tester will examine tyres and wheels while walking around the vehicle and again when he is underneath it.

☐ 23. Front tyres should match each other and rear tyres should match each other, both sets matching in terms of size, aspect ratio and type of structure. For example, you must never fit tyres of different sizes or types, such as cross-ply or radial, on the same 'axle'. If cross-ply or bias belted tyres are fitted to the rear of the car, you must not fit radials to the front. If cross-ply tyres are fitted to the rear, bias belted tyres should not be fitted to the front. (We recommend that you do not mix tyre tyres anywhere on the car.)

☐ 24. Failure of the test can be caused by a cut, lump, tear or bulge in a tyre, exposed ply or cord, a badly seated tyre, a re-cut tyre, a tyre fouling part of the vehicle, or a seriously damaged or misaligned valve stem which could cause sudden deflation of the tyre. To pass the test, the grooves of the tread pattern must be at least 1.6 mm deep throughout a continuous band comprising the central three-quarters of the breadth of tread, and round the entire outer circumference of the tyre.

We are grateful to Dunlop/SP Tyres for all of the following photographs and information in this section.

☐ 24A. Modern vehicles have tread wear indicators built into the tread grooves (usually about eight of them spread equidistantly around the circumference). These appear as continuous bars running across the tread when the original pattern depth has worn down to 1.6 mm. There will be a distinct reduction in wet grip well before the tread wear indicators start to show, and you should replace tyres before they get to this stage, even though this is the legal minimum in the UK.

☐ 24B. Lumps and bulges in the tyre wall usually arise from accidental damage or even because of faults in the tyre construction. You should run your hand all the way around the side wall of the tyre, with the vehicle either jacked off the ground, or moving it half a wheels revolution, so that you can check the part of the tyre that was previously resting on the ground. Since you can't easily check the insides of the tyres in day-to-day use, it is even more important that you spend time carefully checking the inside of each tyre - the MoT tester will certainly do so! Tyres with bulges in them must be scrapped and replaced with new, since they can fail suddenly, causing loss of control of the vehicle.

NEW TYRE — TWI — ILLEGAL TYRE

24A

☐ 24C. Abrasion of the tyre side wall can take place either in conjunction with bulging, or by itself, and this invariably results from an impact, such as the tyre striking the edge of a kerb or a pothole in the road. Once again, the tyre may be at imminent risk or failure and you should take advice from a tyre specialist on whether the abrasion is just superficial, or whether the tyre will need replacement.

24B

24C

24D

24D. All tyres will suffer progressively from cracking, albeit in most cases superficially, due to the effects of sunlight. If old age has caused the tyres on your Land Rover to degrade to this extent, replace them.

24E. If the outer edges of the tread are worn noticeably more than the centre, the tyres have been run under inflated which not only ruins tyres, but causes worse fuel consumption, dangerous handling and is, of course, illegal.

Over-inflation causes the centre part of the tyre to wear more quickly than the outer edges. This is also illegal but in addition, it causes the steering and grip to suffer and the tyre becomes more susceptible to concussion damage.

24E

24F

24F. Incorrect wheel alignment causes one side of the tyre to wear more severely than the other. If your vehicle should ever hit a kerb or large pothole, it is worthwhile having the wheel alignment checked since this costs considerably less than new front tyres!

25. Road wheels must be secure and must not be badly damaged, distorted or cracked, or have badly distorted bead rims (perhaps due to "kerbing"), or loose or missing wheel nuts, studs or bolts.

☐ 26. Check the bodywork for any sharp edges or projections, caused by corrosion or damage, which could prove dangerous to other road users, including pedestrians.

☐ 27. Check that the fuel cap fastens securely and that its sealing washer is neither torn nor deteriorated, or its mounting flange damaged sufficiently to allow fuel to escape (for example, while the vehicle is cornering).

UNDER THE BONNET

☐ 28. The Land Rover should have a Chassis Number or Vehicle Identification Number fitted to the bodywork. The modern VIN plate is required on all vehicles first used on or after 1 August 1980. This should be on a plate secured to the vehicle's bulkhead and will be found etched or stamped on the chassis. See *Chapter 2, Buying Spares* for information on where the vehicle number should be located on your vehicle!

☐ 29. Check the steering box for security by asking your assistant to turn the steering wheel from side to side (with the road wheels on the ground) while you watch what happens under the bonnet. Then, check for free play in the steering assembly as a whole. This is done by turning the steering wheel from side to side as far as possible without moving the road wheels - and measuring how far the steering wheel can be moved in this way. More than 75 mm (approx. 3.0 in.) of free play, on the Land Rover's steering box system, at the perimeter of the steering wheel, due to wear in the steering components, is sufficient grounds for a test failure. Note that the 75 mm criterion is based on a steering wheel of 380 mm (15 in.) diameter and will be less for smaller steering wheels. Also check for the presence and security of retaining and locking devices in the steering column assembly.

☐ 30. While peering under the bonnet check that hydraulic master cylinders and reservoirs are securely mounted and not severely corroded or otherwise damaged. Ensure that caps are present, that fluid levels are satisfactory and that there are no fluid leaks.

☐ 31. Also check that the servo (if fitted) is securely mounted and not damaged or corroded to an extent that would impair its operation. Vacuum pipes should be sound, that is, free from kinks, splits and excessive chafing and not collapsed internally.

☐ 32. Still under the bonnet have a thorough search for evidence of excessive corrosion, severe distortion or fracture in any load bearing panelling within 30 cm (12 in.) of important mounting points such as the master cylinder/servo mounting, front suspension mountings etc. - not likely to be a problem in this area, but see Check 35, below.

UNDER THE LAND ROVER - FRONT END

33. SAFETY FIRST! On some occasions there is no alternative but for your assistant to sit inside while you go beneath. Therefore: 1) Place the ramps as well as axle stands beneath the vehicle's structure so that it cannot fall. 2) Don't allow your assistant to move vigorously or get in or out of the vehicle while you are beneath it. If either of these are problematical, DON'T CARRY OUT THIS CHECK - leave it to your garage.

☐ 34. Have an assistant turn the steering wheel from side to side while you watch for lost movement in the steering unit and then within the ball joints. The ball joint dust covers should also be in sound condition. Ensure that all split pins, locking nuts and so on are in place and correctly fastened, throughout the steering and suspension systems.

☐ 35. Inspect the front springs: Look for excessive rusting of the leaves, cracked or broken leaves, and or misalignment of the individual leaves in relation to each other, or of the springs as a whole in relation to the axle. Check that spring fittings are neither excessively rusted, distorted nor loose. Use a tyre lever (or similar) to move each spring eye in turn while looking for movement of the spring at the shackle bush, indicating wear in the bush. Check that shackle bolts are tight. Also look out for any chassis corrosion, especially within 30 cm (12 in.) of spring shackles and body mountings.

☐ 36. Inspect the shock absorbers: Their upper shrouds (outer casing) tend to rust. Any signs of leaks will cause failure of the test - look for weeping hydraulic fluid just below the lower edge of the upper shroud. Take a firm grip on the upper and lower shroud in turn with both hands and try to twist the damper to check for deterioration in the top and bottom mounting bushes.

☐ 37. Now here's the MoT text theory: With the wheels on the ground again, push down firmly a couple of times at each corner of the vehicle, then let go at the bottom of a stroke. The Land Rover should rise and then fall to approximately its original level. Continuing oscillations will earn you a 'failure' ticket for worn front 'shockers'! On the other hand, if you're strong enough and heavy enough to 'bounce' a Land Rover's springs, you'll deserve to win a coconut.

UNDER THE VEHICLE - REAR SUSPENSION

☐ 38. Check the rear leaf springs (as in paragraph 37 above for the front springs).

☐ 39. A 'bounce' test - says the MoT test regulations! - can be carried out as for the front dampers as an approximate check on how efficient or otherwise the damping effect is.

☐ 40. With the back of the Land Rover raised on axle stands (both rear wheels off the ground), rotate the rear wheels and check, as well as you can, for roughness in the bearings, just as you did at the front.

BRAKES

☐ 41. The MoT brake test is carried out on a special 'rolling road' set-up (except for vehicles such as early Land Rovers which have more than one driving axle permanently engaged), which measures the efficiency in terms of percentage. For the foot brake, the examiner is looking for 50 per cent; the hand brake must measure 25 per cent. Frankly, without a rolling road of your own, there is little that you can do to verify whether or not your vehicle will come up to the required figures. What you can do, though, is carry out an entire check of the brake system, which will also cover all other aspects the examiner will be checking, and be as sure as you can that the system is working efficiently.

IMPORTANT! See *Chapter 3, Service Intervals, Step-by-Step* for important information, including *SAFETY FIRST!* information before working on your Land Rover's brakes.

☐ 42. The MoT examiner will not dismantle any part of the system, but you can do so. So, take off each road wheel in turn, followed by the brake drum, and examine the drum for cracking, ovality and serious scoring, etc. Check the condition of the linings on the brake shoes; renew them if worn down to anywhere near the rivet heads and look for evidence of contamination by hydraulic fluid, oil or grease. Contaminated brake shoes must be replaced because the linings will break up due to the heat if they remain in use - quite apart from the reduction in the brake efficiency due to the contamination. Check the wheel cylinders' dust covers to see whether they contain brake fluid. If so, or if it is obvious that any cylinder has been leaking, replace it.

☐ 43. Ensure that the brake adjusters are free to rotate (i.e. not seized!). If they are stuck fast, apply a little penetrating oil to the backs of the adjusters (but, if possible, only from behind the backplate; if you have to work inside the brake drum, take great care to avoid the risk of getting oil on to the brake shoes), and gently 'work' the adjuster backwards and forwards with a brake adjuster spanner. Eventually the adjusters should free, and a little brake grease can be applied to keep them in this condition. Now rotate the adjuster until the brake shoes contact the drum (preventing the road wheel from turning), then reverse the adjustment just enough to allow the wheel to turn.

☐ 44. A similar procedure can be applied to the transmission brake adjuster. When the shoes have been brought into contact with the drum (by clockwise rotation of the adjuster), turn the adjuster anti-clockwise two clicks - then apply the handbrake firmly to centralise the shoes. Having adjusted this brake, check that the handbrake lever applies the brake fully, well before it reaches the end of its potential range of movement. On some models the handbrake lever can be adjusted by means of a threaded rod in the linkage. This lives beneath a removable panel directly below the drivers seat. Ensure too that the hand brake lever remains locked in the 'on' position when fully applied, even if the lever is knocked sideways.

☐ 45. Closely check the state of ALL visible hydraulic pipework. If any section of the steel tubing shows signs of corrosion, replace it, for safety as well as to gain an MoT pass. Look too for leakage of fluid around pipe joints, and from the master cylinder and servo (if fitted). The fluid level in the master cylinder reservoir must also be at its correct level - if not, find out why and rectify the problem! At the front of the car, bend the flexible hydraulic pipes through 180 degrees (by hand) near each end of each pipe, checking for signs of cracking. If any is evident, or if the pipes have been chafing on the tyres, wheels, steering or suspension components, replace them with new items, re-routing them to avoid future problems.

☐ 46. Have an assistant press down hard on the brake pedal while you check all flexible pipes for bulges. As an additional check, firmly apply the foot brake and hold the pedal down for a few minutes. It should not slowly sink to the floor (if it does, you have a hydraulic system problem). Press and release the pedal a few times - it should not feel 'spongy' (due to the presence of air in the system). Now check the servo (if fitted) by starting the engine while the pedal is being held down. If all is well, as the vacuum servo starts to operate, the pedal should move a short distance towards the floor. Check the condition of the servo unit and its hoses - all MUST be sound. If there is the risk of any problems with the braking system's hydraulics, have a qualified mechanic check it over before using the vehicle.

☐ 47. A test drive should reveal obvious faults (such as pulling to one side, due to a seized wheel cylinder piston, or oiled brakes, for example), but otherwise all will be revealed on the rollers at the MoT station...

BODYWORK STRUCTURE

A structurally deficient Land Rover is a dangerous vehicle, and rust can affect many important areas including the rear cross-member, the entire chassis and its outriggers and the lower parts of the bulkhead. Examine these areas and perhaps especially where the main chassis members curve upwards in front of the rear axle, the outriggers behind the front wheels (where bulkhead mountings will be found), around the forward mountings of the front springs and in front of and behind the fuel tank. In the bulkhead look for rust in the floors, side panels and A posts (the posts to which the drivers and passengers doors are hinged, bearing in mind that if it is within 30 cm (12 in.) of the bulkhead to chassis mountings it could cause a test failure.

☐ 48. Essentially, fractures, cracks or serious corrosion in any load bearing panel or member (to the extent that the affected sections are weakened) needs to be dealt with. In addition, failure will result from any deficiencies in the structural metalwork within 30 cm. (12 in.) of the seat belt mountings, and also the steering and suspension component attachment points. Repairs made to any structural areas must be carried out by 'continuous' seam welding, and the repair should restore the affected section to at least its original strength.

☐ 49. The MoT examiner will be looking for metal which gives way under squeezing pressure between finger and thumb, and will use his wicked little 'Corrosion Assessment Tool' (i.e. a plastic-headed hammer!), which in theory at least should be used for detecting rust by lightly tapping the surface. If scraping the surface of the metal shows weakness beneath, the vehicle will fail.

☐ 50. Note that the security of doors and other openings must also be assessed, including the hinges, locks and catches. Corrosion damage or other weakness in the vicinity of these items can mean failure. It must be possible to open both doors from inside and outside the vehicle. The rust, if any, will be in the Land Rovers steel bulkhead and door frames.

EXTERIOR BODYWORK

☐ 51. Check for another area which can cause problems. Look out for accident damage on the exterior bodywork, which leaves sharp/jagged edges and which may be liable to cause injury. Ideally, repairs should be carried out by welding in new metal, but for non-structural areas, riveting a plate over a hole, bridging the gap with glass fibre/body filler or even taping over the gap can be legally acceptable, at least as far as the MoT test is concerned.

FUEL SYSTEM

☐ 52. Another recent extension of the regulations brings the whole of the fuel system under scrutiny, from the tank to the engine. The system should be examined with and without the engine running, and there must be no leaks from any of the components. The tank must be securely mounted, and the filler cap must fit properly - 'temporary' caps are not permitted.

EMISSIONS

Oh dear! - even the thought of this aspect can cause headaches. In almost every case, a proper 'engine tune' will help to ensure that your Land Rover is running at optimum efficiency, and there should be no difficulty in passing the test, unless your engine, the distributor or the carburettors really are well worn.

☐ 53. For petrol Land Rovers first used before 1 August, 1975, the only test carried out is for 'visual smoke emission'. The engine must be fully warmed up, allowed to idle, then revved slightly. If smoke emitted is regarded by the examiner as being 'excessive', the vehicle will fail. Often smoke emitted during this test is as a result of worn valve stem seals, allowing oil into the combustion chambers during tickover, to be blown out of the exhaust as 'blue smoke' when the engine is revved. In practice, attitudes vary widely between MoT stations on this aspect of the test.

☐ 54. For petrol Land Rovers first used on or after 1 August, 1975, a 'smoke' test also applies. Again, the engine must be fully warmed up, and allowed to idle, before being revved to around 2,500 rpm for 20 seconds (to 'purge' the system). If dense blue or black smoke is emitted for more than five seconds, the Land Rover will fail. In addition, the exhaust gas is analysed. A maximum of 6 per cent carbon monoxide (CO), and 1,200 parts per million (ppm) hydrocarbons is allowable. For vehicles first used on or after 1 August 1983 the carbon monoxide content should not exceed 4.5 per cent. The percentages of these gases are established using an exhaust gas analyser - home user versions are available for testing CO readings.

☐ 55. Exhaust emission tests are carried out on diesel vehicles subject to the tester being satisfied that the engine oil level and pressure is satisfactory and that the engine is safe to be tested up to its maximum speed. For vehicles first used before 1 August 1975 there is a visual test only. Specialised equipment is used for testing later vehicles. Failure of the test will occur if the exhaust smoke or vapour is such that it could obscure the vision of other road users - but some examiners are interpreting this rule far more rigorously than others.

CHAPTER 8 - FACTS & FIGURES

This Chapter serves two main purposes. First, to help you identify which model of Land Rover you are running - which may not be as simple as it seems, especially to a newcomer to Land Rovers. Second, to show which settings you will need to use when servicing your vehicle.

Over the years many Land Rovers have been fitted with "foreign" parts - those from other models of Land Rover - and on some occasions even with parts from other cars! If you're not sure which model of Land Rover you own - and it's essential to know before you set about buying any parts for it - use the model identification section of this chapter to identify it. You will then be able to determine whether specific components are the "right" ones for your car. For instance, some earlier vehicles fitted originally with a dynamo have been converted to alternator, while an early type carburettormay have been changed for one from a later model. The following information should enable you to determine what it is that you've actually got under the bonnet and under the car.

The "Data" sections of this chapter will be essential reading when you prepare to service your Land Rover because you will need to know about valve clearances, the spark plug gap, torque settings and a whole host of other adjustments and measurements and details of particular components.

SECTION 1 - IDENTIFICATION NUMBERS

BMC and British Leyland used to recommend that when parts were being purchased, the correct part numbers were referred to and as we've said earlier, with the passage of time and the possibility of parts being interchanged, this becomes even more important. However, the most important number of all is the vehicles chassis or car number. On some models of Land Rover, this number can be found in alternative positions, see *Chapter 2, Buying Spares* for details and illustrations.

SECTION 2 - WHAT THE NUMBERS MEAN

CHASSIS NUMBERS

To date, throughout the Land Rover's life, a total of seven different chassis number arrangements have been used. The following are the various arrangements and their respective years:

1948 to 1949

Prefixed by an L or R indicating left-hand or right-hand drive, were six or seven digits:
The first digit indicates the year - 8 = 1948 to 1949.

The second digit indicates the type - 6 = Land Rover.

The third digit (applicable only to seven digit numbers) indicates the model: 6 = Basic, 7 = Station Wagon, 8 = Welder.

With the exception of the 866 series, whose serial number started at 3001, the last four digits show the serial number starting with 0001 in each series.

1950 to 1953

Prefixed by an L or R indicating left-hand or right-hand drive, only on 1950 models.

Eight digits: The first digit indicates the year - 0 = 1950, 1 = 1951, 2 = 1952, 3 = 1953.

The second digit indicates the type - 6 = Land Rover.

The third digit indicates the model: 1 = Basic, 2 = Station Wagon, 3 = Welder, 6 = CKD (completely knocked down).

The fourth digit, excluding 1950 models, indicates the destination. 0 = Home Market, 3 = LHD Export, 6 = RHD Export.

With the exception of 1950 models, which have five serial numbers, the last four digits starting at 0001 indicate the serial number.

1954 to 55

An eight digit chassis numbering system:

The first digit indicates the year - 4 = 1954.

The second digit indicates the type - 7 = Land Rover.

The third digit indicates the model - 1 = 86-inch, 2 = 107-inch, 6 = 86-inch CKD, 7 = 107-inch CKD.

The fourth digit indicates the destination - 0 or 1 = Home Market, 3 or 4 = LHD Export, 6 or 7 = RHD Export.

The last four digits starting with 0001 indicate the serial number.

1955

A nine-digit chassis numbering system:

The first digit indicates the type - 1 = Land Rover.

The second digit indicates the model - 7 = 107-inch CKD (for example)

The third digit indicates the destination - 0 = Home Market, 3 = LHD Export, 4 = LHD CKD, 6 = RHD Export, 7 = RHD CKD.

The fourth digit indicates the sanction period - 6 = late 1955 for service purposes.

The last five digits starting with 00001 indicate the serial number.

1956 to 1961

A nine digit chassis numbering system:

The first digit on all models = 1.

The second and third digits are in pairs in the following sequence, indicating model and specification - Series 1 models = 11-35, Series II models = 41-70.

The fourth digit indicates the year - 6 = 1956, 7 = 1957 etc.

The last five digits starting with 00001 indicate the serial number.

1962 to 79

An eight digit chassis numbering system with suffix letters:

The first, second and third digits indicate the model and specification. The sequence 241-354 = Series II models, 901-965 = Series III models. The last five digits starting with 00001 indicate the serial number. Design modifications are shown by the suffix letters which assist when servicing.

NB. The year or model year of manufacture has no identification digit.

1980 to date

All these years have the conventional Vehicle Identification Number (V.I.N.).

SECTION 3 - WHICH MODEL

LAND ROVER SERIES I

Series I, 80 in. (2.051 m.) wheelbase, 1948 to 54

Dimensions and running gear:
Length: 132 in. (3.385 m.)
Height (hood up): 1948 to 51, 70.5 in. (1.808 m.); 1952 to 54, 73.5 in. (1.885 m.)
Width: 61 in. (1.564 m.)
Track: 50 in. (1.282 m.)
Minimum unladen weight: 2,594 lb. (1,178 kg.)
Suspension: Live axles, semi-elliptic springs and hydraulic telescopic dampers front and rear
Brakes: 10 in. x 1.5 in. (254 mm. x 38.1 mm.) hydraulic drum brakes all round and 9 in. drum diameter mechanical transmission brake (handbrake) behind transfer box.
Steering: Recirculating ball, worm and nut
Tyres: 6.00 x 16 or 7.00 x 16

Series I, 86 in. (2.205 m.) wheelbase, 1953 to 57

Dimensions and running gear as Series I, 80 in. (2.051 m.) models except:
Length: 140.7 in. (3.608 m.)
Height (hood up): 76 in. (1.949 m.)
Width: 62.6 in. (1.605 m.)
Unladen weight: 2,702 lb. (1,227 kg.)

Series I, 107 in. (2.744 m.) wheelbase, 1953 to 58

Dimensions and running gear as Series I, 80 in. models except:
Length: 173.5 in. (4.449 m.)
Height (hood up): 83.5 in. (2.141 m.). Station wagon 78 in. (2.0 m.)
Width: 62.6 in. (1.605 m.)
Minimum unladen weight: 3,031 lb. (1,376 kg.). Station wagon 3,444 lb (1,564 kg.) approx
Brakes: 11 in. x 1.5 in. (279.4 mm. x 38.1 mm.) brakes from early 1954
NB. The 107 in (2.744 m.) Station Wagon remained available (with the 1,997 cc petrol engine) until the 109 in Station Wagon became available late in 1958 (some time after other Series II models had been introduced).

Series I, 88 in. (2.256 m.) wheelbase, 1957 to 58

Dimensions and running gear as Series I, 80 in. (2.051 m.) models except:
Length: 140.75 in. (3.609 m.)
Height (hood up): 76 in. (1.949 m.)
Width: 62.6 in. (1.605 m.)
Minimum unladen weight: 2,740 lb. (1,244 kg.) with petrol engine
Minimum unladen weight: 2,935 lb. (1,332 kg.) with diesel engine

Series I, 109 in (2.795 m.) wheelbase, 1957 to 58

Dimensions and running gear as Series I, 88 in (2.256 m.) models except:
Length: 173.5 in. (4.449 m.)
Height (hood up): 83.5 in. (2.141 m.)
Unladen weight: 3,080 lb. (1,398 kg.) with petrol engine
Unladen weight: 3,275 lb. (1,486 kg.) with diesel engine
Brakes: 11 in. x 1.5 in. (279.4 mm. x 38.1 mm.)
Tyres: 7.00 x 16 or 7.50 x 16

1,595 cc Petrol Engine, July 1948 to 1951:

Four-cylinder, three main bearing, overhead inlet and side exhaust valves operated by followers and pushrods, and direct rockers from camshaft respectively. 69.5 mm. bore x 105 mm. stroke Compression ratio 6.8:1. Max. Power (DIN): 50 to 55 bhp @ 4,000 rpm. Max. Torque (DIN): 80 lb.ft. @ 2,000 rpm
Transmission 1948 to 50: Four-wheel drive with freewheel incorporated into the front driveline. 1950 to 54: Freewheel deleted, Permanent four-wheel drive in low range but selectable two or four-wheel drive in high range. Single dry plate clutch, 9 in. diameter. Four-speed and reverse manual gearbox with synchromesh on 3rd and 4th gears. Gear ratios: Reverse - 2.54:1; 1st - 3:1; 2nd - 2.04:1; 3rd - 1.47:1; top - 1:1 (from 1950 P4 gearbox replaced P3 type and 3rd gear ratio changed to 1.38:1.). Transfer gearbox providing a 1.148:1 step down ratio in high range and a 2.89:1 step-down in low range. 4.88:1 front and rear differentials changed to 4.7:1 in mid-1948.

1,997 cc petrol engine August 1951 to 1953 and 1953 to 58:

As for Series I, 1,595 cc petrol engine except 77.8 mm. bore. These two 1,997 cc petrol engines shared the same dimensions except that the later engine had space for cooling water between the bores. Max. Power (DIN): 52 bhp @ 4,000 rpm. Max. Torque (DIN): 101 lb.ft. @ 1,500 rpm

2,052 cc diesel engine 1957 to 1958:

Optional engine on 88 in. model, 1957 to 58. Four-cylinder, three main bearing, overhead valves. 85.7 mm. bore x 88.9 mm. stroke. Compression ratio 22.5:1. CAV fuel injection. Net Power (DIN): 51 bhp @ 3,500 rpm. Max. Torque (DIN): 87 lb.ft. @ 2,000 rpm

LAND ROVER SERIES II

Series II, 88 in (2.256 m) wheelbase, 1958 to 61

Dimensions and running gear as Series I, 88 in (2.256 m.) except:
Length: 142.4 in. (3.651 m.)
Width: 64 in. (1.641 m.)
Maximum height 77.5 in. (1.987 m.)
Track: 51.5 in. (1.321 m.)
Minimum unladen weight: 2,900 lb. (1,317 kg.) with petrol engine
Minimum unladen weight: 3,095 lb. (1,405 kg.) with diesel engine
Tyres: 7.00 x 16 to special order

The 1,997 cc petrol engine (as in the late Series I) was used in Series II 88 in. models at first until existing stocks of this engine were exhausted, then 2,286 cc petrol engine.

2,052 cc diesel engine optional, 1958 to 1961. As Series I
Transmission: As Series I, 88 in. (2.256 m.)

Series II, 109 in. (2.795 m.) wheelbase, 1958 to 61:

Dimensions and running gear as Series II, 88 in. (2.256 m.) models except:
Length: 175 in. (4.487 m.)
Maximum height 81 in. (2.077 m.)
Minimum unladen weight: 3,294 lb. (1,495 kg.) with petrol engine
Minimum unladen weight: 3,489 lb. (1,584 kg.) with diesel engine
Brakes: 11 in. x 2.25 in. (279.4 mm. x 57.15 mm.) drums
Tyres: 7.50 x 16

2,286 cc petrol engine 1958 to 61. Available in 109 in (2.795 m.)

models only at first. Four-cylinder, three main bearing, 90.47 mm. bore x 88.9 mm. stroke. Compression ratio 7.0:1 or 8:1. Solex carburettor. Net. power (7:1): 77 bhp @ 4,250 rpm, (8:1). 81 bhp at 4,250 rpm. Max. Torque (7:1) 124 lb.ft. @ 2,500 rpm

2,052 cc diesel as Series II, 88 in (2.256 m.) models

LAND ROVER SERIES IIA

Series IIA, 88 in. (2.256 m) wheelbase, 1961 to 71

Dimensions and running gear as Series II, 88 in. (2.256 m.) model except:
Minimum unladen weight: 2,953 lb. (1,341 kg.) with petrol engine
Minimum unladen weight: 3,097 lb. (1,406 kg.) with diesel engine

2,286 cc petrol engine as Series II, 88 in. (2.256 m.) models except Zenith carburettor replaced Solex

2,286 cc diesel replaced 2,052 cc. Same specs as 2,286 petrol engine except compression ratio 23:1. CAV fuel injection. Net power output 62 bhp at 4,000 rpm. Maximum torque 103 lb.ft. at 1,800 rpm
Transmission: From 1967 gear ratios changed to 1st 3.6:1, 2nd 2.22:1, 3rd 1.5:1, top 1:1, reverse 3.02:1. Transfer box low range step-down 2.35:1.

Series IIA, 109 in. (2.795 m.) wheelbase, 1961 to 71:

Dimensions and running gear as Series II, 109 in (2.795 m.) model except:
Minimum unladen weight: 3,301 lb. (1,499 kg.) with four-cylinder petrol engine
Minimum unladen weight: 3,445 lb. (1,564 kg.) with diesel engine
Minimum unladen weight: 3,459 lb. (1,570 kg.) with six-cylinder petrol engine

Engines as Series IIA, 88 in. (2.256 m.). Also, 2,625 cc, six-cylinder petrol engine available from April 1967. Seven-bearing crankshaft. Overhead inlet and inclined side exhaust valves. Bore 77.8 mm x 92.1 mm stroke. Compression ratio 7.8:1. SU carburettor initially, replaced by Zenith during 1967. Net power output 83 bhp at 4,500 rpm. Maximum torque 128 lb.ft. at 1,500 rpm

Transmission as Series IIA, 88 in. (2.256 m.)

Brakes: As 109 in. (2.795 m.) Series II except for 11 in. x 3 in. (279.4 mm. x 76.2 mm.) drums on front brakes of six-cylinder models

88 in. Lightweight Military Land Rover, 1968 to 84
Similar specifications to contemporary 88 in. petrol models except when fitted with 24-volt electrical system.

Series IIA, 109 in. (2.795 m.) wheelbase, I ton, 1968 to 71:

Dimensions and running gear as standard Series IIA, 109 in. (2.795 m.) model except:
Minimum unladen weight: 3,886 lb. (1,764 kg.)
Tyres: 9.00 x 16

Engine 2,625 cc petrol only.

Transmission: As standard 109 in (2.795 m.) model except transfer box step-down ratios 1.53:1 (high range) and 3.27:1 (low range) and heavy-duty ENV axles fitted.

LAND ROVER SERIES III

Many new features were introduced with the Series III Land Rovers of which the following are among the more significant from the maintenance point of view. There was a new, all-synchromesh gearbox and a 9.5 in. clutch was standardised across the range. Stronger final drives (half-shafts, swivel bearing housings and stub axles) were used together with stronger front spring mountings and improved brake drums. The battery was moved to under the bonnet and the dynamo was dropped in favour of a 16 ACR alternator (with 18 ACR optional). Four fuses protected the electrical circuits.

The Fairey Overdrive option became available from August 1974 and the 2,286 cc petrol and diesel engines gained five main bearings from 1981.

Series III, 88 in. (2.256 m.) wheelbase, 1971 to 1985:
Dimensions and running gear as Series IIA, 88 in. (2.256 m.) model except
Length: 142.6 in. (3.656 m.)
Width: 66 in. (1.692 m.)
Maximum height 77 in. (1.974 m.)
Minimum unladen weight: 2,953 lb. (1,341 kg.) with petrol engine
Minimum unladen weight: 3,097 lb. (1,406 kg.) with diesel engine

2,286 cc petrol engine as Series IIA, 88 in.

2,286 cc diesel engine as Series IIA, 88 in.

Transmission: As Series IIA, 88 in. except all-synchromesh gearbox. First gear ratio 3.68:1 (3.73:1 later), reverse 4.02:1.

Brakes: Servo-assistance standardised on Station Wagons, otherwise optional.

Series III, 109 in. (2.795 m.) wheelbase, 1971 to 1985:

Dimensions and running gear as Series IIA 109 in. (2.795 m.) model except:
Maximum height: 79 in. (2.026 m.)
Track: 52.5 in. (1.346 m.)
Minimum unladen weight: 3,301 lb. (1,499 kg.) with four-cylinder petrol engine
Minimum unladen weight: 3,445 lb. (1,564 kg.).with diesel engine
Minimum unladen weight: 3,459 lb. (1,570 kg.).with six-cylinder petrol engine

Brakes: As Series III, 88 in. plus servo-assistance standard on six-cylinder models.

Engines: As Series IIA, 109 in.

Transmission: As Series III, 88 in.

Series III, 109 in. (2.795 m.) wheelbase, I ton, 1971 to 80:

Dimensions and running gear as for basic Series III 109 in. (2.795 m.) model except:
Minimum unladen weight: 3,386 lb. (1,537 kg.)
Brakes: Servo assistance standard
Tyres: 9.00 x 16

Engine: 2,625 cc six-cylinder petrol engine only.

Transmission: As for Series IIA, 109 in., I ton.

Series III, 109 in. (2.795 m.) wheelbase, V8, 1979 to 85:

Dimensions and running gear as for basic Series III 109 in. (2.795 m.) model except:
Length: 177 in. (4.538 m.)
Minimum unladen weight: 3,396 lb. (1,542 kg.)

Brakes: Vacuum servo-assistance standard.

Engine: 3,528 cc petrol from February 1979 (export) or 1980 (U.K. market). V8, five main bearings, with a five-bearing camshaft and hydraulically operated tappets. 88.9 mm. bore x 71.12 mm. stroke. Compression ratio 8.13:1 depending on market. Net power output 91 bhp at 3,500 rpm. Maximum torque 166 lb.ft. at 2,000 rpm.

Transmission: Permanent four-wheel drive. Revised ratios for gearbox, transfer box and axles.

SECTION 4 - MAINTENANCE INFORMATION AND SETTINGS

The following information will be required when carrying out certain service jobs. Each Land Rover model is listed in turn followed by the data relating to various parts of the vehicle.

Please note that where compression pressure at cranking speed are listed, these are the manufacturers when new figures. Expect yours to be different, especially if the engine is worn (lower) or if the cylinder head has been skimmed (higher) but these figures are a good guide.

Only the torque wrench settings relating to servicing jobs described in this book are shown here. If you wish to carry out further work, refer to the torque wrench settings shown in the appropriate workshop manual.

CAPACITIES

Air cleaner oil capacity:

Ser. I, 1,595 cc petrol	2 pints (1.13 litres)
Ser. IIA and III, 2,625 cc petrol incl. 1 ton models	1 pint (0.56 litres)
All other Series I/II/III	1.5 pints (0.85 litres)
Ser. III, V8	Not applicable

Coolant capacity:

Ser. I, 1,595 cc petrol	17 pints (9.65 litres)
Ser. I, 1,997 cc petrol	17 pints (9.65 litres)
Ser. I, 2,052 cc diesel	17 pints (9.65 litres)
Ser. II, 2,286 cc petrol	18 pints (10.23 litres)
Ser. II, 2,052 cc diesel	17 pints (9.65 litres)
Ser. IIA, 2,286 cc petrol	18 pints (10.23 litres)
Ser. IIA, 2,286 cc diesel	18 pints (10.23 litres)
Ser. IIA, 2,625 cc petrol	20 pints (11.36 litres)
Ser. III, 2,286 cc petrol	18 pints (10.23 litres)
Ser. III, 2,286 cc diesel	18 pints (10.23 litres)
Ser. III, 2,625 cc petrol	20 pints (11.36 litres)
Ser. III, V8	22.5 pints (12.78 litres)

Engine sump capacity:

Ser. I, 1,595 cc petrol	10 pints (5.68 litres)
Ser. I, 1,997 cc petrol	11 pints (6.25 litres) including filter
Ser. I and II, 2,052 cc diesel	13 pints (7.38 litres) including filter
Ser. II, IIA and III 2,286 cc petrol	11 pints (6.25 litres)
Ser. IIA and III, 2,286 cc diesel	11 pints (6.25 litres)
Ser. IIA and III, 2,625 cc petrol	12 pints (6.81 litres)
Ser. III, V8	9 pints (5.1 litres)

Front/rear axle oil capacity:

1 ton models with ENV type diffs	2.6 pints (1.47 litres)
All other models	3 pints (1.7 litres) - Leyland axle, 4.5 pints (2.5 litres) - Salisbury axle

Gearbox oil capacity:

Ser. I, 1,595 cc petrol	4 pints (2.27 litres)
All other Series I/II/III/ except V8	2.5 pints (1.5 litres)
Series III V8	4.7 pints (2.6 litres)

Front swivel hubs:

All models	1 pint (0.56 litre)

Transfer box oil capacity:

Ser. I, 1,595 cc petrol	6 pints (3.4 litres)
All other Series I/II/III except V8	4.5 pints (2.55 litres)
Series III V8	5.5 pints (3.1 litres)

BRAKING SYSTEM

Fluid type:

All models: Castrol Universal Brake and Clutch Fluid or equivalent and complying with FMVSS 116 DOT3 or SAE J1703 specification.

CLUTCH

Fluid type:

Series II, IIA and III	As for braking system.

COOLING SYSTEM

Pressure cap setting:

Ser. I, 1,595 cc petrol	5 p.s.i. (1.05 kg/cm^2)
Ser. I, 1,997 cc petrol	3.25 to 4.25 p.s.i. (0.22 to 0.29 kg/cm^2)
Ser. I, 2,052 cc diesel	10 p.s.i. (0.703 kg/cm^2)
Ser. II, 2,286 cc petrol	Pressure cap setting: Early models 10 p.s.i. (0.7 kg/cm^2) using cap marked with figure 10. Later models 9 p.s.i. (0.6 kg/cm^2) using cap marked with figure 9. The caps are not interchangeable.
Ser. II, 2,052 cc diesel	10 p.s.i. (0.7 kg/cm^2)
Ser. IIA, 2,286 cc petrol	Pressure cap setting: Early models 10 p.s.i. (0.7 kg/cm^2) using cap marked with figure 10. Later models 9 p.s.i. (0.6 kg/cm^2) using cap marked with figure 9. The caps are not interchangeable.
Ser. IIA, 2,286 cc diesel	Pressure cap setting: Early models 10 p.s.i. (0.7 kg/cm^2) using cap marked with figure 10. Later models 9 p.s.i. (0.6 kg/cm^2) using cap marked with figure 9. The caps are not interchangeable.
Ser. IIA, 2,625 cc petrol	9 p.s.i. (0.6 kg/cm^2)
Ser. III, 2,286 cc petrol	9 p.s.i. (0.6 kg/cm^2)
Ser. III, 2,286 cc diesel	9 p.s.i. (0.6 kg/cm^2)
Ser. III, 2,625 cc petrol	9 p.s.i. (0.6 kg/cm^2)
Ser. III, V8	15 p.s.i. (1.05 kg/cm^2)

ELECTRICAL EQUIPMENT

Alternator:

Series II and IIA models	Optional Lucas 11AC
Series III	Lucas 16ACR (18 ACR optional) or Lucas A115-45

Battery:

All petrol models	1 x 12 volt
All diesel models	2 x 6 volt in series

Battery capacity:

Ser. I, 1,595 cc petrol	51 amp hours
Ser. I, 1,997 cc petrol Ser. II IIA, III petrol models	58 amp hours
All diesel models	120 amp hours

Control box:

Ser. I, 1,595 cc petrol	(Early) Lucas RF96/2, (later) Lucas RF95
Ser. I, 1,997 cc petrol	(Early) Lucas RF96/2, (later) Lucas RF95
Ser. I, 2,052 cc diesel	(Early) Lucas RF96/2, (later) Lucas RF95
Ser. II, 2,286 cc petrol	Lucas RB1106/37182
Ser. II, 2,052 cc diesel	Lucas RB310/37189, (later) RB310/37297

Ser. IIA, 2,286 cc petrol	Lucas RB106/37290
Ser. IIA, 2,286 cc diesel	To vehicle suffix C, Lucas RB310/37472 From vehicle suffix D, Lucas RB340/37387
Ser. IIA, 2,625 cc petrol	Lucas RB340/37517

Dynamo:

Ser. I, 1,595 cc petrol	(Early) Lucas C39P. (Later) Lucas C39PV
Ser. I, 1,997 cc petrol	(Early) Lucas C39P. (Later) Lucas C39PV
Ser. I, 2,052 cc diesel	(Early) Lucas C39P. (Later) Lucas C39PV
Ser. II, 2,286 cc petrol	Lucas C39/PV2
Ser. II, 2,052 cc diesel	Lucas C45/PV5 or C45/PV6
Ser. IIA, 2,286 cc petrol	Lucas C40/1
Ser. IIA, 2,286 cc diesel	Lucas C40/1
Ser. IIA, 2,625 cc petrol	Lucas C42

Fuses:

Series I, all models	1 x 35 amp - horn, windscreen wipers, fuel tank level unit, stoplights.
Series II and IIA models	2 x 35 amp A1-A2 - interior lamps, foglamps etc. A3-A4 - windscreen wiper, fuel tank level unit andstoplights.
Series III models	2 x 35 amp (early models) A1-A2 - interior lamps, foglamps etc. A3-A4 - windscreen wiper, fuel tank level unit and stoplights. 4 x 35 amp (later models) A1-A2 - Lighting circuits. A3-A4 - Not used. A5-A6 - windscreen wiper, direction indicators. A7-A8 - Fuel gauge, temperature gauge, stoplights.

Heater plugs:

Ser. I, 2,052 cc diesel	KLG BRQ1 coil element, 1.7 volts, 36-40 amps
Ser. II, 2,052 cc diesel and Ser. IIA, 2,286 cc diesel	KLG G.F. 210/T coil element, 1.7 volts, 38-42 amps or Champion AG45
Ser. III, 2,286 cc diesel	KLG G.F. 210/T coil element, 1.7 volts, 38-42 amps or Champion AG45

Horns:

All models	Lucas HF1235 or WT618

Polarity:

All Series I and II	Positive earth system.
Series IIA to vehicle suffix C	Positive earth system.
Series IIA from suffix D on	Negative earth system.
Series III	Negative earth system.

Starter motor:

All models	Lucas inertia or pre-engaged type

Windscreen wiper motor:

All models	Lucas CW1 or FW2

ENGINE

Compression pressure at cranking speed (CR = Compression Ratio) :

Ser. I, 1,595 cc petrol	125 psi (8.8 kg/cm^2)
Ser. I, 1,997 cc petrol	125 psi (8.8 kg/cm^2)
Ser. II, IIA and III	
2,286 cc petrol	7:1CR, 145 p.s.i. (10.2 kg/cm^2). 8:1CR, 160 to 170 p.s.i. (11.2 to 11.9 kg/cm^2)
Ser. IIA and III 2,625 cc petrol	7:1CR, 140 p.s.i.. (9.88 kg/cm^2). 7.8:1CR, 170 to 175 p.s.i. (11.95 to 12.3 kg/cm^2)
Ser. III, V8	135 p.s.i. (9.5 kg/cm^2)

Firing order:

All 4-cylinder engines	1, 3, 4, 2.
6-cylinder, 2,625 cc petrol	1, 5, 3, 6, 2, 4.
V8 engines	1, 8, 4, 3, 6, 5, 7, 2.

Number 1 cylinder is the nearest to the radiator in the 4 and 6-cylinder engines, and the nearest to the radiator in the left bank in the V8 engine.

Valve clearances.

All settings are for both inlet and exhaust valves, with engine hot or cold, except where otherwise stated:

Ser. I, 1,595 cc petrol	Inlet 0.010 in. (0.25 mm.), exhaust 0.012 in. (0.30 mm.)
Ser. I, 1,997 cc petrol	Inlet 0.010 in. (0.25 mm.), exhaust 0.012 in. (0.30 mm.)
Ser. I & II, 2,052 cc diesel	0.010 in. (0.25 mm.)
Ser. II and IIA, 2286 cc petrol	0.010 in. (0.25 mm)
Ser. III, 2,286 cc petrol	0.010 in. (0.25 mm.) engine at running temperature.
Ser. IIA and III, 2,286 cc diesel	0.010 in. (0.25 mm.)
Ser. IIA and III, 2,625 cc petrol	Inlet 0.006 in. (0.15 mm.), exhaust 0.010 in. (0.25 mm.)
Ser. III, V8	Hydraulic tappets. Not adjustable.

FUEL SYSTEM

Carburettors:

Ser. I, 1,595 cc petrol	Solex 32 PB1-2 down-draught
Ser. I, 1,997 cc petrol	Solex 32 PB1-2 down-draught
Ser. II, 2,286 cc petrol	Solex PA10-5 or PA10-6 or Zenith 36IV
Ser. IIA, 2,286 cc petrol	Solex PA10-5 or PA10-6 or Zenith 36IV
Ser. IIA, 2,625 cc petrol	Zenith/Stromberg 175CD2S or SUHD6
Ser. III, 2,286 cc petrol	Solex PA10-5 or PA10-6 or Zenith 36IV
Ser. III, 2,625 cc petrol	Zenith/Stromberg 175CD2S or SUHD6
Ser. III, V8	Two Solex 175CDSE (Europe and Australia), 175CD3 (other markets)

Fuel pump:

All models	SU electric or AC mechanical

Injector:

All diesel models	CAV Pintaux

Injection timing:

Ser. I,II 2,052 cc diesel	17° BTDC to engine No. 146900522 (short wheelbase, or 156900285 (long wheelbase). From these engine numbers 16° BTDC
Ser. IIA, III 2,286 cc diesel	Engine suffix K, 16° BTDC Engine suffix L, 15° BTDC

GENERAL DATA

Steering gear - toe-in (otherwise known as wheel alignment or tracking):

All models: 3/64 to 3/32 in. (1.2 to 2.4 mm.)

Tyre pressures:

Ser. I, 1,595 cc petrol 20 p.s.i. (1.4 kg/cm^2) front, 26 p.s.i. (1.8 kg/cm^2) rear.

Ser. I, 1,997 cc petrol and 2,052 cc diesel 25 p.s.i. front and rear, normal road conditions.

When carrying loads in excess of 550 lb (250 kg) increase rear tyre pressures as follows:

86 and 88 in. - 30 p.s.i. (2.1 kg/cm^2)
107 and 109 in. - 32 p.s.i. (2.25 kg/cm^2)

Series II & IIA 88 in. normal road conditions, 25 p.s.i. 1.75 kg/cm^2) front and rear.
88 in. fully laden (load over 250 kg, 550 lb), 25 p.s.i. (1.75 kg/cm^2) front, 30 p.s.i. (2.1 kg/cm^2) rear.
109 in. 7.50 x 16 normal, 25 p.s.i. (1.55 kg/cm^2) front and rear.

7.50 x 16 fully laden (load over 250 kg, 550 lb), 25 p.s.i. (1.8 kg/cm^2) front, 36 p.s.i. (2.5 kg/cm^2) rear.
9.00 x 16 normal, 20 p.s.i. (1.4 kg/cm2) front and rear.
9.00 x 16 fully laden (load over 250 kg, 550 lb), 20 p.s.i. (1.4 kg/cm^2) front, 30 p.s.i. (2.1kg/cm^2) rear.

Series III 88 in. normal road conditions, 6.00, 6.50, 7.00 and 7.50 x 16, 25 p.s.i. (1.76 kg/cm^2) front, 30 p.s.i. (2.11 kg/cm^2) rear.
88 in. normal road conditions, 205 x 16, 25 p.s.i. (1.76 kg/cm^2) front, 35 p.s.i. (2.46 kg/cm^2) rear.
109 in. normal road conditions, 25 p.s.i. (1.76kg/cm^2) front, 36 p.s.i. (2.53 kg/cm^2) rear.
For greater ride comfort rear tyre pressures can be reduced to 25 p.s.i. (1.76 kg/cm^2) in normal road conditions if rear axle load is less than 900 kg.(88 in. models) or 1,050 kg. (109 in. models).

All models For driving in very soft conditions, pressures can be reduced temporarily by up to 30%. Normal pressures must be reinstated as soon as the difficulty has been overcome.

IGNITION SYSTEM

Contact breaker points gap:

Ser. I, 1,595 cc petrol 0.12 in. (0.3 mm.)
Ser. I, 1,997 cc petrol 0.15 in. (0.38 mm.)
All other Ser. II, IIA, III 0.014 to 0.016 in. (0.35 to 0.40 mm.)

Dwell angle:

V8 information only available 26° to 28° at 550 to 650 r.p.m.

Ignition timing (static):

Ser. I, 1,595 cc petrol 15° BTDC
Ser. I, 1,997 cc petrol 8° BTDC 1952 to 53, 10° BTDC 1954 to 58
Ser. II, 2,286 cc petrol 3° BTDC, low-grade fuel, 6° BTDC, normal fuel

Ser. IIA, 2,286 cc petrol (8:1) 0°(TDC), 90 Octane; 3° ATDC, 85 Octane.
(7:1) 3° BTDC, 83 Octane. 0° (TDC), 75 Octane.

Ser. IIA, 2,625 cc petrol (7.8:1) 2° ATDC, 90 Octane; 6° ATDC, 85 Octane.
(7:1) 0° (TDC), 83 Octane; 2° BTDC, 90 Octane.

Ser. III, 2,286 cc petrol (Static and dynamic):
(8:1) 0° (TDC), 90 Octane.
(8:1) 3° ATDC, 85 Octane.
(7:1) 3° BTDC, 83 Octane.
(7:1) 6° BTDC, 90 Octane.

Ser. III, 2,625 cc petrol (7.8:1) 2° ATDC, 90 Octane; 6° ATDC, 85 Octane.
(7:1) 0° (TDC), 83 Octane; 2° BTDC, 90 Octane.

Ser. III, V8 0° (TDC) static, 5° @ 650 rpm.

Spark plugs:

The spark plugs specified by Land Rover for Series I and II vehicles were made by Lodge - who are no longer trading. NGK recommend the following grades of plug, and your supplier will recommend other manufacturers' equivalents if you prefer:

All 4-cylinder engines,
   up to 7:1CR B5ES, gap setting 0.032in. (0.8mm)
   up to 8:1CR BP5ES, gap setting 0.032in. (0.8mm)
All 6-cylinder engines BP6ES, gap setting 0.032in. (0.8mm)
V8 engines BP5ES, gap setting 0.032in. (0.8mm)

LUBRICATION SYSTEM

Oil pressure, engine in unworn condition, (when hot):

Ser. I, 1,595 cc petrol 40 p.s.i. at 30 mph. 75 to 80 p.s.i. if oil cooler fitted in conjunction with special relief valve spring.

Ser. I, 1,997 cc petrol 55 to 65 p.s.i. (3.8 to 4.5 kg/cm2) at 2,000 rpm

Ser. I & II, 2,052 cc diesel 50 to 60 p.s.i. (3.5 to 4.2 kg/cm2) at 2,000 rpm

Ser. II, IIA and III 2,286 cc petrol 45 to 65 p.s.i. (3.16 to 4.57 kg/cm2) at 2,000 rpm

Ser. IIA and III 2,286 cc diesel 45 to 65 p.s.i. (3.16 to 4.57 kg/cm2) at 2,000 rpm

Ser. IIA and III, 2,625 cc petrol 40 to 50 p.s.i. (3.16 to 4.57 kg/cm2)

Ser. III, V8 30 to 40 p.s.i. at 2,400 rpm

TORQUE SETTINGS

Wheel nuts 75 to 85 lb.ft. (10.3 to 11.7 kg.m.)

Spark plugs:

All except V8 engines 25 lb.ft. (3.5 kg.m.)
V8 engines 12 to 15 lb.ft. (1.6 to 2.0 kg.m.)

Track rod end balljoint nuts 30 lb.ft. (4.0 kg.m.)

Spring shackle nuts 60 to 70 lb.ft. (85 to 98 kg.m.)

Propshaft flange bolts 30 to 38 lb.ft. (42 to 53 kg.m.)

Basic maintenance on any vehicle can be carried out using a fairly simple, relatively inexpensive tool kit. There is no need to spend a fortune all at once - most owners who do their own servicing acquire their implements over a long period of time. However, there are some items you simply cannot do without in order to properly carry out the work necessary to keep your vehicle on the road. Therefore, in the following lists, we have concentrated on those items which are likely to be valuable aids to maintaining your car in a good state of tune, and to keep it running sweetly and safely and in addition we have featured some of the tools that are 'nice-to-have' rather than 'must have' because as your tool chest grows, there are some tools that help to make servicing just that bit easier and more thorough to carry out.

One vital point - always buy the best quality tools you can afford. 'Cheap and cheerful' items may look similar to more expensive implements, but experience shows that they often fail when the going gets tough, and some can even be dangerous. With proper care, good quality tools will last a lifetime, and can be regarded as an investment. The extra outlay is well worth it, in the long run.

The following lists are shown under headings indicating the type of use applicable to each group of tools and equipment.

LIFTING: It is inevitable that you will need to raise the car from the ground in order to gain access to the underside of it - and these are heavy vehicles!

SAFETY FIRST! There are, of course, important safety implications when working underneath any vehicle. Sadly, many d-i-y enthusiasts have been killed or seriously injured when maintaining their automotive pride and joy, usually for the want of a few moments' thought. So - THINK SAFETY! In particular, NEVER venture beneath any vehicle supported only by a jack - of ANY type. A jack is ONLY intended to be a means of lifting a vehicle, NOT for holding it 'airborne' while being worked on.

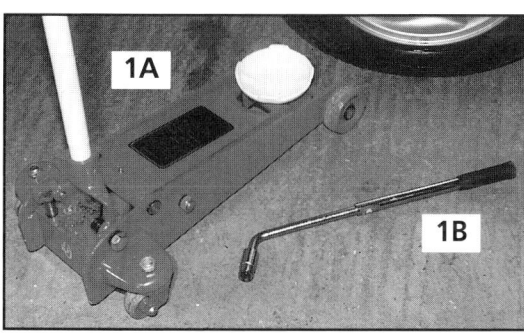

We strongly recommend that you invest in a good quality trolley jack, such as the Kamasa 2 1/4 ton unit shown here (1.A) while alongside is an excellent 'nice-to-have' extendible wheel nut spanner from the same company (1.B). This is also ideal for carrying in the car in case of punctures. If you've ever tried removing a wheel nut tightened by a garage gorilla, you know why this tool is so good!

Having raised the vehicle from the floor, always support it under a sound section of the 'chassis', or, if working at the rear of the car, beneath the rear axle. Use only proper axle stands (2.A), intended for the purpose, with solid wooden blocks on top, if necessary, to spread the load. These Kamasa stands are exceptionally strong and are very rapidly adjusted, using the built-in ratchet stops. Screw-type stands have an infinite amount of adjustments but are fiddly and time-consuming to use. NEVER, NEVER use bricks to support a car - they can crumble without warning, with horrifying results. Always chock all wheels not in the air, to prevent the car from rolling.

Frankly, if you don't need to remove the road wheels for a particular job, the use of car ramps (2.B), which are generally more stable than axle stands - is preferable, in order to gain the necessary working height. However, even then there are dangers. Ensure that the car is 'square' to the ramps before attempting to drive up onto them, and preferably place the ramps on two long lengths of old carpet, extending towards the vehicle. The carpet should help prevent the ramps from sliding as the wheels mount them. If you have an assistant guiding you onto the ramps, be absolutely sure that he/she is well out of the way as you drive forwards. NEVER

Thanks are due to Kamasa Tools for their kind assistance with this chapter.
Almost all of the tools shown here and in Chapter 3 were kindly supplied by them.

allow anyone to stand in front of the car, or immediately beside it - the ramps could tip. Be very careful, too, not to 'overshoot' the ramps. When the car is safely positioned on the ramps, fully apply the handbrake, and firmly chock the pair of wheels still on the ground. See introduction to *Chapter 3, Service Intervals, Step-by-Step*

In conclusion, here's a few more words on using and choosing jacks and supports.

JACKS: Manufacturer's jack - for emergency wheel changing ONLY - NOT to be used when working on the vehicle.

'Bottle' jack - screw or hydraulic types - can be used as a means of lifting the car, in conjunction with axle stands to hold it clear of the ground.

Trolley jack - extremely useful as it is so easily manoeuvrable. Again, use only for lifting the vehicle, in conjunction with axle stands to support it clear of the ground. Ensure that the lifting head of the jack will pass beneath the lowest points on the 'chassis' of your vehicle. Aim for the highest quality jack you can afford. Cheap types seldom last long, and can be VERY dangerous (suddenly allowing a car to drop to ground level, without warning, for example).

AXLE STANDS: Available in a range of sizes. Ensure that those you buy are sturdy, with a good wide base and with a useful range of height adjustment.

CAR RAMPS: Available in several heights - high ones are easier for working beneath the car, but since the Land Rovers is pretty high to start off with this isn't a problem. Do make certain that the ones you buy are capable of supporting your Land Rover's weight.

The ultimate ramps are the 'wind-up' variety - easy to drive onto at their lowest height setting, then raised by means of screw threads to a convenient working height.

SPANNERS: *INSIDE INFORMATION: Many fasteners on the Land Rover have UNF (Unified National Fine) threads, compatible with AF (American Fine) or SAE threads but earliest vehicles were predominantly BSF. Some parts have UNC (Unified National Coarse) threads, and a very few use the BSF or BSW (British Standard Fine, and British Standard Whitworth - coarse, respectively). BA (British Association) screws are also employed, as are BSP (British Standard Pipe) threads, in the fuel, lubrication and cooling systems. Metric threads were used on Lucas electrical components from 1969, and on may more components as the years went by. Thread types vary enormously - and can even vary on the same vehicle. However, for most jobs, spanners in 'AF' sizes, measured across the flats of the spanner in fractions of an inch, will be required, with some items requiring the use of implements designed for the other systems mentioned above.*

This Kamasa spanner set (3.A) is very unusual in that it includes the more unusual types of spanner size in the same set. There are also 'stubby' ratchet handles available (3.B) for that cramped engine bay!

Note - in every case, ring spanners provide a more positive grip on a nut/bolt head than open-ended types, which can spread and/or slip when used on tight fasteners. Similarly, 'impact' type socket spanners with hexagonal apertures give better grip on a tight fastener than the normal 12 point 'bi-hex' variety.

Open-ended spanners - set(s) covering the range 3/8 to 15/16in AF.

Ring spanners - set(s) covering the range 3/8 to 15/16in AF (alternatively, combination spanner set(s) (with one ring end, and one 'open' end of the same AF size, for each spanner) covering the same range.

Socket spanners - 3/8in and 1/2in square drive, covering the same range.

A long extension bar is a typical 'nice-to-have' tool. (4.C)

Adjustable spanner - nine inch, to start off with. (8.F)

Allen key set. (4.D)

Spark plug spanner, with rubber 'plug grip' insert either for use with the ratchet set (3.A) or the harder to use T-bar type. (4B)

Rear axle drain plug spanner. (4.E)

Brake adjuster spanner.

Torque wrench. This is very nearly a 'must-have' item and for any serious mechan-

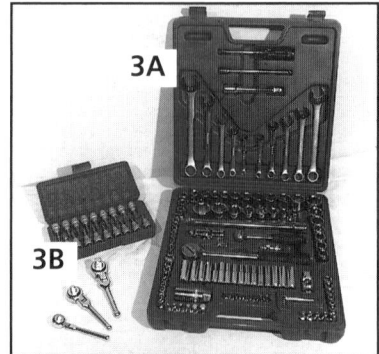

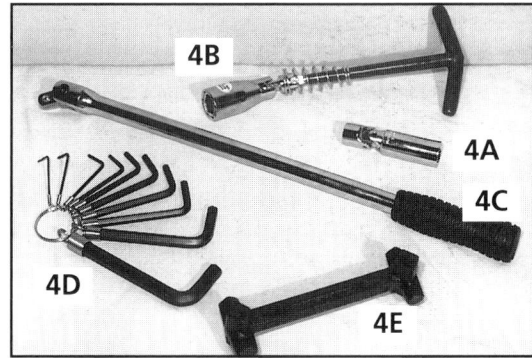

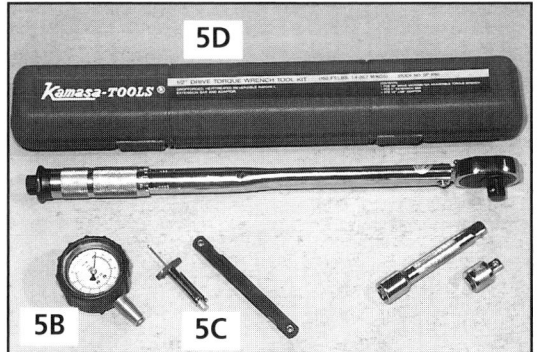

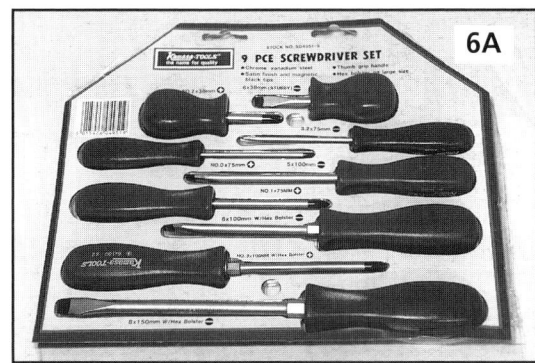

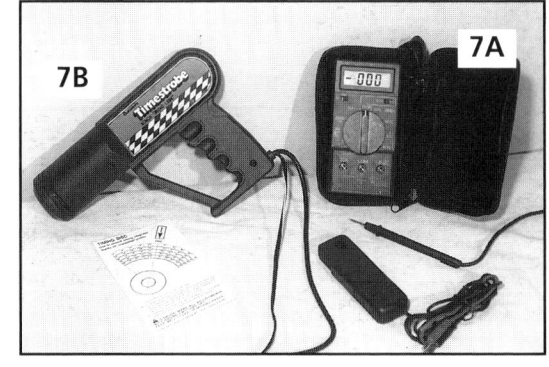

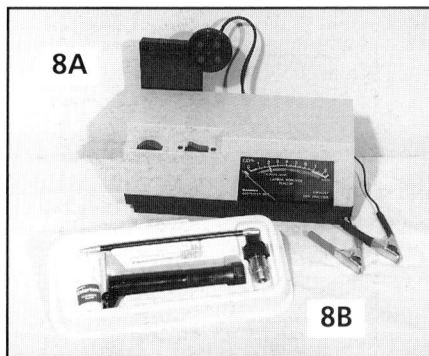

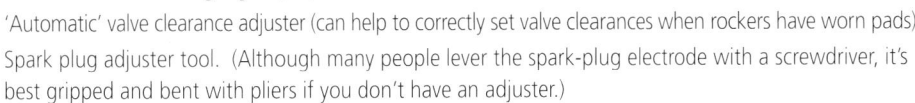

ic, it becomes a 'must-have' once you have one. Prevents overtightening and shearing. (5.D)

SCREWDRIVERS

General-purpose set of cross-head variety and set of flat-bladed variety. (All available in various-sized sets.) (6.A)

Impact driver (useful for releasing seized screws in brake drums, etc.). (12.A)

'TUNING' AIDS:

Depending on how much of the servicing you want to carry out yourself, you'll need all of these - see Chapter 3, Service Intervals, Step-by-Step for information on how to use them. The more expensive can be purchased gradually, as you save more money by doing your own servicing!

Compression gauge, preferably screw-in, rather than 'push-in' variety.

Set of feeler gauges. (5C)

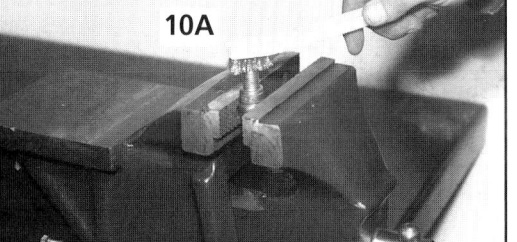

'Automatic' valve clearance adjuster (can help to correctly set valve clearances when rockers have worn pads).

Spark plug adjuster tool. (Although many people lever the spark-plug electrode with a screwdriver, it's best gripped and bent with pliers if you don't have an adjuster.)

Dwell meter/multi-meter (preferably with built-in tachometer). (7.A)

Xenon stroboscopic timing light (neon types can be used, but the orange light produced is less bright than the white light produced by the xenon lamps, so that the timing marks are correspondingly less easy to see). This is one of several from the highly regarded Gunson range. (7.B)

Carburettor balancing/adjusting tool.

Simple CO meter. Gunson have now introduced an accurate exhaust gas analyser that is expensive but affordable. (8.A)

Colortune. This enables you to see the spark - which changes colour as you adjust the carburettor and to set the carburation accordingly. (8B)

SUNDRY ITEMS:

Tool box - steel types are sturdiest.

Extension lead.

Small/medium ball pein hammer this one part of the huge Kamasa range. (9.A)

Soft-faced hammer (available here, from Kamasa Tools, as a set). (9.B)

Special, brass bristle wire brush for cleaning spark plugs. (10A)

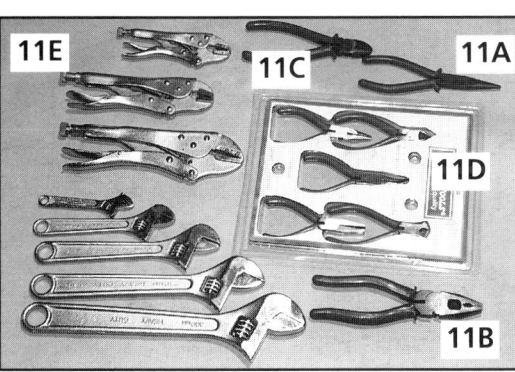

12 volt test lamp (can be made using 12 volt bulb, bulb holder, two short lengths of cable and two small crocodile clips).

Copper-based anti-seize compound - useful during assembly of threaded components, including spark plugs, to make future dismantling easier!

Grease gun.

Oil can (with 15W/50 multigrade oil, for general purpose lubrication).

Water dispellant 'electrical' aerosol spray.

Pair of pliers ('standard' jaw). (11.A)

Pair of 'long-nosed' pliers. (11.B)

Pair of 'side cutters'. (11.C)

Kamasa also sell pliers in sets, as this shoal indicates. (11.D)

Self-grip wrench or -preferably - set of three. (11.E)

Junior hacksaw. (9.C)

Oil filter removal tool.

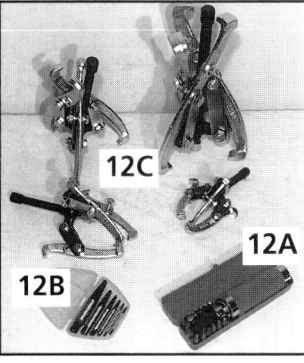

Stud removing tools. A 'nice-to-have' when studs shear and all else fails. (12B)

Tyre pump.

Tyre tread depth gauge. (5.B)

Tyre pressure gauge. (5.C)

Drifts - a set is an extremely useful 'nice-to-have'. (9.D)

Hub pullers, useful when you go beyond the straightforward servicing stage. (12.C)

Electric drill. Not a servicing tool as such but a 'must-have' nevertheless. The Kamasa rechargeable drill (13A) is superb, enabling you to reach tight spots without trailing leads - and much safer out of doors. Recommended!

APPENDIX 1
RECOMMENDED CASTROL LUBRICANTS

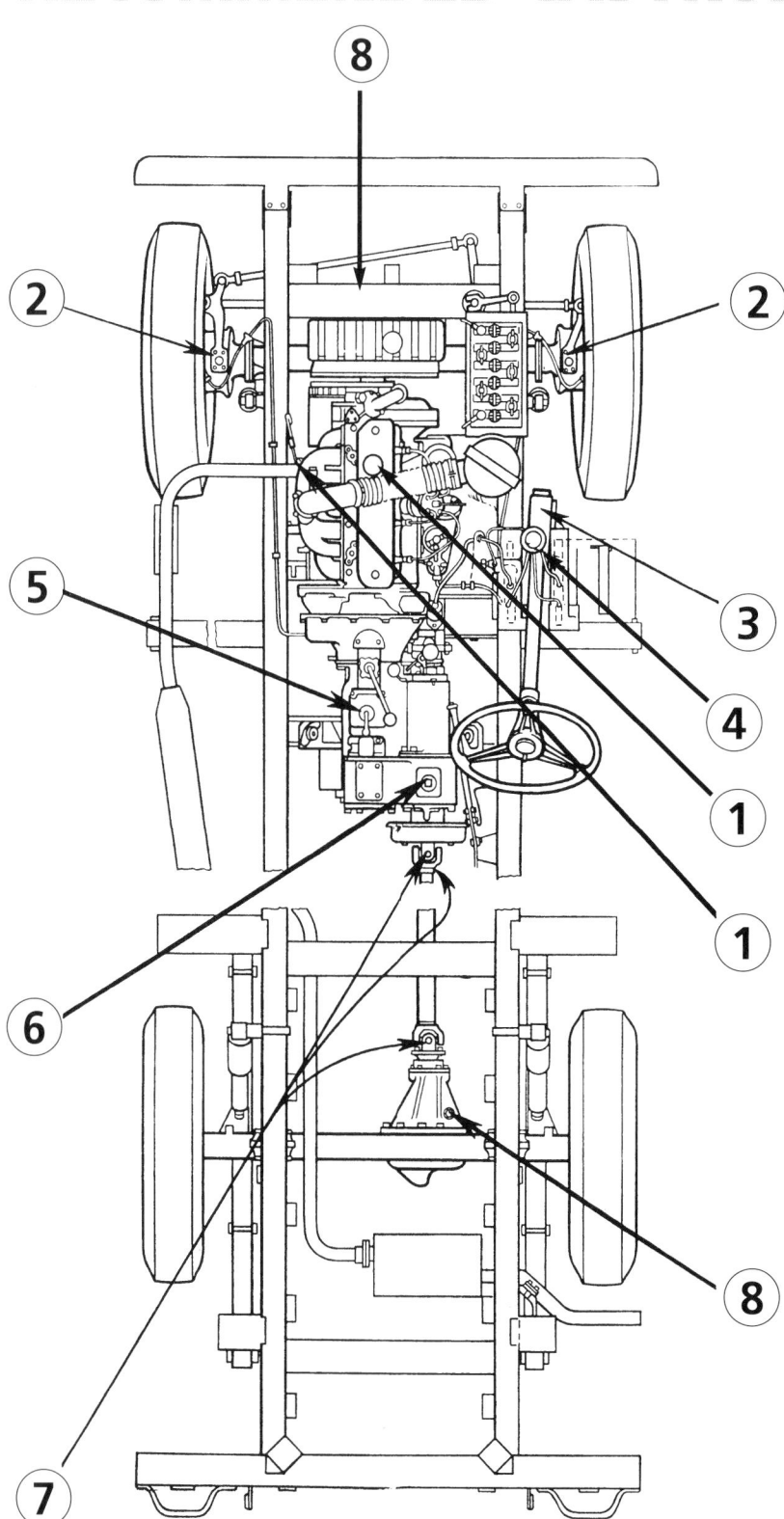

1 = Engine
See Jobs 1, and 28 to 32
Castrol GTX
Overseas For territories with regular air temperatures below 5° C, there are various grades of Castrol lubricants available. Consult your local supplier.

2 = Front swivel pin housings
See Jobs 50 and 157
Castrol EPX 80W/90 Gear Oil

3 = Steering box
See Job 43
Castrol EPX 80W/90 Gear Oil
SI 2 SAE140 (Pennti)

4 = Brake and Clutch Fluid
See Jobs 2, 3 and 153
Castrol Universal Brake and Clutch Fluid

5 = Main gearbox
See Jobs 59 and 135
Castrol EPX 80W/90 Gear Oil

6 = Transfer box
See Jobs 60 and 134
Castrol EPX 80W/90 Gear Oil

7 = Propshaft U/Js and sliding splines
See Jobs 54, 66, 67 and 156
Castrol LM Grease

8 = Front and rear axles
See Jobs 53, 65, 136 and 141
Castrol EPX 80W/90 Gear Oil

Brake Mechanism - areas of metal-to-metal contact
See Jobs 100, 107 and 155
Proprietary brand of high melting point brake grease, such as Castrol PH Grease

General greasing
Castrol LM Grease

General lubricating
Castrol Flick Easing Oil (aerosol)
Castrol Everyman Oil (in a can)

NB Not every model will have all the grease points shown here. In general, the later the model, the fewer the grease nipples.

Issued by Castrol (UK) Limited, Burmah Castrol House, Pipers Way, Swindon SN3 1RE Tel: 0793 452222

APPENDIX 2
AMERICAN AND BRITISH TERMS

It was Mark Twain who described the British and the Americans as, "two nations divided by a common language". such cynicism has no place here but we do acknowledge that our common language evolves in different directions. We hope that this glossary of terms, commonly encountered when servicing your car, will be of assistance to American owners and, in some cases, English speaking owners in other parts of the world, too.

American	British
Antenna	Antenna
Axleshaft	Halfshaft
Back-up	Reverse
Carburetor	Carburettor
Cotter pin	Split pin
Damper	Shock absorber
DC Generator	Dynamo
Defog	Demist
Drive line	Transmission
Driveshaft	Propeller shaft
Fender	Wing or mudguard
Firewall	Bulkhead
First gear	Bottom gear
Float bowl	Float chamber
Freeway, turnpike	Motorway
Frozen	Seized
Gas tank	Petrol tank
Gas pedal	Accelerator or throttle pedal
Gasoline, Gas or Fuel	Petrol or fuel
Ground (electricity)	Earth
Hard top	Fast back
Header	Exhaust manifold
Headlight dimmer	Headlamp dipswitch
High gear	Top gear
Hood	Bonnet
Industrial Alcohol or Denatured Alcohol	Methylated spirit
Kerosene	Paraffin
Lash	Free-play
License plate	Number plate
Lug nut	Wheel nut
Mineral spirit	White spirit
Muffler	Silencer
Oil pan	Sump
Panel wagon/van	Van
Parking light	Side light
Parking brake	Hand brake
'Pinging'	'Pinking'
Quarter window	Quarterlight
Recap (tire)	Remould or retread
Rocker panel	Sill panel

American	British
Rotor or disk (brake)	Disc
Sedan	Saloon
Sheet metal	Bodywork
Shift lever	Gear lever
Side marker lights, side turn signal or position indicator	Side indicator lights
Soft-top	Hood
Spindle arm	Steering arm
Stabiliser or sway bar	Anti-roll bar
Throw-out bearing	Release or thrust bearing
Tie-rod (or connecting rod)	Track rod (or steering)
Tire	Tyre
Transmission	Drive line
Trouble shooting	Fault finding/diagnosis
Trunk	Boot
Turn signal	Indicator
Valve lifter	Tappet
Valve cover	Rocker cover
Valve lifter or tappet	Cam follower or tappet
Vise	Vice
Windshield	Windscreen
Wrench	Spanner

Useful conversions:

	Multiply by
US gallons to Litres	3.785
Litres to US gallons	0.2642
UK gallons to US gallons	1.20095
US gallons to UK gallons	0.832674

Fahrenheit to Celsius (Centigrade) -
Subtract 32, multiply by 0.5555

Celsius to Fahrenheit -
Multiply by 1.8, add 32

APPENDIX 3
SPECIALISTS & SUPPLIERS

All of the products and specialists listed below have contributed in various ways to this book. All of the consumer products used are available through regular high street outlets.

Autoline (Dinitrol), Eagle House, Redstone Industrial Estate, Boston, Lincs, PE21 8EA. Tel: 0205 354500
Rust prevention treatment in various grades.

Automotive Chemicals Ltd, Bevis Green Works, Wallmersley, Bury, Lancs, BL9 8RE. Tel: 061 797 5899
Aerosol spray paint.

Automotive Products, Tachbrook Road, Leamington Spa, Warwicks, CV31 3ER. Tel: 0926 472251
Manufacturers of A P Lockheed 'original equipment' brakes.

Castrol (UK) Ltd, Burmah House, Pipers Way, Swindon, Wiltshire, SN3 1RE. Tel: 0793 452222
Contact Castrol's Consumer Technical Department Help Line on the above number for assistance with lubrication recommendations.

Keith Gott, Greenwood Farm, Old Odiham Road, Alton, Hampshire Tel:(0420) 544330 sales and 543210 for parts.
Carried out much of the work featured in this book.

Gunson Ltd, Pudding Mill Lane, Stratford, London, E15 2PJ   Tel: 081 555 7421
Electrical and electronic engine tuning equipment.

Holden Vintage and Classic Ltd, Linton Trading Estate, Bromyard, Hfds. HR7 4QT Tel: 0885 488000
'Period' Lucas electrical components for every age of Land Rover.

Kamasa Tools, Saxon Industries, Lower Everland Road, Hungerford, Berkshire, RG17 0DX
Wide range of hand and power tools, used throughout this book.

Land Rover Series I Club, East Foldhay, Zeal Monachorum, Crediton, Devon, EX17 6DH. Tel: 0363 82666 (9-5pm)
Caters for owners and enthusiasts of Series One Land Rovers up to 1958. The club provides a magazine every two months which includes information on spares, specialists and gives technical advice.

Land-Rover Series II Club, PO Box 1750, Bridport, Dorset DT6 5YJ.
This club organises various events, provides a quarterly newsletter and provides technical information and assistance to members.

Land-Rover Series III Owners Club - Frank King, 16 Holly Street, Cannock, Staffordshire WS11 2RU.
The club organises meetings and other events, informs owners about relevant specialists, offers spares supply and technical advice services to members and provides a monthly newsletter which contains much useful information plus trade and private advertisements.

NGK Spark Plugs (UK) Ltd, 7-8-9 Garrick Industrial Centre, Hendon, London, NW9 6AQ. Tel: 081 202 2151
Top quality spark plugs.

Partco. See Yellow Pages for your local Partco centre (look under Motor Factors).
Suppliers of most types of consumable and regular service items used in automotive repair.

SP Tyres UK Ltd, Fort Dunlop, Birmingham, B24 9QT. Tel: 021 384 4444
Manufacturers of Dunlop tyres in both modern and 'period' patterns.

W David & Sons Ltd (Isopon), Ridgemount House, 1 Totteridge Lane, Whetstone, London, N20 0EY. Tel: 081 445 0372
Manufacturers of the top-quality body repair materials used in this book.

APPENDIX 4
SERVICE HISTORY

This Chapter helps you keep track of all the servicing carried out on your Land Rover and can even save you money! A vehicle with a 'service history' is always worth more than one without. Although this book's main purpose is to give invaluable advice to anyone carrying out his or her own servicing, you could make full use of this section, even if you have a garage or mechanic carry out the work for you. It enables you to specify the jobs you want to have carried out to your Land Rover and, once again, it enables you to keep that all-important service history. And even if your Land Rover doesn't have a 'history' going back to when it was new, keeping this Chapter complete will add to it's value when you come to sell it. Mind you, it obviously won't be enough to just to tick the boxes: keep all your receipts when you buy oil, filters and other consumables or parts. That way, you'll also be able to return any faulty parts if needs be.

IMPORTANT NOTE! The Service Jobs listed here are intended as a check list and a means of keeping a record of your Land Rover's service history. It is most important that you refer to *Chapter 3, Service Intervals, Step-by-Step* for full details of how to carry out each Job listed here and for essential SAFETY information, all of which will be essential when you come to carry out the work.

Before carrying out a service, you will need to purchase the right parts. Please refer to *Chapter 2, Buying Spares* for information on how to buy the right parts at the right prices and for the location of your vehicle's 'chassis number', and *Chapter 8, Facts and Figures* for information on how to find your vehicle's model type, identify components and so on: information that you will need in order to buy the right parts, first time!

Wherever possible, the Jobs listed in this section have been placed in a logical order or placed into groups that will help you make progress quickly. We have tried to save you too much in the way of unnecessary movement by grouping Jobs around areas of the vehicle and also - most important, this! - into groups of jobs that apply when the Land Rover is on the ground, when one front wheel is removed, when the front or rear is off the ground, and so on. Therefore, at each Service Interval, you will see the work grouped into Jobs that need carrying out in the Engine Bay, Around the Vehicle or Under the Vehicle and another division into Bodywork and Interior Jobs, and Mechanical and Electrical Jobs.

You'll also see space at each Service Interval for you to write down the date, price and seller's name every time you buy consumables or accessories. And once again, do remember to *keep your receipts!* There's also space for you to date and sign the Service Record or for a garage's stamp to be applied.

As you move through the Service Intervals, you will notice that the work carried out at, say, *1,500 Miles or Every Month, Whichever Comes First,* is repeated at each one of the following Service Intervals. The same applies to the *6,000 Miles or Six Months* Interval: much of it is repeated at *12,000 Miles or Twelve Months.* Every time a Job or set of Jobs is 'repeated' from an earlier Interval, we show it in a tinted area on the page. You can then see more clearly which jobs are unique to the level of Service Interval that you are on. And you may be surprised to find that all the major Intervals, right up to *36,000 Miles or Thirty Six Months* contain Jobs that are unique to that Service Interval. That's why we have continued this Service History right up to the 3 Year Interval. There are sufficient Service History sheets for you to keep a record of your servicing for three years, and when that is full, you can purchase a set of continuation sheets from Porter Publishing at the address and telephone number shown at the end of this Chapter. If you keep your Land Rover and wish to continue your service record, you will be able to start the 3 year sequence all over again, in the knowledge that your vehicle has been serviced as well as anyone could wish for!

500 MILES, WEEKLY, OR BEFORE A LONG JOURNEY

This list is shown, complete, only once. It would have been a bit much to have provided the list 52 times over for use once a week throughout the year! They are, however, included with every longer Service list from 3,000 miles/Three Months-on so that each of the 'weekly' Jobs is carried out as part of every Service.

500 Mile Mechanical and Electrical - The Engine Bay

Job 1. Engine oil level.

Job 2. NOT SERIES I VEHICLES Clutch fluid level.

Job 3. Brake fluid level.

Job 4. Battery electrolyte.

Job 5. Washer reservoir.

Job 6. Cooling system.

500 Mile, Mechanical and Electrical - Around the Vehicle

Job 7. Check horns.

Job 8. Windscreen washers.

Job 9. Windscreen wipers.

Job 10. Tyre pressures.

Job 11. Check headlamps.

Job 12. Check front sidelamps.

Job 13. Check rear sidelamps.

Job 14. Number plate lamps.

Job 15. Reversing lamps.

Job 16. Interior lights.

500 Mile Bodywork and Interior - Around the Vehicle

Job 17. Clean bodywork.

1,500 MILES - OR EVERY MONTH, whichever comes first

These Jobs are similar to the 500 Mile Jobs but don't need carrying out quite so regularly. Once again, these Jobs are not shown with a separate listing for each 1,500 miles/1 Month interval but they are included as part of every 3,000 miles/Three Month Service list and for every longer Service interval.

1,500 Mile Mechanical and Electrical - The Engine Bay

Job 18. DIESEL MODELS ONLY Drain sedimenter.

Job 19. DIESEL MODELS ONLY Drain fuel filter.

1,500 Mile Mechanical and Electrical - Around the Vehicle

Job 20. Check tyres.

Job 21. Check spare tyre.

Job 22. Tighten wheel nuts.

1,500 Mile Bodywork and Interior - Around the Vehicle

Job 23. Touch-up paintwork.

Job 24. Aerial/antenna.

Job 25. Clean out interior.

Job 26. Improve visibility!

1,500 Mile Bodywork - Under the Vehicle

Job 27. Clean mud traps.

3,000 MILES - OR EVERY THREE MONTHS, whichever comes first

All the Service Jobs in the tinted area have been carried forward from earlier service intervals and are to be repeated at this Service.

3,000 Mile Mechanical and Electrical - The Engine Bay

First carry out all the Jobs listed under earlier Service Intervals as applicable.

☐ Job 1. Engine oil level.

☐ Job 2. NOT SERIES I VEHICLES Clutch fluid level.

☐ Job 3. Brake fluid level.

☐ Job 4. Battery electrolyte.

☐ Job 5. Washer reservoir.

☐ Job 6. Cooling system.

☐ Job 18. DIESEL MODELS ONLY Drain sedimenter.

☐ Job 19. DIESEL MODELS ONLY Drain fuel filter.

☐ Job 28. Drain engine oil.

☐ Job 29. Remove engine oil filter.

☐ Job 30. Fit new oil filter.

☐ Job 31. Pour fresh engine oil.

☐ Job 32. Check oil level.

☐ Job 33. Clean oil bath air cleaner.

☐ Job 34. Adjust spark plugs.

☐ Job 35. Check distributor cap and rotor arm.

☐ Job 36. Check HT Circuit.

☐ Job 37. Check CB points.

☐ Job 38. Lubricate distributor.

☐ Job 39. Check drive belts.

☐ Job 40. 6-CYLINDER MODELS ONLY Check air pump drivebelt.

☐ Job 41. Pipes and hoses.

☐ Job 42. Lubricate accelerator controls.

☐ Job 43. V8 ENGINES ONLY Check heated air intake valve.

☐ Job 44. Set carburettors.

3,000 Mile Mechanical and Electrical - Around the Vehicle

First carry out all the Jobs listed under earlier Service Intervals as applicable.

☐ Job 7. Check horns.

☐ Job 8. Windscreen washers.

☐ Job 9. Windscreen wipers.

☐ Job 10. Tyre pressures.

☐ Job 11. Check headlamps.

☐ Job 12. Check front sidelamps.

☐ Job 13. Check rear sidelamps.

☐ Job 14. Number plate lamps.

☐ Job 15. Reversing lamps.

☐ Job 16. Interior lights.

☐ Job 20. Check tyres.

☐ Job 21. Check spare tyre.

☐ Job 22. Tighten wheel nuts.

☐ Job 45. Check fuel pipes.

☐ Job 46. Fuel filler pipe.

☐ Job 47. Top-up steering relay.

☐ Job 48. SPECIALIST SERVICE Front wheel alignment.

3,000 Mile Mechanical and Electrical - Under the Vehicle

☐ Job 49. Check wheel hubs.

☐ Job 50. Top-up swivel pin housings.

☐ Job 51. Steering joints.

☐ Job 52. Adjust front brakes.

☐ Job 53. Top-up front axle oil.

☐ Job 54. Grease front propshaft U/Js.

☐ Job 55. Check for oil leaks.

☐ Job 56. Check front brake pipes.

☐ Job 57. Check clutch pipes.

☐ Job 58. Drain flywheel housing.

☐ Job 59. Top-up gearbox and overdrive oil.

☐ Job 60. Top-up transfer box.

☐ Job 61. Adjust handbrake.

☐ Job 62. Adjust clutch pedal.

☐ Job 63. SERIES I VEHICLES Grease pedal shafts.

☐ Job 64. Check rear brake pipes.

☐ Job 65. Top-up rear axle oil.

☐ Job 66. Grease rear propshaft U/Js.

☐ Job 67. Grease rear propshaft splines.

☐ Job 68. Adjust rear brakes.

☐ Job 69. Change wheel positions.

3,000 Mile Mechanical and Electrical - Road Test

☐ Job 70. Clean controls.

☐ Job 71. Check instrumentation.

☐ Job 72. Throttle pedal.

☐ Job 73. Hand brake function.

☐ Job 74. Brakes and steering.

3,000 Mile Bodywork and Interior - Around the Vehicle

First carry out all the Jobs listed under earlier Service Intervals as applicable.

☐ Job 17. Clean bodywork.

☐ Job 23. Touch-up paintwork.

☐ Job 24. Aerial/antenna.

☐ Job 25. Clean out interior.

☐ Job 26. Improve visibility!

☐ Job 75. Wiper blades and arms.

☐ Job 76. Check windscreen seals.

☐ Job 77. Check windscreen.

☐ Job 78. Check mirrors.

3,000 Mile Bodywork - Under the Vehicle

First carry out all the Jobs listed under earlier Service Intervals as applicable.

☐ Job 27. Clean mud traps.

☐ Job 79. Inspect underside.

Date serviced:...

Carried out by:..
Garage Stamp or signature:

Parts/Accessories purchased (date, parts,

source) ....

....

....

....

6,000 MILES - OR EVERY SIX MONTHS, whichever comes first

All the Service Jobs in the tinted area have been carried forward from earlier service intervals are to be repeated at this Service.

6,000 Mile Mechanical and Electrical - The Engine Bay

First carry out all the Jobs listed under earlier Service Intervals as applicable.

☐ Job 1. Engine oil level.

☐ Job 2. NOT SERIES I VEHICLES Clutch fluid level.

☐ Job 3. Brake fluid level.

☐ Job 4. Battery electrolyte.

☐ Job 5. Washer reservoir.

☐ Job 6. Cooling system.

☐ Job 18. DIESEL MODELS ONLY Drain sedimenter.

☐ Job 19. DIESEL MODELS ONLY Drain fuel filter.

☐ Job 28. Drain engine oil.

☐ Job 29. Remove engine oil filter.

☐ Job 30. Fit new oil filter.

☐ Job 31. Pour fresh engine oil.

☐ Job 32. Check oil level.

☐ Job 33. Clean oil bath air cleaner.

☐ Job 34. Adjust spark plugs.

☐ Job 35. Check distributor cap and rotor arm.

☐ Job 36. Check HT Circuit.

☐ Job 37. Check CB points.

☐ Job 38. Lubricate distributor.

☐ Job 39. Check drive belts.

☐ Job 40. 6-CYLINDER MODELS ONLY Check air pump drivebelt.

☐ Job 41. Pipes and hoses.

☐ Job 42. Lubricate accelerator controls.

☐ Job 43. V8 ENGINES ONLY Check heated air intake valve.

☐ Job 44. Set carburettors.

☐ Job 80. Clean engine breather filters.

☐ Job 81. OPTIONAL Renew spark plugs.

☐ Job 82. Renew CB points.

☐ Job 83. NOT V8 MODELS Adjust valve clearances.

- [ ] Job 84. Rocker cover gasket.
- [ ] Job 85. Cooling system.
- [ ] Job 86. Coolant check.
- [ ] Job 87. Heater valve.
- [ ] Job 88. Check water pump.
- [ ] Job 89. Battery terminals.
- [ ] Job 90. Top-up carburettor dashpots.
- [ ] Job 91. Adjust ignition timing.
- [ ] Job 92. Distributor advance.
- [ ] Job 93. Brake servo hose.
- [ ] Job 94. **SPECIALIST SERVICE** Exhaust emissions check.

6,000 Mile Mechanical and Electrical - Around the Vehicle

First carry out all the Jobs listed under earlier Service Intervals as applicable.

- [ ] Job 7. Check horns.
- [ ] Job 8. Windscreen washers.
- [ ] Job 9. Windscreen wipers.
- [ ] Job 10. Tyre pressures.
- [ ] Job 11. Check headlamps.
- [ ] Job 12. Check front sidelamps.
- [ ] Job 13. Check rear sidelamps.
- [ ] Job 14. Number plate lamps.
- [ ] Job 15. Reversing lamps.
- [ ] Job 16. Interior lights.
- [ ] Job 20. Check tyres.
- [ ] Job 21. Check spare tyre.
- [ ] Job 22. Tighten wheel nuts.
- [ ] Job 45. Check fuel pipes.
- [ ] Job 46. Fuel filler pipe.
- [ ] Job 47. Top-up steering relay.
- [ ] Job 48. **SPECIALIST SERVICE** Front wheel alignment.

- [ ] Job 95. **SPECIALIST SERVICE** Adjust headlamps.
- [ ] Job 96. Bonnet release.
- [ ] Job 97. Locks and hinges.

6,000 Mile Mechanical and Electrical - Under the Vehicle

First carry out all the Jobs listed under earlier Service Intervals as applicable.

- [ ] Job 49. Check wheel hubs.
- [ ] Job 50. Top-up swivel pin housings.
- [ ] Job 51. Steering joints.
- [ ] Job 52. Adjust front brakes.
- [ ] Job 53. Top-up front axle oil.
- [ ] Job 54. Grease front propshaft U/Js.
- [ ] Job 55. Check for oil leaks.
- [ ] Job 56. Check front brake pipes.
- [ ] Job 57. Check clutch pipes.
- [ ] Job 58. Drain flywheel housing.
- [ ] Job 59. Top-up gearbox and overdrive oil.
- [ ] Job 60. Top-up transfer box.
- [ ] Job 61. Adjust handbrake.
- [ ] Job 62. Adjust clutch pedal.
- [ ] Job 63. **SERIES I VEHICLES** Grease pedal shafts.
- [ ] Job 64. Check rear brake pipes.
- [ ] Job 65. Top-up rear axle oil.
- [ ] Job 66. Grease rear propshaft U/Js.
- [ ] Job 67. Grease rear propshaft splines.
- [ ] Job 68. Adjust rear brakes.
- [ ] Job 69. Change wheel positions.

- [ ] Job 98. Lubricate steering box.
- [ ] Job 99. Check and adjust steering box.
- [ ] Job 100. Inspect front brakes.
- [ ] Job 101. Inspect front wheel cylinders.
- [ ] Job 102. Front hub/swivel assemblies.
- [ ] Job 103. Check steering balljoints.
- [ ] Job 104. Front shock absorbers.
- [ ] Job 105. Oil front springs.
- [ ] Job 106. Lubricate hand brake linkage.
- [ ] Job 107. Inspect rear brakes.
- [ ] Job 108. Inspect rear wheel cylinders.
- [ ] Job 109. Check exhaust system.
- [ ] Job 110. Rear shock absorbers.
- [ ] Job 111. Oil rear springs.

6,000 Mile Mechanical and Electrical - Road Test

Carry out all the Jobs listed under earlier Service Intervals.

- [ ] Job 70. Clean controls.
- [ ] Job 71. Check instrumentation.
- [ ] Job 72. Throttle pedal.
- [ ] Job 73. Hand brake function.
- [ ] Job 74. Brakes and steering.

6,000 Mile Bodywork and Interior - Around the Vehicle

First carry out all the Jobs listed under earlier Service Intervals as applicable.

- [ ] Job 17. Clean bodywork.
- [ ] Job 23. Touch-up paintwork.
- [ ] Job 24. Aerial/antenna.
- [ ] Job 25. Clean out interior.
- [ ] Job 26. Improve visibility!
- [ ] Job 75. Wiper blades and arms.
- [ ] Job 76. Check windscreen seals.
- [ ] Job 77. Check windscreen.
- [ ] Job 78. Check mirrors.

- [ ] Job 112. Seats and seat belts.
- [ ] Job 113. Inertia reel mechanisms.

6,000 Mile Bodywork - Under the Vehicle

First carry out all the Jobs listed under earlier Service Intervals as applicable.

- [ ] Job 27. Clean mud traps.
- [ ] Job 79. Inspect underside.

- [ ] Job 114. Rustproof underbody.

Date serviced:..

Carried out by:..
Garage Stamp or signature:

Parts/Accessories purchased (date, parts, source) ....
....
....
....

9,000 MILES - OR EVERY NINE MONTHS, whichever comes first

All the Service Jobs at this Service Interval have been carried forward from earlier service intervals and are to be repeated at this Service as applicable.

9,000 Mile Mechanical and Electrical - The Engine Bay

- [ ] Job 1. Engine oil level.
- [ ] Job 2. **NOT SERIES I VEHICLES** Clutch fluid level.
- [ ] Job 3. Brake fluid level.
- [ ] Job 4. Battery electrolyte.
- [ ] Job 5. Washer reservoir.
- [ ] Job 6. Cooling system.
- [ ] Job 18. **DIESEL MODELS ONLY** Drain sedimenter.
- [ ] Job 19. **DIESEL MODELS ONLY** Drain fuel filter.
- [ ] Job 28. Drain engine oil.
- [ ] Job 29. Remove engine oil filter.
- [ ] Job 30. Fit new oil filter.
- [ ] Job 31. Pour fresh engine oil.
- [ ] Job 32. Check oil level.
- [ ] Job 33. Clean oil bath air cleaner.
- [ ] Job 34. Adjust spark plugs.
- [ ] Job 35. Check distributor cap and rotor arm.
- [ ] Job 36. Check HT Circuit.
- [ ] Job 37. Check CB points.
- [ ] Job 38. Lubricate distributor.
- [ ] Job 39. Check drive belts.
- [ ] Job 40. **6-CYLINDER MODELS ONLY** Check air pump drivebelt.
- [ ] Job 41. Pipes and hoses.
- [ ] Job 42. Lubricate accelerator controls.
- [ ] Job 43. **V8 ENGINES ONLY** Check heated air intake valve.
- [ ] Job 44. Set carburettors.

9,000 Mile Mechanical and Electrical - Around the Vehicle

First carry out all the Jobs listed under earlier Service Intervals as applicable.

- [ ] Job 7. Check horns.
- [ ] Job 8. Windscreen washers.
- [ ] Job 9. Windscreen wipers.
- [ ] Job 10. Tyre pressures.
- [ ] Job 11. Check headlamps.
- [ ] Job 12. Check front sidelamps.
- [ ] Job 13. Check rear sidelamps.
- [ ] Job 14. Number plate lamps.
- [ ] Job 15. Reversing lamps.
- [ ] Job 16. Interior lights.
- [ ] Job 20. Check tyres.
- [ ] Job 21. Check spare tyre.
- [ ] Job 22. Tighten wheel nuts.
- [ ] Job 45. Check fuel pipes.
- [ ] Job 46. Fuel filler pipe.
- [ ] Job 47. Top-up steering relay.
- [ ] Job 48. **SPECIALIST SERVICE** Front wheel alignment.

9,000 Mile Mechanical and Electrical - Under the Vehicle

First carry out all the Jobs listed under earlier Service Intervals as applicable.

- [ ] Job 49. Check wheel hubs.
- [ ] Job 50. Top-up swivel pin housings.
- [ ] Job 51. Steering joints.
- [ ] Job 52. Adjust front brakes.
- [ ] Job 53. Top-up front axle oil.
- [ ] Job 54. Grease front propshaft U/Js.
- [ ] Job 55. Check for oil leaks.
- [ ] Job 56. Check front brake pipes.
- [ ] Job 57. Check clutch pipes.
- [ ] Job 58. Drain flywheel housing.
- [ ] Job 59. Top-up gearbox and overdrive oil.
- [ ] Job 60. Top-up transfer box.
- [ ] Job 61. Adjust handbrake.
- [ ] Job 62. Adjust clutch pedal.
- [ ] Job 63. **SERIES I VEHICLES** Grease pedal shafts.
- [ ] Job 64. Check rear brake pipes.
- [ ] Job 65. Top-up rear axle oil.
- [ ] Job 66. Grease rear propshaft U/Js.
- [ ] Job 67. Grease rear propshaft splines.
- [ ] Job 68. Adjust rear brakes.
- [ ] Job 69. Change wheel positions.

9,000 Mile Mechanical and Electrical - Road Test

Carry out all the Jobs listed under earlier Service Intervals.

- [ ] Job 70. Clean controls.
- [ ] Job 71. Check instrumentation.
- [ ] Job 72. Throttle pedal.
- [ ] Job 73. Hand brake function.
- [ ] Job 74. Brakes and steering.

9,000 Mile Bodywork and Interior - Around the Vehicle

First carry out all the Jobs listed under earlier Service Intervals as applicable.

- [ ] Job 17. Clean bodywork.
- [ ] Job 23. Touch-up paintwork.
- [ ] Job 24. Aerial/antenna.
- [ ] Job 25. Clean out interior.
- [ ] Job 26. Improve visibility!
- [ ] Job 75. Wiper blades and arms.
- [ ] Job 76. Check windscreen seals.
- [ ] Job 77. Check windscreen.
- [ ] Job 78. Check mirrors.

9,000 Mile Bodywork - Under the Vehicle

First carry out all the Jobs listed under earlier Service Intervals as applicable.

- [ ] Job 27. Clean mud traps.
- [ ] Job 79. Inspect underside.

Date serviced:...

Carried out by: ....
Garage Stamp or signature:

Parts/Accessories purchased (date, parts, source) ....
....
....
....
....

12,000 MILES - OR EVERY TWELVE MONTHS, whichever comes first

All the Service Jobs in the tinted area have been carried forward from earlier service intervals and are to be repeated at this Service.

12,000 Mile Mechanical and Electrical - Emission Control Equipment

☐ Job 115. 6-CYLINDER AND V8 MODELS ONLY Renew crankcase breather flame trap.

☐ Job 116. EARLY 4-CYLINDER AND ALL 6-CYLINDER MODELS ONLY Crankcase breather valve.

☐ Job 117. SPECIFIC EXPORT 6-CYL. MODELS ONLY Check air injection system.

☐ Job 118. SPECIFIC EXPORT 6-CYL. MODELS ONLY Replace air pump belt.

☐ Job 119. SPECIFIC EXPORT 6-CYL. MODELS ONLY Test check valve.

☐ Job 120. SPECIFIC EXPORT 6-CYL. MODELS ONLY AND SPECIALIST SERVICE Emission system.

12,000 Mile Mechanical and Electrical - The Engine Bay

First carry out all the Jobs listed under earlier Service Intervals as applicable.

☐ Job 1. Engine oil level.

☐ Job 2. NOT SERIES I VEHICLES Clutch fluid level.

☐ Job 3. Brake fluid level.

☐ Job 4. Battery electrolyte.

☐ Job 5. Washer reservoir.

☐ Job 6. Cooling system.

☐ Job 18. DIESEL MODELS ONLY Drain sedimenter.

☐ Job 19. DIESEL MODELS ONLY Drain fuel filter.

☐ Job 28. Drain engine oil.

☐ Job 29. Remove engine oil filter.

☐ Job 30. Fit new oil filter.

☐ Job 31. Pour fresh engine oil.

☐ Job 32. Check oil level.

☐ Job 33. Clean oil bath air cleaner.

☐ Job 34. Adjust spark plugs.

☐ Job 35. Check distributor cap and rotor arm.

☐ Job 36. Check HT Circuit.

☐ Job 37. Check CB points.

☐ Job 38. Lubricate distributor.

☐ Job 39. Check drive belts.

☐ Job 40. 6-CYLINDER MODELS ONLY Check air pump drivebelt.

☐ Job 41. Pipes and hoses.

☐ Job 42. Lubricate accelerator controls.

☐ Job 43. V8 ENGINES ONLY Check heated air intake valve.

☐ Job 44. Set carburettors.

☐ Job 80. Clean engine breather filters.

☐ Job 81. OPTIONAL Renew spark plugs.

☐ Job 82. Renew CB points.

☐ Job 83. NOT V8 MODELS Adjust valve clearances.

☐ Job 84. Rocker cover gasket.

☐ Job 85. Cooling system.

☐ Job 86. Coolant check.

☐ Job 87. Heater valve.

☐ Job 88. Check water pump.

☐ Job 89. Battery terminals.

☐ Job 90. Top-up carburettor dashpots.

☐ Job 91. Adjust ignition timing.

☐ Job 92. Distributor advance.

☐ Job 93. Brake servo hose.

☐ Job 94. SPECIALIST SERVICE Exhaust emissions check.

☐ Job 121. Cabin heater and hoses.

☐ Job 122. DIESEL MODELS ONLY and SPECIALIST SERVICE Check injectors.

☐ Job 123. DIESEL MODELS ONLY Diesel heater plug wiring.

☐ Job 124. V8 MODELS ONLY Renew air cleaner element.

☐ Job 125. PETROL MODELS ONLY Cylinder compressions.

☐ Job 126. Lubricate dynamo.

☐ Job 127. Clean fuel sediment bowl.

☐ Job 128. 6-CYLINDER PETROL MODELS ONLY Renew bulkhead fuel filter.

☐ Job 129. DIESEL MODELS ONLY Clean fuel sedimenter.

☐ Job 130. DIESEL MODELS ONLY Renew fuel filter element.

☐ Job 131. DIESEL MODELS ONLY Bleed fuel system.

12,000 Mile Mechanical and Electrical - Around the Vehicle

First carry out all the Jobs listed under earlier Service Intervals as applicable.

☐ Job 7. Check horns.

☐ Job 8. Windscreen washers.

☐ Job 9. Windscreen wipers.

☐ Job 10. Tyre pressures.

☐ Job 11. Check headlamps.

☐ Job 12. Check front sidelamps.

☐ Job 13. Check rear sidelamps.

☐ Job 14. Number plate lamps.

☐ Job 15. Reversing lamps.

☐ Job 16. Interior lights.

☐ Job 20. Check tyres.

☐ Job 21. Check spare tyre.

☐ Job 22. Tighten wheel nuts.

☐ Job 45. Check fuel pipes.

☐ Job 46. Fuel filler pipe.

☐ Job 47. Top-up steering relay.

☐ Job 48. SPECIALIST SERVICE Front wheel alignment.

☐ Job 95. SPECIALIST SERVICE Adjust headlamps.

☐ Job 96. Bonnet release.

☐ Job 97. Locks and hinges.

☐ Job 132. Toolkit and jack.

☐ Job 133. Test shock absorbers.

12,000 Mile Mechanical and Electrical - Under the Vehicle

First carry out all the Jobs listed under earlier Service Intervals as applicable.

☐ Job 49. Check wheel hubs.

☐ Job 50. Top-up swivel pin housings.

☐ Job 51. Steering joints.

☐ Job 52. Adjust front brakes.

☐ Job 53. Top-up front axle oil.

☐ Job 54. Grease front propshaft U/Js.

☐ Job 55. Check for oil leaks.

☐ Job 56. Check front brake pipes.

☐ Job 57. Check clutch pipes.

☐ Job 58. Drain flywheel housing.

☐ Job 59. Top-up gearbox and overdrive oil.

- [ ] Job 60. Top-up transfer box.
- [ ] Job 61. Adjust handbrake.
- [ ] Job 62. Adjust clutch pedal.
- [ ] Job 63. **SERIES I VEHICLES** Grease pedal shafts.
- [ ] Job 64. Check rear brake pipes.
- [ ] Job 65. Top-up rear axle oil.
- [ ] Job 66. Grease rear propshaft U/Js.
- [ ] Job 67. Grease rear propshaft splines.
- [ ] Job 68. Adjust rear brakes.
- [ ] Job 69. Change wheel positions.
- [ ] Job 98. Lubricate steering box.
- [ ] Job 99. Check and adjust steering box.
- [ ] Job 100. Inspect front brakes.
- [ ] Job 101. Inspect front wheel cylinders.
- [ ] Job 102. Front hub/swivel assemblies.
- [ ] Job 103. Check steering balljoints.
- [ ] Job 104. Front shock absorbers.
- [ ] Job 105. Oil front springs.
- [ ] Job 106. Lubricate hand brake linkage.
- [ ] Job 107. Inspect rear brakes.
- [ ] Job 108. Inspect rear wheel cylinders.
- [ ] Job 109. Check exhaust system.
- [ ] Job 110. Rear shock absorbers.
- [ ] Job 111. Oil rear springs.

- [ ] Job 134. Renew transfer box oil.
- [ ] Job 135. Renew gearbox oil and overdrive oil (if fitted).
- [ ] Job 136. Renew front axle oil.
- [ ] Job 137. Front axle breather.
- [ ] Job 138. Front suspension security.
- [ ] Job 139. Check front propshaft U/Js.
- [ ] Job 140. Service freewheeling hubs.
- [ ] Job 141. Renew rear axle oil.
- [ ] Job 142. Rear axle breather.
- [ ] Job 143. Rear suspension security.
- [ ] Job 144. Check rear propshaft U/Js.
- [ ] Job 145. **SERIES II & IIA ONLY** Check/lubricate door hinges.

Parts/Accessories purchased (date, parts, source)

....

....

....

12,000 Mile Mechanical and Electrical - Road Test

Carry out all the Jobs listed under earlier Service Intervals.

- [ ] Job 70. Clean controls.
- [ ] Job 71. Check instrumentation.
- [ ] Job 72. Throttle pedal.
- [ ] Job 73. Hand brake function.
- [ ] Job 74. Brakes and steering.

12,000 Mile Bodywork and Interior - Around the Vehicle

First carry out all the Jobs listed under earlier Service Intervals as applicable.

- [ ] Job 17. Clean bodywork.
- [ ] Job 23. Touch-up paintwork.
- [ ] Job 24. Aerial/antenna.
- [ ] Job 25. Clean out interior.
- [ ] Job 26. Improve visibility!
- [ ] Job 75. Wiper blades and arms.
- [ ] Job 76. Check windscreen seals.
- [ ] Job 77. Check windscreen.
- [ ] Job 78. Check mirrors.
- [ ] Job 112. Seats and seat belts.
- [ ] Job 113. Inertia reel mechanisms.

12,000 Mile Bodywork - Under the Vehicle

First carry out all the Jobs listed under earlier Service Intervals as applicable.

- [ ] Job 27. Clean mud traps.
- [ ] Job 79. Inspect underside.
- [ ] Job 114. Rustproof underbody.

- [ ] Job 146. Tighten wing and body bolts.
- [ ] Job 147. Top-up rustproofing.

Date serviced:..

Carried out by:...

Garage Stamp or signature:

15,000 MILES - OR EVERY FIFTEEN MONTHS, whichever comes first

All the Service Jobs at this Service Interval have been carried forward from earlier service intervals and are to be repeated at this Service.

15,000 Mile Mechanical and Electrical - The Engine Bay

- [ ] Job 1. Engine oil level.
- [ ] Job 2. **NOT SERIES I VEHICLES** Clutch fluid level.
- [ ] Job 3. Brake fluid level.
- [ ] Job 4. Battery electrolyte.
- [ ] Job 5. Washer reservoir.
- [ ] Job 6. Cooling system.
- [ ] Job 18. **DIESEL MODELS ONLY** Drain sedimenter.
- [ ] Job 19. **DIESEL MODELS ONLY** Drain fuel filter.
- [ ] Job 28. Drain engine oil.
- [ ] Job 29. Remove engine oil filter.
- [ ] Job 30. Fit new oil filter.
- [ ] Job 31. Pour fresh engine oil.
- [ ] Job 32. Check oil level.
- [ ] Job 33. Clean oil bath air cleaner.
- [ ] Job 34. Adjust spark plugs.
- [ ] Job 35. Check distributor cap and rotor arm.
- [ ] Job 36. Check HT Circuit.
- [ ] Job 37. Check CB points.
- [ ] Job 38. Lubricate distributor.
- [ ] Job 39. Check drive belts.
- [ ] Job 40. **6-CYLINDER MODELS ONLY** Check air pump drivebelt.
- [ ] Job 41. Pipes and hoses.
- [ ] Job 42. Lubricate accelerator controls.
- [ ] Job 43. **V8 ENGINES ONLY** Check heated air intake valve.
- [ ] Job 44. Set carburettors.

15,000 Mile Mechanical and Electrical - Around the Vehicle

First carry out all the Jobs listed under earlier Service Intervals as applicable.

- [ ] Job 7. Check horns.
- [ ] Job 8. Windscreen washers.

Job 9. Windscreen wipers.

Job 10. Tyre pressures.

Job 11. Check headlamps.

Job 12. Check front sidelamps.

Job 13. Check rear sidelamps.

Job 14. Number plate lamps.

Job 15. Reversing lamps.

Job 16. Interior lights.

Job 20. Check tyres.

Job 21. Check spare tyre.

Job 22. Tighten wheel nuts.

Job 45. Check fuel pipes.

Job 46. Fuel filler pipe.

Job 47. Top-up steering relay.

Job 48. **SPECIALIST SERVICE** Front wheel alignment.

15,000 Mile Mechanical and Electrical - Under the Vehicle

First carry out all the Jobs listed under earlier Service Intervals as applicable.

Job 49. Check wheel hubs.

Job 50. Top-up swivel pin housings.

Job 51. Steering joints.

Job 52. Adjust front brakes.

Job 53. Top-up front axle oil.

Job 54. Grease front propshaft U/Js.

Job 55. Check for oil leaks.

Job 56. Check front brake pipes.

Job 57. Check clutch pipes.

Job 58. Drain flywheel housing.

Job 59. Top-up gearbox and overdrive oil.

Job 60. Top-up transfer box.

Job 61. Adjust handbrake.

Job 62. Adjust clutch pedal.

Job 63. **SERIES I VEHICLES** Grease pedal shafts.

Job 64. Check rear brake pipes.

Job 65. Top-up rear axle oil.

Job 66. Grease rear propshaft U/Js.

Job 67. Grease rear propshaft splines.

Job 68. Adjust rear brakes.

Job 69. Change wheel positions.

15,000 Mile Mechanical and Electrical - Road Test

Carry out all the Jobs listed under earlier Service Intervals.

Job 70. Clean controls.

Job 71. Check instrumentation.

Job 72. Throttle pedal.

Job 73. Hand brake function.

Job 74. Brakes and steering.

15,000 Mile Bodywork and Interior - Around the Vehicle

First carry out all the Jobs listed under earlier Service Intervals as applicable.

Job 17. Clean bodywork.

Job 23. Touch-up paintwork.

Job 24. Aerial/antenna.

Job 25. Clean out interior.

Job 26. Improve visibility!

Job 75. Wiper blades and arms.

Job 76. Check windscreen seals.

Job 77. Check windscreen.

Job 78. Check mirrors.

15,000 Mile Bodywork - Under the Vehicle

First carry out all the Jobs listed under earlier Service Intervals as applicable.

Job 27. Clean mud traps.

Job 79. Inspect underside.

Date serviced:...

Carried out by: ....
Garage Stamp or signature:

Parts/Accessories purchased (date, parts,

source) ....

....

....

....

....

18,000 MILES - OR EVERY EIGHTEEN MONTHS, whichever comes first

All the Service Jobs at this Service Interval have been carried forward from earlier service intervals and are to be repeated at this Service.

18,000 Mile Mechanical and Electrical - The Engine Bay

First carry out all the Jobs listed under earlier Service Intervals as applicable.

Job 1. Engine oil level.

Job 2. **NOT SERIES I VEHICLES** Clutch fluid level.

Job 3. Brake fluid level.

Job 4. Battery electrolyte.

Job 5. Washer reservoir.

Job 6. Cooling system.

Job 18. **DIESEL MODELS ONLY** Drain sedimenter.

Job 19. **DIESEL MODELS ONLY** Drain fuel filter.

Job 28. Drain engine oil.

Job 29. Remove engine oil filter.

Job 30. Fit new oil filter.

Job 31. Pour fresh engine oil.

Job 32. Check oil level.

Job 33. Clean oil bath air cleaner.

Job 34. Adjust spark plugs.

Job 35. Check distributor cap and rotor arm.

Job 36. Check HT Circuit.

Job 37. Check CB points.

Job 38. Lubricate distributor.

Job 39. Check drive belts.

Job 40. **6-CYLINDER MODELS ONLY** Check air pump drivebelt.

Job 41. Pipes and hoses.

Job 42. Lubricate accelerator controls.

Job 43. **V8 ENGINES ONLY** Check heated air intake valve.

Job 44. Set carburettors.

Job 80. Clean engine breather filters.

Job 81. **OPTIONAL** Renew spark plugs.

Job 82. Renew CB points.

Job 83. **NOT V8 MODELS** Adjust valve clearances.

- [ ] Job 84. Rocker cover gasket.
- [ ] Job 85. Cooling system.
- [ ] Job 86. Coolant check.
- [ ] Job 87. Heater valve.
- [ ] Job 88. Check water pump.
- [ ] Job 89. Battery terminals.
- [ ] Job 90. Top-up carburettor dashpots.
- [ ] Job 91. Adjust ignition timing.
- [ ] Job 92. Distributor advance.
- [ ] Job 93. Brake servo hose.
- [ ] Job 94. **SPECIALIST SERVICE** Exhaust emissions check.

18,000 Mile Mechanical and Electrical - Around the Vehicle

First carry out all the Jobs listed under earlier Service Intervals as applicable.

- [ ] Job 7. Check horns.
- [ ] Job 8. Windscreen washers.
- [ ] Job 9. Windscreen wipers.
- [ ] Job 10. Tyre pressures.
- [ ] Job 11. Check headlamps.
- [ ] Job 12. Check front sidelamps.
- [ ] Job 13. Check rear sidelamps.
- [ ] Job 14. Number plate lamps.
- [ ] Job 15. Reversing lamps.
- [ ] Job 16. Interior lights.
- [ ] Job 20. Check tyres.
- [ ] Job 21. Check spare tyre.
- [ ] Job 22. Tighten wheel nuts.
- [ ] Job 45. Check fuel pipes.
- [ ] Job 46. Fuel filler pipe.
- [ ] Job 47. Top-up steering relay.
- [ ] Job 48. **SPECIALIST SERVICE** Front wheel alignment.
- [ ] Job 95. **SPECIALIST SERVICE** Adjust headlamps.
- [ ] Job 96. Bonnet release.
- [ ] Job 97. Locks and hinges.

18,000 Mile Mechanical and Electrical - Under the Vehicle

First carry out all the Jobs listed under earlier Service Intervals as applicable.

- [ ] Job 49. Check wheel hubs.
- [ ] Job 50. Top-up swivel pin housings.
- [ ] Job 51. Steering joints.
- [ ] Job 52. Adjust front brakes.
- [ ] Job 53. Top-up front axle oil.
- [ ] Job 54. Grease front propshaft U/Js.
- [ ] Job 55. Check for oil leaks.
- [ ] Job 56. Check front brake pipes.
- [ ] Job 57. Check clutch pipes.
- [ ] Job 58. Drain flywheel housing.
- [ ] Job 59. Top-up gearbox and overdrive oil.
- [ ] Job 60. Top-up transfer box.
- [ ] Job 61. Adjust handbrake.
- [ ] Job 62. Adjust clutch pedal.
- [ ] Job 63. **SERIES I VEHICLES** Grease pedal shafts.
- [ ] Job 64. Check rear brake pipes.
- [ ] Job 65. Top-up rear axle oil.
- [ ] Job 66. Grease rear propshaft U/Js.
- [ ] Job 67. Grease rear propshaft splines.
- [ ] Job 68. Adjust rear brakes.
- [ ] Job 69. Change wheel positions.
- [ ] Job 98. Lubricate steering box.
- [ ] Job 99. Check and adjust steering box.
- [ ] Job 100. Inspect front brakes.
- [ ] Job 101. Inspect front wheel cylinders.
- [ ] Job 102. Front hub/swivel assemblies.
- [ ] Job 103. Check steering balljoints.
- [ ] Job 104. Front shock absorbers.
- [ ] Job 105. Oil front springs.
- [ ] Job 106. Lubricate hand brake linkage.
- [ ] Job 107. Inspect rear brakes.
- [ ] Job 108. Inspect rear wheel cylinders.
- [ ] Job 109. Check exhaust system.
- [ ] Job 110. Rear shock absorbers.
- [ ] Job 111. Oil rear springs.

18,000 mile Mechanical and Electrical - Road Test

Carry out all the Jobs listed under earlier Service Intervals.

- [ ] Job 70. Clean controls.
- [ ] Job 71. Check instrumentation.
- [ ] Job 72. Throttle pedal.
- [ ] Job 73. Hand brake function.
- [ ] Job 74. Brakes and steering.

18,000 Mile Bodywork and Interior - Around the Vehicle

First carry out all the Jobs listed under earlier Service Intervals as applicable.

- [ ] Job 17. Clean bodywork.
- [ ] Job 23. Touch-up paintwork.
- [ ] Job 24. Aerial/antenna.
- [ ] Job 25. Clean out interior.
- [ ] Job 26. Improve visibility!
- [ ] Job 75. Wiper blades and arms.
- [ ] Job 76. Check windscreen seals.
- [ ] Job 77. Check windscreen.
- [ ] Job 78. Check mirrors.
- [ ] Job 112. Seats and seat belts.
- [ ] Job 113. Inertia reel mechanisms.

18,000 Mile Bodywork - Under the Vehicle

First carry out all the Jobs listed under earlier Service Intervals as applicable.

- [ ] Job 27. Clean mud traps.
- [ ] Job 79. Inspect underside.
- [ ] Job 114. Rustproof underbody.

Date serviced:...................................

Carried out by:................................
Garage Stamp or signature:

Parts/Accessories purchased (date, parts, source) ....

....

....

....

....

....

....

....

....

21,000 MILES - OR EVERY TWENTY ONE MONTHS, whichever comes first

All the Service Jobs at this Service Interval have been carried forward from earlier service intervals and are to be repeated at this Service.

21,000 Mile Mechanical and Electrical - The Engine Bay

- [ ] Job 1. Engine oil level.
- [ ] Job 2. **NOT SERIES I VEHICLES** Clutch fluid level.
- [ ] Job 3. Brake fluid level.
- [ ] Job 4. Battery electrolyte.
- [ ] Job 5. Washer reservoir.
- [ ] Job 6. Cooling system.
- [ ] Job 18. **DIESEL MODELS ONLY** Drain sedimenter.
- [ ] Job 19. **DIESEL MODELS ONLY** Drain fuel filter.
- [ ] Job 28. Drain engine oil.
- [ ] Job 29. Remove engine oil filter.
- [ ] Job 30. Fit new oil filter.
- [ ] Job 31. Pour fresh engine oil.
- [ ] Job 32. Check oil level.
- [ ] Job 33. Clean oil bath air cleaner.
- [ ] Job 34. Adjust spark plugs.
- [ ] Job 35. Check distributor cap and rotor arm.
- [ ] Job 36. Check HT Circuit.
- [ ] Job 37. Check CB points.
- [ ] Job 38. Lubricate distributor.
- [ ] Job 39. Check drive belts.
- [ ] Job 40. **6-CYLINDER MODELS ONLY** Check air pump drivebelt.
- [ ] Job 41. Pipes and hoses.
- [ ] Job 42. Lubricate accelerator controls.
- [ ] Job 43. **V8 ENGINES ONLY** Check heated air intake valve.
- [ ] Job 44. Set carburettors.

21,000 Mile Mechanical and Electrical - Around the Vehicle

First carry out all the Jobs listed under earlier Service Intervals as applicable.

- [ ] Job 7. Check horns.
- [ ] Job 8. Windscreen washers.

- [ ] Job 9. Windscreen wipers.
- [ ] Job 10. Tyre pressures.
- [ ] Job 11. Check headlamps.
- [ ] Job 12. Check front sidelamps.
- [ ] Job 13. Check rear sidelamps.
- [ ] Job 14. Number plate lamps.
- [ ] Job 15. Reversing lamps.
- [ ] Job 16. Interior lights.
- [ ] Job 20. Check tyres.
- [ ] Job 21. Check spare tyre.
- [ ] Job 22. Tighten wheel nuts.
- [ ] Job 45. Check fuel pipes.
- [ ] Job 46. Fuel filler pipe.
- [ ] Job 47. Top-up steering relay.
- [ ] Job 48. **SPECIALIST SERVICE** Front wheel alignment.

21,000 Mile Mechanical and Electrical - Under the Vehicle

First carry out all the Jobs listed under earlier Service Intervals as applicable.

- [ ] Job 49. Check wheel hubs.
- [ ] Job 50. Top-up swivel pin housings.
- [ ] Job 51. Steering joints.
- [ ] Job 52. Adjust front brakes.
- [ ] Job 53. Top-up front axle oil.
- [ ] Job 54. Grease front propshaft U/Js.
- [ ] Job 55. Check for oil leaks.
- [ ] Job 56. Check front brake pipes.
- [ ] Job 57. Check clutch pipes.
- [ ] Job 58. Drain flywheel housing.
- [ ] Job 59. Top-up gearbox and overdrive oil.
- [ ] Job 60. Top-up transfer box.
- [ ] Job 61. Adjust handbrake.
- [ ] Job 62. Adjust clutch pedal.
- [ ] Job 63. **SERIES I VEHICLES** Grease pedal shafts.
- [ ] Job 64. Check rear brake pipes.
- [ ] Job 65. Top-up rear axle oil.
- [ ] Job 66. Grease rear propshaft U/Js.
- [ ] Job 67. Grease rear propshaft splines.
- [ ] Job 68. Adjust rear brakes.
- [ ] Job 69. Change wheel positions.

21,000 Mile Mechanical and Electrical - Road Test

Carry out all the Jobs listed under earlier Service Intervals.

- [ ] Job 70. Clean controls.
- [ ] Job 71. Check instrumentation.
- [ ] Job 72. Throttle pedal.
- [ ] Job 73. Hand brake function.
- [ ] Job 74. Brakes and steering.

21,000 Mile Bodywork and Interior - Around the Vehicle

First carry out all the Jobs listed under earlier Service Intervals as applicable.

- [ ] Job 17. Clean bodywork.
- [ ] Job 23. Touch-up paintwork.
- [ ] Job 24. Aerial/antenna.
- [ ] Job 25. Clean out interior.
- [ ] Job 26. Improve visibility!
- [ ] Job 75. Wiper blades and arms.
- [ ] Job 76. Check windscreen seals.
- [ ] Job 77. Check windscreen.
- [ ] Job 78. Check mirrors.

21,000 Mile Bodywork - Under the Vehicle

First carry out all the Jobs listed under earlier Service Intervals as applicable.

- [ ] Job 27. Clean mud traps.
- [ ] Job 79. Inspect underside.

Date serviced:...

Carried out by:...
Garage Stamp or signature:

Parts/Accessories purchased (date, parts,

source) ....

....

....

....

....

24,000 MILES - OR EVERY TWENTY FOUR MONTHS, whichever comes first

All the Service Jobs in the tinted area have been carried forward from earlier service intervals and are to be repeated at this Service.

24,000 Mile Mechanical and Electrical - Emission Control Equipment

Carry out all the Jobs listed under earlier Service Intervals.

- [ ] Job 115. 6-CYLINDER AND V8 MODELS ONLY Renew crankcase breather flame trap.
- [ ] Job 116. EARLY 4-CYLINDER AND ALL 6-CYLINDER MODELS ONLY Crankcase breather valve.
- [ ] Job 117. SPECIFIC EXPORT 6-CYL. MODELS ONLY Check air injection system.
- [ ] Job 118. SPECIFIC EXPORT 6-CYL. MODELS ONLY Replace air pump belt.
- [ ] Job 119. SPECIFIC EXPORT 6-CYL. MODELS ONLY Test check valve.
- [ ] Job 120. SPECIFIC EXPORT 6-CYL. MODELS ONLY AND SPECIALIST SERVICE Emission system.

24,000 Miles, Mechanical and Electrical - The Engine Bay

First carry out all the Jobs listed under earlier Service Intervals as applicable.

- [ ] Job 1. Engine oil level.
- [ ] Job 2. NOT SERIES I VEHICLES Clutch fluid level.
- [ ] Job 3. Brake fluid level.
- [ ] Job 4. Battery electrolyte.
- [ ] Job 5. Washer reservoir.
- [ ] Job 6. Cooling system.
- [ ] Job 18. DIESEL MODELS ONLY Drain sedimenter.
- [ ] Job 19. DIESEL MODELS ONLY Drain fuel filter.
- [ ] Job 28. Drain engine oil.
- [ ] Job 29. Remove engine oil filter.
- [ ] Job 30. Fit new oil filter.
- [ ] Job 31. Pour fresh engine oil.
- [ ] Job 32. Check oil level.
- [ ] Job 33. Clean oil bath air cleaner.
- [ ] Job 34. Adjust spark plugs.

- [ ] Job 35. Check distributor cap and rotor arm.
- [ ] Job 36. Check HT Circuit.
- [ ] Job 37. Check CB points.
- [ ] Job 38. Lubricate distributor.
- [ ] Job 39. Check drive belts.
- [ ] Job 40. 6-CYLINDER MODELS ONLY Check air pump drivebelt.
- [ ] Job 41. Pipes and hoses.
- [ ] Job 42. Lubricate accelerator controls.
- [ ] Job 43. V8 ENGINES ONLY Check heated air intake valve.
- [ ] Job 44. Set carburettors.
- [ ] Job 80. Clean engine breather filters.
- [ ] Job 81. OPTIONAL Renew spark plugs.
- [ ] Job 82. Renew CB points.
- [ ] Job 83. NOT V8 MODELS Adjust valve clearances.
- [ ] Job 84. Rocker cover gasket.
- [ ] Job 85. Cooling system.
- [ ] Job 86. Coolant check.
- [ ] Job 87. Heater valve.
- [ ] Job 88. Check water pump.
- [ ] Job 89. Battery terminals.
- [ ] Job 90. Top-up carburettor dashpots.
- [ ] Job 91. Adjust ignition timing.
- [ ] Job 92. Distributor advance.
- [ ] Job 93. Brake servo hose.
- [ ] Job 94. SPECIALIST SERVICE Exhaust emissions check.
- [ ] Job 121. Cabin heater and hoses.
- [ ] Job 122. DIESEL MODELS ONLY and SPECIALIST SERVICE Check injectors.
- [ ] Job 123. DIESEL MODELS ONLY Diesel heater plug wiring.
- [ ] Job 124. V8 MODELS ONLY Renew air cleaner element.
- [ ] Job 125. PETROL MODELS ONLY Cylinder compressions.
- [ ] Job 126. Lubricate dynamo.
- [ ] Job 127. Clean fuel sediment bowl.
- [ ] Job 128. 6-CYLINDER PETROL MODELS ONLY Renew bulkhead fuel filter.
- [ ] Job 129. DIESEL MODELS ONLY Clean fuel sedimenter.
- [ ] Job 130. DIESEL MODELS ONLY Renew fuel filter element.
- [ ] Job 131. DIESEL MODELS ONLY Bleed fuel system.

☐ Job 148. Engine mountings.

☐ Job 149. Refill cooling system.

☐ Job 150. Radiator pressure cap.

☐ Job 151. Renew drive belts.

24,000 Mile Mechanical and Electrical - Around the Vehicle

First carry out all the Jobs listed under earlier Service Intervals as applicable.

☐ Job 7. Check horns.

☐ Job 8. Windscreen washers.

☐ Job 9. Windscreen wipers.

☐ Job 10. Tyre pressures.

☐ Job 11. Check headlamps.

☐ Job 12. Check front sidelamps.

☐ Job 13. Check rear sidelamps.

☐ Job 14. Number plate lamps.

☐ Job 15. Reversing lamps.

☐ Job 16. Interior lights.

☐ Job 20. Check tyres.

☐ Job 21. Check spare tyre.

☐ Job 22. Tighten wheel nuts.

☐ Job 45. Check fuel pipes.

☐ Job 46. Fuel filler pipe.

☐ Job 47. Top-up steering relay.

☐ Job 48. **SPECIALIST SERVICE** Front wheel alignment.

☐ Job 95. **SPECIALIST SERVICE** Adjust headlamps.

☐ Job 96. Bonnet release.

☐ Job 97. Locks and hinges.

☐ Job 132. Toolkit and jack.

☐ Job 133. Test shock absorbers.

24,000 Mile Mechanical and Electrical - Under the Vehicle

First carry out all the Jobs listed under earlier Service Intervals as applicable.

☐ Job 49. Check wheel hubs.

☐ Job 50. Top-up swivel pin housings.

☐ Job 51. Steering joints.

☐ Job 52. Adjust front brakes.

☐ Job 53. Top-up front axle oil.

☐ Job 54. Grease front propshaft U/Js.

☐ Job 55. Check for oil leaks.

☐ Job 56. Check front brake pipes.

☐ Job 57. Check clutch pipes.

☐ Job 58. Drain flywheel housing.

☐ Job 59. Top-up gearbox and overdrive oil.

☐ Job 60. Top-up transfer box.

☐ Job 61. Adjust handbrake.

☐ Job 62. Adjust clutch pedal.

☐ Job 63. **SERIES I VEHICLES** Grease pedal shafts.

☐ Job 64. Check rear brake pipes.

☐ Job 65. Top-up rear axle oil.

☐ Job 66. Grease rear propshaft U/Js.

☐ Job 67. Grease rear propshaft splines.

☐ Job 68. Adjust rear brakes.

☐ Job 69. Change wheel positions.

☐ Job 98. Lubricate steering box.

☐ Job 99. Check and adjust steering box.

☐ Job 100. Inspect front brakes.

☐ Job 101. Inspect front wheel cylinders.

☐ Job 102. Front hub/swivel assemblies.

☐ Job 103. Check steering balljoints.

☐ Job 104. Front shock absorbers.

☐ Job 105. Oil front springs.

☐ Job 106. Lubricate hand brake linkage.

☐ Job 107. Inspect rear brakes.

☐ Job 108. Inspect rear wheel cylinders.

☐ Job 109. Check exhaust system.

☐ Job 110. Rear shock absorbers.

☐ Job 111. Oil rear springs.

☐ Job 134. Renew transfer box oil.

☐ Job 135. Renew gearbox oil and overdrive oil (if fitted).

☐ Job 136. Renew front axle oil.

☐ Job 137. Front axle breather.

☐ Job 138. Front suspension security.

☐ Job 139. Check front propshaft U/Js.

☐ Job 140. Service freewheeling hubs.

☐ Job 141. Renew rear axle oil.

☐ Job 142. Rear axle breather.

☐ Job 143. Rear suspension security.

☐ Job 144. Check rear propshaft U/Js.

☐ Job 145. **SERIES II & IIA ONLY** Check/lubricate door hinges.

☐ Job 152. Engine Flushing Oil.

☐ Job 153. Change brake fluid.

☐ Job 154. Check brake drums.

☐ Job 155. Brake back plates.

☐ Job 156. Grease front propeller shaft splines.

☐ Job 157 Drain swivel pin housings.

24,000 mile Bodywork and Interior - Around the car

First carry out all the Jobs listed under earlier Service Intervals as applicable.

☐ Job 17. Clean bodywork.

☐ Job 23. Touch-up paintwork.

☐ Job 24. Aerial/antenna.

☐ Job 25. Clean out interior.

☐ Job 26. Improve visibility!

☐ Job 75. Wiper blades and arms.

☐ Job 76. Check windscreen seals.

☐ Job 77. Check windscreen.

☐ Job 78. Check mirrors.

☐ Job 112. Seats and seat belts.

☐ Job 113. Inertia reel mechanisms.

☐ Job 158. Lamp seals.

24,000 Mile Bodywork - Under the Vehicle

First carry out all the Jobs listed under earlier Service Intervals as applicable.

☐ Job 27. Clean mud traps.

☐ Job 79. Inspect underside.

☐ Job 114. Rustproof underbody.

☐ Job 146. Tighten wing and body bolts.

☐ Job 147. Top-up rustproofing.

Date serviced:..

Carried out by:...
Garage Stamp or signature:

Parts/Accessories purchased (date, parts, source)..
....
....

27,000 MILES - OR EVERY TWENTY SEVEN MONTHS, whichever comes first

All the Service Jobs at this Service Interval have been carried forward from earlier service intervals and are to be repeated at this Service as applicable.

27,000 Mile Mechanical and Electrical - The Engine Bay

- [ ] Job 1. Engine oil level.
- [ ] Job 2. NOT SERIES I VEHICLES Clutch fluid level.
- [ ] Job 3. Brake fluid level.
- [ ] Job 4. Battery electrolyte.
- [ ] Job 5. Washer reservoir.
- [ ] Job 6. Cooling system.
- [ ] Job 18. DIESEL MODELS ONLY Drain sedimenter.
- [ ] Job 19. DIESEL MODELS ONLY Drain fuel filter.
- [ ] Job 28. Drain engine oil.
- [ ] Job 29. Remove engine oil filter.
- [ ] Job 30. Fit new oil filter.
- [ ] Job 31. Pour fresh engine oil.
- [ ] Job 32. Check oil level.
- [ ] Job 33. Clean oil bath air cleaner.
- [ ] Job 34. Adjust spark plugs.
- [ ] Job 35. Check distributor cap and rotor arm.
- [ ] Job 36. Check HT Circuit.
- [ ] Job 37. Check CB points.
- [ ] Job 38. Lubricate distributor.
- [ ] Job 39. Check drive belts.
- [ ] Job 40. 6-CYLINDER MODELS ONLY Check air pump drivebelt.
- [ ] Job 41. Pipes and hoses.
- [ ] Job 42. Lubricate accelerator controls.
- [ ] Job 43. V8 ENGINES ONLY Check heated air intake valve.
- [ ] Job 44. Set carburettors.

27,000 Mile Mechanical and Electrical - Around the Vehicle

First carry out all the Jobs listed under earlier Service Intervals as applicable.

- [ ] Job 7. Check horns.
- [ ] Job 8. Windscreen washers.
- [ ] Job 9. Windscreen wipers.
- [ ] Job 10. Tyre pressures.
- [ ] Job 11. Check headlamps.
- [ ] Job 12. Check front sidelamps.
- [ ] Job 13. Check rear sidelamps.
- [ ] Job 14. Number plate lamps.
- [ ] Job 15. Reversing lamps.
- [ ] Job 16. Interior lights.
- [ ] Job 20. Check tyres.
- [ ] Job 21. Check spare tyre.
- [ ] Job 22. Tighten wheel nuts.
- [ ] Job 45. Check fuel pipes.
- [ ] Job 46. Fuel filler pipe.
- [ ] Job 47. Top-up steering relay.
- [ ] Job 48. SPECIALIST SERVICE Front wheel alignment.

27,000 Mile Mechanical and Electrical - Under the Vehicle

First carry out all the Jobs listed under earlier Service Intervals as applicable.

- [ ] Job 49. Check wheel hubs.
- [ ] Job 50. Top-up swivel pin housings.
- [ ] Job 51. Steering joints.
- [ ] Job 52. Adjust front brakes.
- [ ] Job 53. Top-up front axle oil.
- [ ] Job 54. Grease front propshaft U/Js.
- [ ] Job 55. Check for oil leaks.
- [ ] Job 56. Check front brake pipes.
- [ ] Job 57. Check clutch pipes.
- [ ] Job 58. Drain flywheel housing.
- [ ] Job 59. Top-up gearbox and overdrive oil.
- [ ] Job 60. Top-up transfer box.
- [ ] Job 61. Adjust handbrake.
- [ ] Job 62. Adjust clutch pedal.
- [ ] Job 63. SERIES I VEHICLES Grease pedal shafts.
- [ ] Job 64. Check rear brake pipes.
- [ ] Job 65. Top-up rear axle oil.
- [ ] Job 66. Grease rear propshaft U/Js.
- [ ] Job 67. Grease rear propshaft splines.
- [ ] Job 68. Adjust rear brakes.
- [ ] Job 69. Change wheel positions.

27,000 Mile Mechanical and Electrical - Road Test

Carry out all the Jobs listed under earlier Service Intervals.

- [ ] Job 70. Clean controls.
- [ ] Job 71. Check instrumentation.
- [ ] Job 72. Throttle pedal.
- [ ] Job 73. Hand brake function.
- [ ] Job 74. Brakes and steering.

27,000 Mile Bodywork and Interior - Around the Vehicle

First carry out all the Jobs listed under earlier Service Intervals as applicable.

- [ ] Job 17. Clean bodywork.
- [ ] Job 23. Touch-up paintwork.
- [ ] Job 24. Aerial/antenna.
- [ ] Job 25. Clean out interior.
- [ ] Job 26. Improve visibility!
- [ ] Job 75. Wiper blades and arms.
- [ ] Job 76. Check windscreen seals.
- [ ] Job 77. Check windscreen.
- [ ] Job 78. Check mirrors.

27,000 Mile Bodywork - Under the Vehicle

First carry out all the Jobs listed under earlier Service Intervals as applicable.

- [ ] Job 27. Clean mud traps.
- [ ] Job 79. Inspect underside.

Date serviced:..

Carried out by: ....
Garage Stamp or signature:

Parts/Accessories purchased (date, parts, source) ....
....
....
....
....

30,000 MILES - OR EVERY THIRTY MONTHS, whichever comes first

All the Service Jobs at this Service Interval have been carried forward from earlier service intervals and are to be repeated at this Service.

30,000 Mile Mechanical and Electrical - The Engine Bay

First carry out all the Jobs listed under earlier Service Intervals as applicable.

- [ ] Job 1. Engine oil level.
- [ ] Job 2. **NOT SERIES I VEHICLES** Clutch fluid level.
- [ ] Job 3. Brake fluid level.
- [ ] Job 4. Battery electrolyte.
- [ ] Job 5. Washer reservoir.
- [ ] Job 6. Cooling system.
- [ ] Job 18. **DIESEL MODELS ONLY** Drain sedimenter.
- [ ] Job 19. **DIESEL MODELS ONLY** Drain fuel filter.
- [ ] Job 28. Drain engine oil.
- [ ] Job 29. Remove engine oil filter.
- [ ] Job 30. Fit new oil filter.
- [ ] Job 31. Pour fresh engine oil.
- [ ] Job 32. Check oil level.
- [ ] Job 33. Clean oil bath air cleaner.
- [ ] Job 34. Adjust spark plugs.
- [ ] Job 35. Check distributor cap and rotor arm.
- [ ] Job 36. Check HT Circuit.
- [ ] Job 37. Check CB points.
- [ ] Job 38. Lubricate distributor.
- [ ] Job 39. Check drive belts.
- [ ] Job 40. **6-CYLINDER MODELS ONLY** Check air pump drivebelt.
- [ ] Job 41. Pipes and hoses.
- [ ] Job 42. Lubricate accelerator controls.
- [ ] Job 43. **V8 ENGINES ONLY** Check heated air intake valve.
- [ ] Job 44. Set carburettors.
- [ ] Job 80. Clean engine breather filters.
- [ ] Job 81. **OPTIONAL** Renew spark plugs.
- [ ] Job 82. Renew CB points.
- [ ] Job 83. **NOT V8 MODELS** Adjust valve clearances.

- [ ] Job 84. Rocker cover gasket.
- [ ] Job 85. Cooling system.
- [ ] Job 86. Coolant check.
- [ ] Job 87. Heater valve.
- [ ] Job 88. Check water pump.
- [ ] Job 89. Battery terminals.
- [ ] Job 90. Top-up carburettor dashpots.
- [ ] Job 91. Adjust ignition timing.
- [ ] Job 92. Distributor advance.
- [ ] Job 93. Brake servo hose.
- [ ] Job 94. **SPECIALIST SERVICE** Exhaust emissions check.

30,000 Mile Mechanical and Electrical - Around the Vehicle

First carry out all the Jobs listed under earlier Service Intervals as applicable.

- [ ] Job 7. Check horns.
- [ ] Job 8. Windscreen washers.
- [ ] Job 9. Windscreen wipers.
- [ ] Job 10. Tyre pressures.
- [ ] Job 11. Check headlamps.
- [ ] Job 12. Check front sidelamps.
- [ ] Job 13. Check rear sidelamps.
- [ ] Job 14. Number plate lamps.
- [ ] Job 15. Reversing lamps.
- [ ] Job 16. Interior lights.
- [ ] Job 20. Check tyres.
- [ ] Job 21. Check spare tyre.
- [ ] Job 22. Tighten wheel nuts.
- [ ] Job 45. Check fuel pipes.
- [ ] Job 46. Fuel filler pipe.
- [ ] Job 47. Top-up steering relay.
- [ ] Job 48. **SPECIALIST SERVICE** Front wheel alignment.
- [ ] Job 95. **SPECIALIST SERVICE** Adjust headlamps.
- [ ] Job 96. Bonnet release.
- [ ] Job 97. Locks and hinges.

30,000 Mile Mechanical and Electrical - Under the Vehicle

First carry out all the Jobs listed under earlier Service Intervals as applicable.

- [ ] Job 49. Check wheel hubs.
- [ ] Job 50. Top-up swivel pin housings.
- [ ] Job 51. Steering joints.
- [ ] Job 52. Adjust front brakes.
- [ ] Job 53. Top-up front axle oil.
- [ ] Job 54. Grease front propshaft U/Js.
- [ ] Job 55. Check for oil leaks.
- [ ] Job 56. Check front brake pipes.
- [ ] Job 57. Check clutch pipes.
- [ ] Job 58. Drain flywheel housing.
- [ ] Job 59. Top-up gearbox and overdrive oil.
- [ ] Job 60. Top-up transfer box.
- [ ] Job 61. Adjust handbrake.
- [ ] Job 62. Adjust clutch pedal.
- [ ] Job 63. **SERIES I VEHICLES** Grease pedal shafts.
- [ ] Job 64. Check rear brake pipes.
- [ ] Job 65. Top-up rear axle oil.
- [ ] Job 66. Grease rear propshaft U/Js.
- [ ] Job 67. Grease rear propshaft splines.
- [ ] Job 68. Adjust rear brakes.
- [ ] Job 69. Change wheel positions.
- [ ] Job 98. Lubricate steering box.
- [ ] Job 99. Check and adjust steering box.
- [ ] Job 100. Inspect front brakes.
- [ ] Job 101. Inspect front wheel cylinders.
- [ ] Job 102. Front hub/swivel assemblies.
- [ ] Job 103. Check steering balljoints.
- [ ] Job 104. Front shock absorbers.
- [ ] Job 105. Oil front springs.
- [ ] Job 106. Lubricate hand brake linkage.
- [ ] Job 107. Inspect rear brakes.
- [ ] Job 108. Inspect rear wheel cylinders.
- [ ] Job 109. Check exhaust system.
- [ ] Job 110. Rear shock absorbers.
- [ ] Job 111. Oil rear springs.

30,000 Mile Mechanical and Electrical - Road Test

Carry out all the Jobs listed under earlier Service Intervals.

- [ ] Job 70. Clean controls.
- [ ] Job 71. Check instrumentation.
- [ ] Job 72. Throttle pedal.
- [ ] Job 73. Hand brake function.
- [ ] Job 74. Brakes and steering.

30,000 Mile Bodywork and Interior - Around the Vehicle

First carry out all the Jobs listed under earlier Service Intervals as applicable.

- [ ] Job 17. Clean bodywork.
- [ ] Job 23. Touch-up paintwork.
- [ ] Job 24. Aerial/antenna.
- [ ] Job 25. Clean out interior.
- [ ] Job 26. Improve visibility!
- [ ] Job 75. Wiper blades and arms.
- [ ] Job 76. Check windscreen seals.
- [ ] Job 77. Check windscreen.
- [ ] Job 78. Check mirrors.
- [ ] Job 112. Seats and seat belts.
- [ ] Job 113. Inertia reel mechanisms.

30,000 Mile Bodywork - Under the Vehicle

First carry out all the Jobs listed under earlier Service Intervals as applicable.

- [ ] Job 27. Clean mud traps.
- [ ] Job 79. Inspect underside.
- [ ] Job 114. Rustproof underbody.

Date serviced:...

Carried out by: ....
Garage Stamp or signature:

Parts/Accessories purchased (date, parts,

source) ....

....

....

....

....

....

....

....

33,000 MILES - OR EVERY THIRTY THREE MONTHS, whichever comes first

All the Service Jobs at this Service Interval have been carried forward from earlier service intervals and are to be repeated at this Service as applicable.

33,000 Mile Mechanical and Electrical - The Engine Bay

- [ ] Job 1. Engine oil level.
- [ ] Job 2. **NOT SERIES I VEHICLES** Clutch fluid level.
- [ ] Job 3. Brake fluid level.
- [ ] Job 4. Battery electrolyte.
- [ ] Job 5. Washer reservoir.
- [ ] Job 6. Cooling system.
- [ ] Job 18. **DIESEL MODELS ONLY** Drain sedimenter.
- [ ] Job 19. **DIESEL MODELS ONLY** Drain fuel filter.
- [ ] Job 28. Drain engine oil.
- [ ] Job 29. Remove engine oil filter.
- [ ] Job 30. Fit new oil filter.
- [ ] Job 31. Pour fresh engine oil.
- [ ] Job 32. Check oil level.
- [ ] Job 33. Clean oil bath air cleaner.
- [ ] Job 34. Adjust spark plugs.
- [ ] Job 35. Check distributor cap and rotor arm.
- [ ] Job 36. Check HT Circuit.
- [ ] Job 37. Check CB points.
- [ ] Job 38. Lubricate distributor.
- [ ] Job 39. Check drive belts.
- [ ] Job 40. **6-CYLINDER MODELS ONLY** Check air pump drivebelt.
- [ ] Job 41. Pipes and hoses.
- [ ] Job 42. Lubricate accelerator controls.
- [ ] Job 43. **V8 ENGINES ONLY** Check heated air intake valve.
- [ ] Job 44. Set carburettors.

33,000 Mile Mechanical and Electrical - Around the Vehicle

First carry out all the Jobs listed under earlier Service Intervals as applicable.

- [ ] Job 7. Check horns.
- [ ] Job 8. Windscreen washers.

- [ ] Job 9. Windscreen wipers.
- [ ] Job 10. Tyre pressures.
- [ ] Job 11. Check headlamps.
- [ ] Job 12. Check front sidelamps.
- [ ] Job 13. Check rear sidelamps.
- [ ] Job 14. Number plate lamps.
- [ ] Job 15. Reversing lamps.
- [ ] Job 16. Interior lights.
- [ ] Job 20. Check tyres.
- [ ] Job 21. Check spare tyre.
- [ ] Job 22. Tighten wheel nuts.
- [ ] Job 45. Check fuel pipes.
- [ ] Job 46. Fuel filler pipe.
- [ ] Job 47. Top-up steering relay.
- [ ] Job 48. **SPECIALIST SERVICE** Front wheel alignment.

33,000 Mile Mechanical and Electrical - Under the Vehicle

First carry out all the Jobs listed under earlier Service Intervals as applicable.

- [ ] Job 49. Check wheel hubs.
- [ ] Job 50. Top-up swivel pin housings.
- [ ] Job 51. Steering joints.
- [ ] Job 52. Adjust front brakes.
- [ ] Job 53. Top-up front axle oil.
- [ ] Job 54. Grease front propshaft U/Js.
- [ ] Job 55. Check for oil leaks.
- [ ] Job 56. Check front brake pipes.
- [ ] Job 57. Check clutch pipes.
- [ ] Job 58. Drain flywheel housing.
- [ ] Job 59. Top-up gearbox and overdrive oil.
- [ ] Job 60. Top-up transfer box.
- [ ] Job 61. Adjust handbrake.
- [ ] Job 62. Adjust clutch pedal.
- [ ] Job 63. **SERIES I VEHICLES** Grease pedal shafts.
- [ ] Job 64. Check rear brake pipes.
- [ ] Job 65. Top-up rear axle oil.
- [ ] Job 66. Grease rear propshaft U/Js.
- [ ] Job 67. Grease rear propshaft splines.
- [ ] Job 68. Adjust rear brakes.
- [ ] Job 69. Change wheel positions.

33,000 Mile Mechanical and Electrical - Road Test

Carry out all the Jobs listed under earlier Service Intervals.

- [ ] Job 70. Clean controls.
- [ ] Job 71. Check instrumentation.
- [ ] Job 72. Throttle pedal.
- [ ] Job 73. Hand brake function.
- [ ] Job 74. Brakes and steering.

33,000 Mile Bodywork and Interior - Around the Vehicle

First carry out all the Jobs listed under earlier Service Intervals as applicable.

- [ ] Job 17. Clean bodywork.
- [ ] Job 23. Touch-up paintwork.
- [ ] Job 24. Aerial/antenna.
- [ ] Job 25. Clean out interior.
- [ ] Job 26. Improve visibility!
- [ ] Job 75. Wiper blades and arms.
- [ ] Job 76. Check windscreen seals.
- [ ] Job 77. Check windscreen.
- [ ] Job 78. Check mirrors.

33,000 Mile Bodywork - Under the Vehicle

First carry out all the Jobs listed under earlier Service Intervals as applicable.

- [ ] Job 27. Clean mud traps.
- [ ] Job 79. Inspect underside.

Date serviced:..

Carried out by:..
Garage Stamp or signature:

Parts/Accessories purchased (date, parts, source) ....
....
....
....
....

36,000 MILES - OR EVERY THIRTY SIX MONTHS, whichever comes first.

All the Service Jobs in the tinted area have been carried forward from earlier service intervals and are to be repeated at this Service.

36,000 Mile Mechanical and Electrical - Emission Control Equipment

Carry out all the Jobs listed under earlier Service Intervals.

- [ ] Job 115. **6-CYLINDER AND V8 MODELS ONLY** Renew crankcase breather flame trap.
- [ ] Job 116. **EARLY 4-CYLINDER AND ALL 6-CYLINDER MODELS ONLY** Crankcase breather valve.
- [ ] Job 117. **SPECIFIC EXPORT 6-CYL. MODELS ONLY** Check air injection system.
- [ ] Job 118. **SPECIFIC EXPORT 6-CYL. MODELS ONLY** Replace air pump belt.
- [ ] Job 119. **SPECIFIC EXPORT 6-CYL. MODELS ONLY** Test check valve.
- [ ] Job 120. **SPECIFIC EXPORT 6-CYL. MODELS ONLY AND SPECIALIST SERVICE** Emission system.

36,000 Mile Mechanical and Electrical - The Engine Bay

First carry out all the Jobs listed under earlier Service Intervals as applicable.

- [ ] Job 1. Engine oil level.
- [ ] Job 2. **NOT SERIES I VEHICLES** Clutch fluid level.
- [ ] Job 3. Brake fluid level.
- [ ] Job 4. Battery electrolyte.
- [ ] Job 5. Washer reservoir.
- [ ] Job 6. Cooling system.
- [ ] Job 18. **DIESEL MODELS ONLY** Drain sedimenter.
- [ ] Job 19. **DIESEL MODELS ONLY** Drain fuel filter.
- [ ] Job 28. Drain engine oil.
- [ ] Job 29. Remove engine oil filter.
- [ ] Job 30. Fit new oil filter.
- [ ] Job 31. Pour fresh engine oil.
- [ ] Job 32. Check oil level.
- [ ] Job 33. Clean oil bath air cleaner.
- [ ] Job 34. Adjust spark plugs.

- [ ] Job 35. Check distributor cap and rotor arm.
- [ ] Job 36. Check HT Circuit.
- [ ] Job 37. Check CB points.
- [ ] Job 38. Lubricate distributor.
- [ ] Job 39. Check drive belts.
- [ ] Job 40. **6-CYLINDER MODELS ONLY** Check air pump drivebelt.
- [ ] Job 41. Pipes and hoses.
- [ ] Job 42. Lubricate accelerator controls.
- [ ] Job 43. **V8 ENGINES ONLY** Check heated air intake valve.
- [ ] Job 44. Set carburettors.
- [ ] Job 80. Clean engine breather filters.
- [ ] Job 81. **OPTIONAL** Renew spark plugs.
- [ ] Job 82. Renew CB points.
- [ ] Job 83. **NOT V8 MODELS** Adjust valve clearances.
- [ ] Job 84. Rocker cover gasket.
- [ ] Job 85. Cooling system.
- [ ] Job 86. Coolant check.
- [ ] Job 87. Heater valve.
- [ ] Job 88. Check water pump.
- [ ] Job 89. Battery terminals.
- [ ] Job 90. Top-up carburettor dashpots.
- [ ] Job 91. Adjust ignition timing.
- [ ] Job 92. Distributor advance.
- [ ] Job 93. Brake servo hose.
- [ ] Job 94. **SPECIALIST SERVICE** Exhaust emissions check.
- [ ] Job 121. Cabin heater and hoses.
- [ ] Job 122. **DIESEL MODELS ONLY and SPECIALIST SERVICE** Check injectors.
- [ ] Job 123. **DIESEL MODELS ONLY** Diesel heater plug wiring.
- [ ] Job 124. **V8 MODELS ONLY** Renew air cleaner element.
- [ ] Job 125. **PETROL MODELS ONLY** Cylinder compressions.
- [ ] Job 126. Lubricate dynamo.
- [ ] Job 127. Clean fuel sediment bowl.
- [ ] Job 128. **6-CYLINDER PETROL MODELS ONLY** Renew bulkhead fuel filter.
- [ ] Job 129. **DIESEL MODELS ONLY** Clean fuel sedimenter.
- [ ] Job 130. **DIESEL MODELS ONLY** Renew fuel filter element.
- [ ] Job 131. **DIESEL MODELS ONLY** Bleed

- [ ] Job 159. Overhaul ignition.
- [ ] Job 160. Clean float chambers.
- [ ] Job 161. **SPECIALIST SERVICE** Renew brake servo filter.

36,000 Mile Mechanical and Electrical - Around the Vehicle

First carry out all the Jobs listed under earlier Service Intervals as applicable.

- [ ] Job 7. Check horns.
- [ ] Job 8. Windscreen washers.
- [ ] Job 9. Windscreen wipers.
- [ ] Job 10. Tyre pressures.
- [ ] Job 11. Check headlamps.
- [ ] Job 12. Check front sidelamps.
- [ ] Job 13. Check rear sidelamps.
- [ ] Job 14. Number plate lamps.
- [ ] Job 15. Reversing lamps.
- [ ] Job 16. Interior lights.
- [ ] Job 20. Check tyres.
- [ ] Job 21. Check spare tyre.
- [ ] Job 22. Tighten wheel nuts.
- [ ] Job 45. Check fuel pipes.
- [ ] Job 46. Fuel filler pipe.
- [ ] Job 47. Top-up steering relay.
- [ ] Job 48. **SPECIALIST SERVICE** Front wheel alignment.
- [ ] Job 95. **SPECIALIST SERVICE** Adjust headlamps.
- [ ] Job 96. Bonnet release.
- [ ] Job 97. Locks and hinges.
- [ ] Job 132. Toolkit and jack.
- [ ] Job 133. Test shock absorbers.

36,000 Mile Mechanical and Electrical - Under the Vehicle

First carry out all the Jobs listed under earlier Service Intervals as applicable.

- [ ] Job 49. Check wheel hubs.
- [ ] Job 50. Top-up swivel pin housings.
- [ ] Job 51. Steering joints.
- [ ] Job 52. Adjust front brakes.
- [ ] Job 53. Top-up front axle oil.
- [ ] Job 54. Grease front propshaft U/Js.

- [ ] Job 55. Check for oil leaks.
- [ ] Job 56. Check front brake pipes.
- [ ] Job 57. Check clutch pipes.
- [ ] Job 58. Drain flywheel housing.
- [ ] Job 59. Top-up gearbox and overdrive oil.
- [ ] Job 60. Top-up transfer box.
- [ ] Job 61. Adjust handbrake.
- [ ] Job 62. Adjust clutch pedal.
- [ ] Job 63. **SERIES I VEHICLES** Grease pedal shafts.
- [ ] Job 64. Check rear brake pipes.
- [ ] Job 65. Top-up rear axle oil.
- [ ] Job 66. Grease rear propshaft U/Js.
- [ ] Job 67. Grease rear propshaft splines.
- [ ] Job 68. Adjust rear brakes.
- [ ] Job 69. Change wheel positions.
- [ ] Job 98. Lubricate steering box.
- [ ] Job 99. Check and adjust steering box.
- [ ] Job 100. Inspect front brakes.
- [ ] Job 101. Inspect front wheel cylinders.
- [ ] Job 102. Front hub/swivel assemblies.
- [ ] Job 103. Check steering balljoints.
- [ ] Job 104. Front shock absorbers.
- [ ] Job 105. Oil front springs.
- [ ] Job 106. Lubricate hand brake linkage.
- [ ] Job 107. Inspect rear brakes.
- [ ] Job 108. Inspect rear wheel cylinders.
- [ ] Job 109. Check exhaust system.
- [ ] Job 110. Rear shock absorbers.
- [ ] Job 111. Oil rear springs.
- [ ] Job 134. Renew transfer box oil.
- [ ] Job 135. Renew gearbox oil and over-drive oil (if fitted).
- [ ] Job 136. Renew front axle oil.
- [ ] Job 137. Front axle breather.
- [ ] Job 138. Front suspension security.
- [ ] Job 139. Check front propshaft U/Js.
- [ ] Job 140. Service freewheeling hubs.
- [ ] Job 141. Renew rear axle oil.
- [ ] Job 142. Rear axle breather.
- [ ] Job 143. Rear suspension security.
- [ ] Job 144. Check rear propshaft U/Js.
- [ ] Job 145. **SERIES II & IIA ONLY** Check/lubricate door hinges.

☐ Job 162. **6-CYL. & V8 MODELS ONLY**
Clean electric fuel pump filter.

☐ Job 163. **SPECIALIST SERVICE** Braking system seals.

36,000 Mile Mechanical and Electrical - Road Test

Carry out all the Jobs listed under earlier Service Intervals.

☐ Job 70. Clean controls.

☐ Job 71. Check instrumentation.

☐ Job 72. Throttle pedal.

☐ Job 73. Hand brake function.

☐ Job 74. Brakes and steering.

36,000 Mile Bodywork and Interior - Around the Vehicle

First carry out all the Jobs listed under earlier Service Intervals as applicable.

☐ Job 17. Clean bodywork.

☐ Job 23. Touch-up paintwork.

☐ Job 24. Aerial/antenna.

☐ Job 25. Clean out interior.

☐ Job 26. Improve visibility!

☐ Job 75. Wiper blades and arms.

☐ Job 76. Check windscreen seals.

☐ Job 77. Check windscreen.

☐ Job 78. Check mirrors.

☐ Job 112. Seats and seat belts.

☐ Job 113. Inertia reel mechanisms.

36,000 Mile Bodywork - Under the Vehicle

First carry out all the Jobs listed under earlier Service Intervals as applicable.

☐ Job 27. Clean mud traps.

☐ Job 79. Inspect underside.

☐ Job 114. Rustproof underbody.

☐ Job 146. Tighten wing and body bolts.

☐ Job 147. Top-up rustproofing.

Date serviced:...

Carried out by:...
Garage Stamp or signature:

Parts/Accessories purchased (date, parts, source)..

....

....

....

....

YOU HAVE NOW COMPLETED ALL OF THE SERVICE JOBS LISTED IN THIS SERVICE GUIDE, 'THE LONGEST' INTERVAL BETWEEN ANY JOBS BEING 36,000 MILES OR THREE YEARS. WHEN YOU HAVE FILLED IN EACH OF THE SERVICE INTERVALS SHOWN HERE, YOU MAY PURCHASE CONTINUATION SHEETS TO ENABLE YOU TO CONTINUE AND COMPLETE YOUR SERVICE HISTORY FOR AS LONG AS YOU OWN THE CAR.

PLEASE CONTACT

PORTER PUBLISHING
The Storehouse
Little Hereford Street
Bromyard
Hereford
HR7 4DE
England
Tel: 01885 488800